GW01459298

ADVENTURE IN DEPTH

Commander William King

ADVENTURE IN DEPTH

G. P. Putnam's Sons, New York

FOUNDED 1838

GPPS

C OPYRIGHT © 1975 by COMMANDER WILLIAM KING

All rights reserved. This book, or parts thereof,
must not be reproduced in any form without permission.
Published simultaneously in Canada
by Longman Canada Limited, Toronto.

SBN: 399-11493-9

Library of Congress Catalog
Card Number: 74-30558

Grateful acknowledgment is made to the
Nautical Publishing Company Ltd for
permission to use passages from
Capsize *by Commander King.*

PRINTED IN THE UNITED STATES OF AMERICA

Part 1

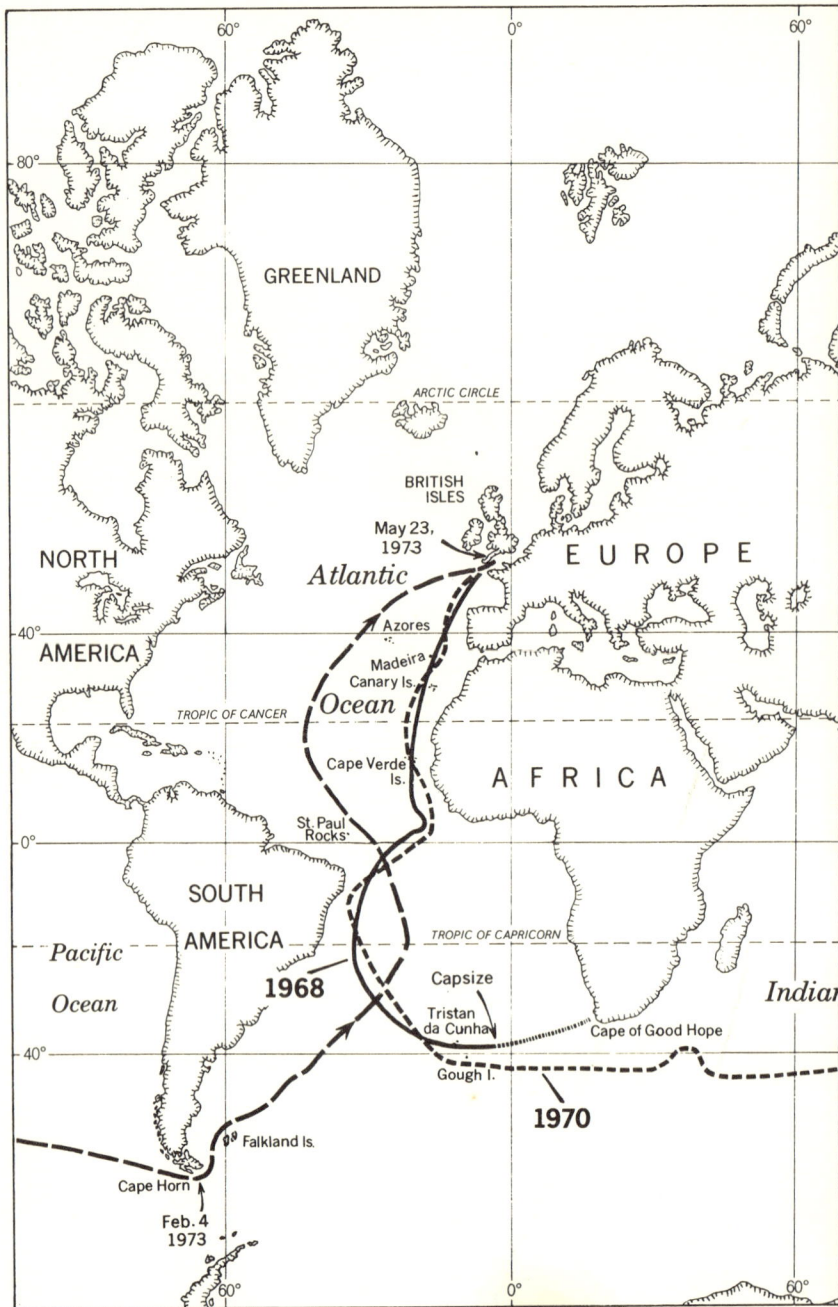

60°   0°   60°

80°

GREENLAND

ARCTIC CIRCLE

BRITISH
ISLES

May 23,
1973

Atlantic

NORTH

E U R O P E

40°

AMERICA

Azores

Madeira
Canary Is.

Ocean

TROPIC OF CANCER

Cape Verde
Is.

A F R I C A

St. Paul
Rocks·

0°

SOUTH

AMERICA

TROPIC OF CAPRICORN

1968

Capsize

Pacific

Tristan
da Cunha

India

Ocean

Cape of Good Hope

40°

Gough I.

1970

Falkland Is.

Cape Horn

Feb. 4
1973

60°   0°   60°

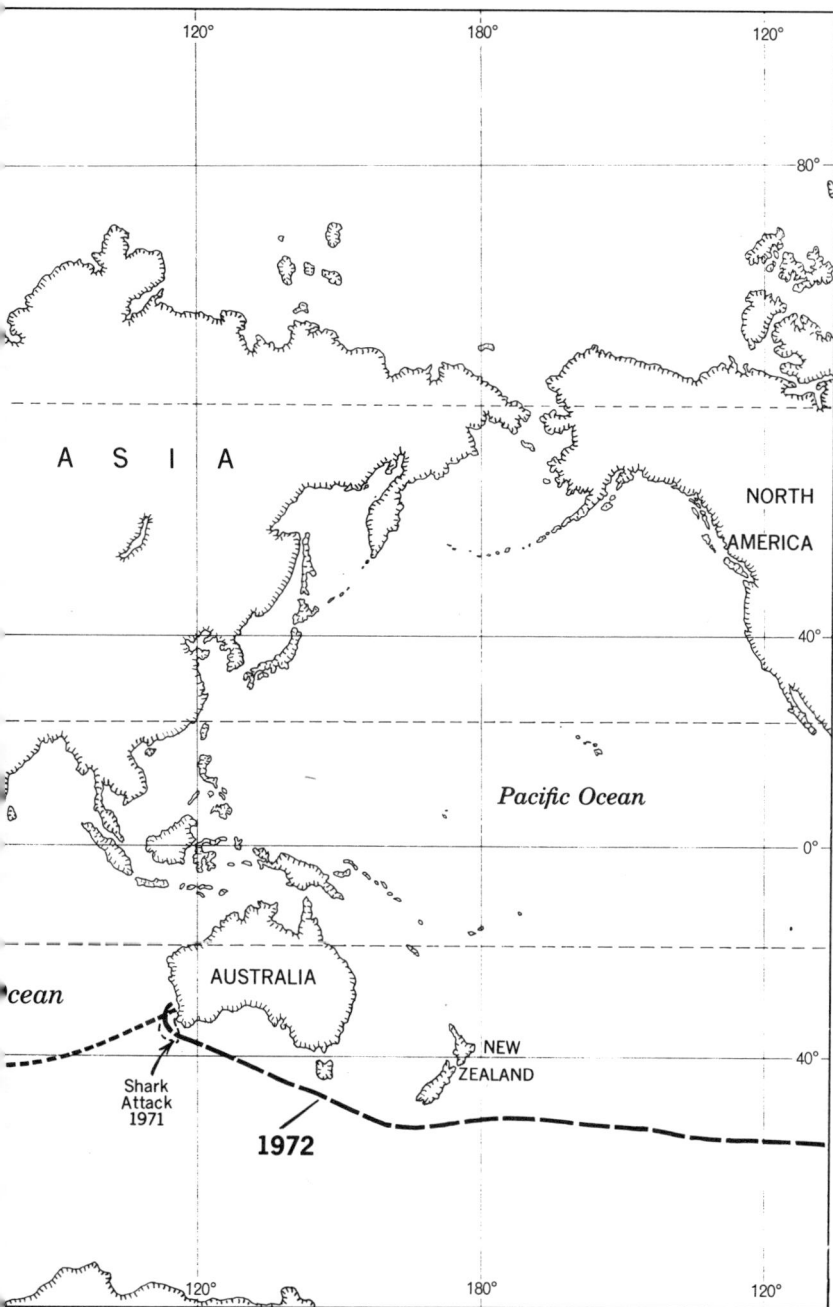

120°   180°   120°

80°

A S I A

NORTH
AMERICA

40°

Pacific Ocean

0°

AUSTRALIA

cean

NEW
ZEALAND

40°

Shark
Attack
1971

1972

120°   180°   120°

CHAPTER 1

Farewell to War

THE gray line on the horizon meant Plymouth. I shouted revolution orders into the mouthpiece of the copper voice pipe leading to th helmsman below in the control room, and the engine throb slowed its beat.

My submarine turned her nose toward the great harbor, and the wings of spray that had risen high above her gray sides all the way from the Pacific, dropped and folded as a bird folds its wings. Past the breakwater we looked up at the Hoe where Drake had played his famous game of bowls. The green hill rose proudly beside the smashed old city; cobbled streets and medieval houses had been bombed to rubble. The naval base survived. "Stop engines. Out engine clutches. Finished with main engines," I called. Electric motors now took over and H.M.S. *Telemachus* slowed to a glide. Ahead of us lay her kennel—a basin of water about two-hundred feet square into which a submarine goes for a refit. I turned her across the tide, shot into the basin with a bit of a flourish, and stopped the motors. From this moment onward the dockyard hands had to take control. With shore capstans, wires, ropes, and a motor tug they were supposed to warp her round into an allotted corner. At this precise moment a siren blew for dinner hour, and as usual every man jack disappeared, leaving *Telemachus*, which had been fighting in hellish conditions for eighteen months, sitting in the basin entrance waiting expectantly to be towed to her berth.

She was the third submarine I had commanded and we

3

were weary from the China seas. It had been an onerous period, entailing fifty-day patrols in stifling conditions. After I had managed to sink a Japanese submarine outside Singapore, we were employed landing commandos on the jungle coast and trying to control the prickly heat on our skins. For so many nights I had slept or curled up on the deck of the control tower that now my face showed a permanent crease down the right side, and it had not been easy to keep a British crew contented in the Pacific during 1945 when they saw that American submarines were bigger and much faster. It was like reaching the finals of a motor rally in a Model T Ford!

Standing, therefore, on my submarine, regarding the deserted shore of that basin, I made a swift decision. I did not care if I scraped her side. This was the end of my war. I had no intention of remaining in a peacetime Navy. I was just damned if I'd tolerate this reception. Dinner hour indeed!

It looked almost impossible to move a submarine by propellers in such a confined space, but there was just room to advance and swing her stern round missing a granite wall by two feet. I stationed officers fore and aft to shout distances and in a flurry of foam, moving ahead and then astern at full power, I cajoled *Telemachus* back and forth until her bows were locked into a corner of the basin. Then we turned her tail 180 degrees and then a further 90 degrees to nudge into our berth.

Somewhat to my surprise we did all this without a scrape. When the dockyard hands rolled up later with their bellies full, *Telemachus* sat innocently moored in her correct position. My crew enjoyed viewing the dropped jaws and incredulous expressions.

As I walked across the gangplank to depart on leave, I looked back at the sea which had been my home since I was fourteen years old—a hideous home for the last six years, yet so alluring, so part of me. I would get back to

her I felt sure. In a different way I would get back to her,
on top of the waves not underneath. I had not finished
with the sea, I would turn back to her for resuscitation.
Later on, I thought, a little later on.

CHAPTER 2

Background Music

ACTUALLY, it was twenty-three years later that I would set forth from Plymouth in my junk-rigged schooner to sail alone around the world. While waiting for fog to lift and the keen westerly wind to change to east, thus making my getaway through the crowded shipping lanes of the Western Approaches less hazardous, I went for long walks through the Cornish lanes with my wife Anita, and one day, while waiting for the hour of the special weather report, we sat down in the sun and stared across the harbor to Plymouth Naval Base. "What are those odd-looking objects?" she asked, pointing across the water to the submarine basins. I laughed, remembering the summer of 1945 when I had driven a submarine in there for the last time. Even from this distance of time it gave me a feeling of satisfaction to recall the manner in which I had successfully parked H.M.S. *Telemachus* and amazed the dockhands back from dinner hour.

And here I was again. The wheel had come full circle and brought me back to Plymouth, this time with my own boat and with an expedition of my own choice looming ahead. Surely the springs which get wound tight in all submarine captains and which even a happy family life in Ireland had not really loosened would now be released—in the absolute freedom, the violent beauty of battling above, not under, the waves.

I found it a little difficult to answer the questions which friends were always putting to me. Why do you want to do it? What drives you to set sail in a little boat alone?

There were several answers. I loved sailing. I had always wanted to sail around Cape Horn. Bringing a boat alone through the fierce Southern Ocean and the Roaring Forties represented a challenge for which I thought myself particularly well fitted.

These simple explanations were received in puzzled silence. The vital reason, mixed deep with all others, was impossible for me to express at the time. Five years of wartime submarining had created a kind of blockage in my mind, which Irish country life could enamel as an oyster can enamel a piece of grit in a pearl. But I wanted to dig the grit out. My animal instincts led me to the sea for healing. I was, in fact, intent on doing a "cure" in the manner which, for me, though not for many, would be thrilling and enjoyable. It is not easy to opt out of ordinary life and embark on such a venture. My experience as a seaman made it easier. So did the fact that my wife understood the urge.

After the war things had gone remarkably well for me. It took a long time to get out of the Navy, yet since the evening of an alcoholic farewell party in the mess, since the day soon after that, when I married the girl I had chased to her home in County Monaghan, few men could have lived more exactly in the pattern of their choice.

I was mad about organic farming and able to breed cattle and sheep and horses in the west of Ireland. In fact, I was an ecologist before I had even heard the word. My children ate bread made from wheat grown in our own fields and drank milk from our own cows and ran wild beside Galway Bay. They grew up rosy, if a trifle wild. I also enjoyed skiing and mountaineering, as well as farming, and could get away for this with my former flotilla commander, the famous "Ruckers"* who had built himself an idyllic chalet in Kitzbühel. What more

*Vice-Admiral Philip Ruck-Keene, C.B., C.B.E., D.S.O.

could I desire? Only to clear that small section of my
mind which had grown tense and resentful during the
war. I had not always been like this. Perhaps the
memories of a lighthearted youth made me particularly
irritated by an irritation. My father had been killed in the
1914 war; a professional soldier who experimented with
the first balloons and fighting planes, he was killed by a
shell just before returning to England on leave. My
mother was waiting expectantly for him at her garden
gate when the telegram arrived. Left with a small son and
daughter, she had us educated in the conventional
English way and I never returned to County Galway
where my grandfather's home had been. Instead, our
holidays were passed in the Scottish Highlands where *her*
father, old Fraser Mackenzie, finished his days.
Grandma Mackenzie was an indomitable old lady who
horrified her family by her astonishing sporting widow-
hood—learning to ski in her seventies and skippering
her own yacht *Imatra,** a fifty-ton yawl with a paid crew
of five, around the stormy coast of Western Scotland.
She had a shiny pink face and was never seasick. Perhaps
I inherited this lucky trait from her. Certainly my lovely
flowerlike mother was constitutionally constructed on
different lines. She grew pale and suffered horribly in
rough seas. I can remember a few smart "yachting
parties" when the ladies retired below and pathetic pleas
to make for harbor were sent up the hatch via the crew.
But Granny, who enjoyed taking the tiller herself, kept
right on sailing hard on the wind. As ghastly sounds
emanated from below all she said was "Hark at the
wonderful gurgle of water on the bow!"
    Not only did Grandma never feel seasick, but she
seemed impervious to cold. When we were living at the

---

*Built in 1899, *Imatra* was splendidly constructed and is still sailing
around New Zealand. Her dark wood interior, built in the Victorian style
with corridors and little private cabins, is now regarded as a museum pice
and her present owner has kept the yawl unaltered.

big house in the Grampian range it was her pleasure to go up into the mountains with a portable campstool and easel to paint watercolors on the snowline. I did not, alas, inherit this trait. I *always* felt the cold.

The only part of my childhood I detested was boarding school. In the heartless English fashion I was packed off at eight to what my gentle mother had been told was "the nicest prep school in England." Here the food was abominable and the headmaster seemed to enjoy beating little boys. Needless to add, the fees were enormous!

At fourteen I entered the Royal Naval College at Dartmouth, thrilled at having passed all the mental and physical tests. and became technically a sailor. The long grim training could not quench my spirits, though I think I did hate it more than many of the boys, so perhaps I was a sensitive type. Among my chums was one who would spend two years as a Japanese prisoner working on the Burma Railroad. When I met him after this experience, he said, "Dartmouth was splendid training for being a POW. You just felt you were back at school again, bullied and starved and generally ill-treated."

At seventeen I went to sea in H.M.S. *Nelson*, a brand-new battleship, the most powerful in the Navy. The ward room contained the royal Duke of Kent and the gun room resounded with great names. We humble cadets flitted around on our duties, wildly anxious not to put a foot wrong.

Six months later we were swept away to be subjected to a fresh rigorous training, which would turn us into midshipmen, on board an elderly battleship H.M.S. *Resolution*. For two years we sailed around the Mediterranean. Under iron discipline we were smelted into the kind of men considered suitable to eventually command a ship in what was then the world's greatest Navy. More or less conscientious, more or less ambitious, each according to his nature, we were all single-minded in our belief in the British Empire as a force for good and in our own Navy as a force to sustain that good. In 1927 the glory of being a serving officer was very real to me.

Gibraltar, Malta, Majorca, Alexandria, Athens, and Constantinople were the ports to which H.M.S. *Resolution* took us and we read their history briefly before tearing away to play polo, golf, and tennis. Unfortunately for me I was discovered to have the makings of a long-distance runner and whenever sports were organized, I had to represent my ship. I must have run hundreds of miles along those Mediterranean shores where only too often it was insufferably hot! I grew to intensely dislike the starting officers—invariably large, rather fat men with red faces who enjoyed after-dinner port—their rich, throaty voices seemed to dispatch us with a horrid satisfaction on ten miles or so across country. "Ready, boys—one, two, three, go!" Then it was back to the bar for them.

Thus two years passed in the Mediterranean—the iron decks, the polished brass, the gray clean paint, the oil-smelling engines, the big guns silhouetted against the dawn and night sky—this was our nursery.

We returned to England full-fledged senior midshipmen, a rank which seemed to us exceedingly important, almost heroic, although still far down in the hierarchy of the gods.

Grandma, whom I had not seen for so long, was now eighty and, according to all the family, "worse than ever." My mother had opted out of all cruising invitations and so had most of her friends. Apart from the paid hands, Granny now had to be content with tough young men as company, the type who advertise in the personal columns as "ready for anything, money no consideration."

The submarine service was, in general, manned by volunteers, but when my class came up to the point of determining the branch which we served, there were no volunteers. There had been too many in the previous class, but instead of picking some from their overflow three months older than ourselves the Admiralty replied, "The following *will* volunteer for submarines. . .!" With six other young men who had chosen surface ships on which to develop their talents I lined up for the medical examination which was even stricter than for normal naval entry. We all thought up some disability, easy to simulate. I felt quite confident of failing the test because only the previous week I had developed a limp, and a jolly red-faced surgeon commander, himself a great man with the bottle, had diagnosed gout and adjured me to be more temperate in my habits. Five of my companions were bowled out, but I hobbled cockily into this new doctor and thought I was on a very good wicket when I announced, "Gout," for I knew that any form of rheumatic disease blocked you for submarines. I don't know if he was irritated or amused, but all he said was "Left turn. Quick march." And so, at the age of twenty-one, I marched into submarines. It was the march of historic events which kept me in this branch for fifteen years instead of spending the usual two periods of eighteen months in the general service. When my first period for general service was due, the Abyssinian War blew up; and when I reached the second, there came the Great War.

I arrived in Hong Kong to join a 1,500-ton submarine H.M.S. *Orpheus*, which carried five officers and fifty-two seamen. Here I continued to learn my trade under the brilliant guidance of Captain Bill Barry. I can remember that in the torpedo-loading competition (which involved loading six two-ton steel monsters into their tubes) we completed the exercise in six minutes and the next best ship took twelve. Bill Barry not only taught me how to fight a submarine (under him we practiced our major function in war—that is, torpedo attack on surface ships with absolute precision), but also taught me the difference between a leader and other men. It lies not only in the ceaseless pursuit of perfection but in a magnetic quality which inspires those around you. He never flapped, he never raised his voice, he simply drew the best out of everyone.

We glimpsed what we could of China—visiting the Great Wall and the Altar of Heaven in Peking and tramping off on expeditions through the countryside where we talked in pidgin fashion to the peasants and grew to love their humor and humanness. We were hard and fit so that wherever we landed we could walk miles and get the "feel" of the people. Taking a two-day trip to Harbin, a couple of us on leave found we could communicate in a form of Russian Chinese and we walked for miles around the city. In the evenings we stuffed caviar at one shilling* a plateful in the nightclubs.

Since my great uncle had been governor of Burma and Bengal I had several letters of introduction to interesting friends in the Far East, but with the contrariness of youth I scorned social circles recommended by my family. Fear of "respectability" induced me to lay out my own entertainment campaign. As a result, I ended up, after seeing Tsingtao nightlife, lying in the Chinese bazaar, having been hit on the head and robbed. As in the dawn light I came painfully back to consciousness, I heard a loud buzzing, as of bees in lime trees on a summer day in England. These proved to be flies on the open wound on my scalp! Sitting up I discovered my coat and wallet missing. I could only find a handkerchief to staunch the blood flow from my scalp. Coolies walked by, expressionless, and those stall owners who were setting up their booths paying no attention whatsoever to the "white lord" fallen low. I staggered to my feet and summoned a rickshaw to the quayside where a sampan man I knew took over. He paid the rickshaw and delivered me safely to the Depot Ship where I hastened

---

*Five modern pence, or 10 cents.

to the showers and combed my wet hair like a toupee over the scalp wound before reporting for duty.

How congenial and humorous the Chinese were—the only real gulf between us lay, I think, in the different values we placed on human life. Although ready to kill in battle, we Europeans regard each life as precious. On one occasion when a Chinese had fallen into the sea and drowned, our commanding officer stormed up, "Why the devil didn't you do anything to help him?" The dead man's companions just shook with laughter. "Head look so funny—up and down like coconut!" Then one day when three of us were bathing at Repulse Bay, a glamorous resort built up by a Chinese millionaire, we noticed from the raft on which we lay sunning ourselves that a mighty splashing was taking place near the shore. Strong swimmers, we all dived in and streaked for the commotion. We found a large fat Chinese apparently drowning in his own depth of water while watched by other Chinese who only had to *wade* out to pull him in. We dragged the man unconscious onto the sand and held him upside down enabling a gallon or so of wine and expensive lunch from the Repulse Bay Hotel to flow out. Then we practiced the artificial respiration we knew so well. His fellow Chinese on the beach appeared to come of the rich middle class and their utter indifference or rather want of action could only be attributable to the widely held superstition that if a drowning man is rescued his soul sits on his helper's shoulders throughout the afterlife. Language barriers made it impossible for us to pursue the subject. One can talk quite freely in pidgin Chinese with laborers but not philosophize with the upper class. We went off baffled. Had we not happened to notice all the splashing that man would have drowned in four feet of water.

The Chinese we knew and liked best were the peasants. We used to go out from Weihaiwei to fire practice salvoes and to dive, after which each torpedo (an intricate mechanical object costing some 3,000 pounds) had to be recovered. The steel cylinder (without, of course, any explosive head) was supposed to pass under the target and rise to the surface, but if a certain stop-valve was not opened it could sink to the bottom and be lost—an expensive loss which aroused wrath in higher circles. During the period when I was torpedo officer on *Orpheus* I did not always personally inspect the stop-valve of each torpedo; I merely asked the torpedo gunner's mate. When a morning came on which we could not find a torpedo floating on the surface, I knew myself to be absolutely responsible, for I had not checked the stop-valve with my own eyes. All day long we combed the ocean in squares, hoping to sight that precious metal cylinder. Our search proved vain. Having owned up to the fact that I had accepted a seaman's word without actually inspecting it, I gloomily awaited the "official inquiry." The sea had been so choppy at the time that I continued to hope against hope that the gunner's mate had answered correctly and that we might yet find that torpedo, but the repeated searches (which ruined everyone else's afternoons) yielded no results. Two months passed before rumors reached us that a strange long shiny object, possibly a phallic totem from the gods, had been washed up on an island one hundred and eighty miles away. A naval party in a destroyer hurriedly set forth to investigate. They landed by whaler on an open beach to be greeted by fisher folk whose expectancy of increased fertility had put them in most cheerful humor. Yes indeed, a wonderful object, phallic in appearance, had been washed ashore by the kind sea. To us it seemed unbelievable that a steel tube weighing over a ton could, as they said, be carried inland by singing men, but enthusiasm can work wonders. Chattering merrily, the islanders led our naval party along jungle tracks to a village three miles inland. And there in its own little temple of woven palm leaves stood my lost torpedo!

The people seemed to well understand how anxious the British must be to recover such a very special *objet d'art*, and after remuneration and great jollifications they offered to transport our great "emblem" back to the shore. With much talk and laughter they slung that fifteen-foot-long steel torpedo between big bamboo poles and with twelve men aside carried it back to the shore singing as they marched. Wide-eyed with interest, they watched it being towed out to sea and hoisted onto the awaiting destroyer. We never learned how successfully the magic had worked, but no "official inquiry" had to dampen my spirits that summer and never again did I fail to examine each valve for myself!

Two and a half years on the China station must change any man, for the Confucian philosophy lies not only in books—it permeates the very atmosphere. And certainly the simple people knew that war was coming when apparently neither London nor Washington did. I remember my delightful sampan man who would smilingly row me twelve miles or so for a day's duck shooting on the mainland, looking back at the wooded swamps and saying, "Two years—Japanese come." They did and they killed him cruelly for having taken British officers to their sport.

In Manila we met the American Navy, and among the friends I made among the submarine officers was one magnificent six-footer who could drink most men under the table. One night we gave a dance on the depot ship, and Star, as he was called, turned up with about the most beautiful girl I had ever set eyes on. Astonishingly, she seemed able to knock back whisky as imperturbably as her escort, and her face did not appear to fall to pieces as usually occurs when women drink hard. However, when the time came for the party to end, Star did have to march her somewhat unsteadily to the gangplank, and he may had dropped a word of admonition in her ear because she suddenly straightened, landed him a black

eye, and fell unconscious into his arms. Manfully he laid
the lady over his arm in the manner in which one carries
a mackintosh and continued his way over the gangplank.
(He was boxing champion of the Asiatic Fleet and fit as a
fiddle, but nonetheless this was an astonishing feat.) I
happened to be officer of the watch that night, and with
admiration I watched as the side-party accorded the
honors usual to a departing officer of a foreign navy.
Pipes shrilled and we all stood to attention. Not a flicker
of expression crossed that magnificent countenance as
he returned the salute and boarded the awaiting launch.
Nor was there a twitch from the body draped on his arm.
It was the most impressive piping-off we ever witnessed.

After a long leave in England and some fox hunting in
Ireland, I was posted as second-in-command to H.M.S.
Narwhal, the most modern of our submarine fleet. This
splendid new ship was sent off on a recruiting campaign,
and in view of recent events in Northern Ireland it may
be interesting to recall our visit to what was then the
peaceful city of Belfast. As usual on these excursions, we
opened the submarine to the public and long queues
formed to see her interior. In order to do this people had
to walk across the depot ship and then climb down
through the submarine's hatch and out the other end.
(As a very fat lady had once got stuck in the hatches,
those on the plump side had to pass through a wooden
testing ring first!) This was the first time I had ever been
to Northern Ireland and I recall my surprise on seeing
that the police, the Royal Ulster Constabulary, were
armed. Toward the end of the day we announced "closing time." The remainder of the queue would not take
this and immediately rioted angrily. To our amazement
they tried to throw off mooring ropes and set the depot
ship adrift. Violence lay so near the surface even then.
This simply never occurred in docile England.

Narwhal was a beautiful ship, and her crew took an
extraordinary pride in her. When Edward VIII, during

his brief reign, came to inspect her, the sailors worked long after duty hours and even gave up their leave to burnish every fitting. She gleamed almost like a great jewel on the day that England's king, still looking like a fresh-faced youth, came to see her. He had just been on a visit to the Welsh mines and had caused parliamentary criticism by saying, "Something must be done—the conditions are appalling." The sailors adored him. None of us had ever heard of Mrs. Simpson, but the following weekend when I went to London I heard of nothing else, and a few months later the abdication took place. My sailors were downcast—in their eyes he was the golden boy who could do no wrong. The utterances of Mr. Stanley Baldwin and the Archbishop of Canterbury appeased them not at all. "Why shouldn't 'e 'ave any woman—divorced or not—" Middle-class England felt differently.

Soon I left *Narwhal* to attend the qualifying courses for submarine commanding officers. Many first-class men fail to pass these particular tests and go on to command surface ships with brilliance. To attain exactitude with a submarine requires a certain flair which these examinations are intended to reveal. I cannot say that I am glad that I passed. Looking back, I hope impartially, I think I had talent and a certain eye but not the real touch of genius. During the next six years, however, our submarines would be decimated by aircraft and depth charges, whether commanded by geniuses or not. And no virtuoso of a captain could attack with the swift power of German and American captains because British submarines did not possess equipment enabling torpedoes to be fired in all directions. Our submarines all had fixed gyros and they could fire only from a certain position. Maybe my secret lack of conceit in my own ability in this extraordinarily difficult form of attack helped me to bring three submarines through the war. Over-confidence can be lethal, and I tried to make up what I

lacked in attacking brilliance by absolute perfection and
attention to detail. I made the crew work even more
quietly than most. I became known as a cautious captain.
This, I think, gives men more confidence when under
water, rather than the reverse.

Normally, submarine officers reverted to the general
service at certain fixed points in their careers, but
whenever my number came up for this transfer, a new
threat of war had arisen. Experienced officers were then
too few to withdraw from submarines, and so I remained
continuously a submariner.

Anyway, I reached 1945 in the manner related, and by
1968 after many years of happy family life in Ireland I
was back in Plymouth facing the sea again, intent on
absolving some shadow that lurked around me still.

CHAPTER 3

Motivation

SINCE the whole project of sailing around the world depended entirely on my wife's acceptance of the idea, perhaps the real beginning of the story of my lone sailing should begin with our courtship. As I look back, it does indeed seem that the sequence of circumstances which allowed my great personal adventure to materialize started in 1943 in the Lebanon Mountains when lucky chance caused Captain Ruck-Keene to summon me from a somewhat exhausting "inter-submarine rest" in Malta to his submarine flotilla based at Beirut. There it was that I met Anita. How, one might ask, does a submarine CO find a wife on the snow-covered peak of Jebel Sanin in the very middle of the war? That story goes back—link by link right through my naval career. Perhaps it should start not in 1943 but in the summer of 1939 when I got command of my first submarine H.M.S. *Snapper* and found myself serving under the dynamic "Ruckers"—a man who we all knew was determined to prepare proper-ly for war—*if* it came. I had wildly hoped to be allotted to his flotilla, and on the day when *Snapper's* departing CO muttered, "She's all yours, old boy," and I stood for the first time on my own ship, this ambition came true. Already a legend for his outbursts of rage, his realistic concepts, and his original ideas, Ruckers either loved or hated you. He radiated *joie de vivre* and could not hide his fury at those who were not aware of life and danger to life. I think it was because he cared so much for beauty that he grew so angry at the possibility of "muffing it" in war. Because he never bothered to hide his opinions, even of senior officers, he was not always popular. He was the man I'd prayed to get as flotilla commander and now I had him—his vitality and realistic views inspired. We accepted any dressing down from this man because his roars were heartfelt and we knew we deserved them; also, one didn't *forget* a reprimand from Ruckers—it was the experience of a lifetime.

How strange it is to recall those dreamlike months of 1939 in the Mediterranean—the sunlit exercises in the blue sea, the knowledge that war *must* come!

Two submarine disasters stunned the peacetime world that summer, and we took careful note of the tiny errors which had resulted in such heavy loss of life.

Back in England submarine M.2 was sunk while catapulting a seaplane and Ruckers was recalled to investigate the disaster. Eventually it had to be surmised that the captain's order "Blow [tanks] three and four" had been heard as "Open hanger door." This phonetic mistake sent M.2 to the bottom and the Admiralty altered the words of command.

Then we were all talking about the latest T-class submarine, whose prototype *Thetis* was being built at Cammell Laird's at Birkenhead. Great hopes were pinned to this new design and worldwide publicity attended her first trial run in Liverpool Bay. She carried on board for her first dive, not only her own crew of five officers and forty-eight ratings but also nine observer officers, including the flotilla captain and forty-one experts and technicians. This meant that one hundred and three men instead of fifty-three were breathing within her hull. When *Thetis* reached her diving position in the bay, she appeared to have difficulty in getting under, until suddenly she submerged very fast and there was a suspicious splash of air from under the bow. "I don't like the look of it," said an officer in the accompanying tug. *Thetis* never came up again. At low tide her stern projected a few feet above the water, but her forward compartments appeared to have been flooded and she could not rise to the surface. At length four men got out by using the Davis escape apparatus, but they were in a confused state owing to carbon-dioxide poisoning, and in any case little could be done to help direct the baffled rescue teams. Within forty-eight hours, ninety-nine men, all of vital importance to England, had died, and later the toll reached a hundred when a diver passed out on the hull. Exactly what had happened?

A submarine's forward torpedo tube has two apertures, each closed by a movable door: the rear door past which the torpedo is loaded, and the bow cap which is opened for firing. If the bow cap was left open the tube would be flooded, and if the inner door was then opened, the water would be channeled straight into the submarine. To avoid the possibility of this lethal occurrence, a small pencil-sized vent hole existed and we had all done countless hours of torpedo-reloading drill in which the vital safety measure of opening that vent had to be taken to see if water came out of the empty torpedo tube because by some error it had remained open. On *Thetis* the initial error was made. An outer bow cap *was* open, but the test produced a false answer because a small blob of paint had stuck to the inside of the tiny vent hole. No water leaked out. Logically, this was meant to prove the tube empty. The rear door was opened. In gushed the sea and the submarine was flooded in her forward compartments. She sank head down, her bows weighted by tons of water. No radio can transmit under water. Aerials to rise above the surface had not been devised, so the men trapped in the steel hull of *Thetis* had to die without communication with the outside world.

Thetis would, in fact, win unhappy renown as the only British submarine in our era to be sunk twice. Having been salvaged, reconditioned and renamed *Thunderbolt*, she went off to war eighteen months later. Under the brilliant command of young Cecil Crouch she cut a swath of dazzling successes through the enemy before meeting her second death under a rain of depth charges off Sicily. This time she went down like a warrior in battle, mourned, but her fate was expected and accepted. On both occasions I lost close friends.

When, in September, war came, the S-class flotilla lingered on in the Mediterranean—*Snapper, Shark, Sealion,* and *Salmon,* which was commanded by a live wire, Edward Bickford, who was Ruckers' delight and the dread of every mama with a pretty daughter in Alexandria. Then our four submarines returned to England. We reached the misty channel in line abreast to be charged and nearly rammed by a patrol boat—bravely wirelessing "Four U-boats on the service"!

While the flotilla was being formed up, Bickford and I were ordered to Sheerness with orders to patrol the North Sea. It was November, and since the binoculars issued were not too good and were always getting flooded, I sent off to a shop in Bond Street where my family had always purchased theirs for racing!

Can any man forget his first wartime patrol? I was twenty-nine. I had commanded *Snapper* for six months. I hoped to use her swiftly, ambitiously in her own specialized way, and to return with prizes. When at sea a submarine captain hardly sleeps. He lives between the bridge and the chart table and the periscope. He never undresses. He never ceases to be on the alert. Unlike the captains of surface ships, he is not in direct communication with his superiors. He carries sealed orders. Every decision is made by him alone. One had indeed known a very real pride in the honors accorded to the skipper of a submarine when he was piped on board ships in the same way as much older captains of destroyers and cruisers, but alone on the bridge in a murky night setting out into fifteen-day patrol in the North Sea, a terrible isolation had to enfold each of us who were so entirely responsible for our men's lives and our ship's prowess.

On the first patrol, the area allotted to *Snapper* was a *square* off the Dutch coast, lined by the German-mine barriers which barred the way to Heligoland Bight.

I stood on the bridge, battling with the dark, tense with excitement, almost ill with it. I did not know that this was but the beginning of six years of almost ceaseless submarine patrols—of days spent hiding below the water and nights spent perilously taking in air on the surface. The damp fug would be freezing in northern waters and hellishly hot in the tropics while the smell of diesel oil, chlorine, and unwashed bodies remained the same.

But even on this first patrol I knew the tension which links a crew in constant peril with their captain, and the grip of unseen fangs tightened in my spine. When wintry dawn showed, we dived, but it was too rough to keep periscope depth. *Snapper* rolled even when down to sixty feet, where I could not see but could only listen for enemy ships by lowering the bubblelike device which contained the asdic dome. For two weeks the gale never abated and we never saw or heard a ship. "The enemy wouldn't be such a bloody fool as to come out in this—sir!" remarked a lookout. We could not expect to meet the enemy in such weather, but we had to remain out for our allotted time. At least one did not have to fear being spotted while recharging batteries each night; but because a submarine when surfaced remains two-thirds under water and has to be kept beam-on to the wind so as to be able to dive quickly, the violent rolling in bad weather is very hard on the crew. The diesel engines vibrate with incredible din, and this noise and the oil-smell on top of seasickness reduce some men to absolute misery.

Night after night I wedged myself on the bridge, trying to avoid the waves and keep the sextant dry so that if for a second the clouds parted I could get a star-sight to give us a clue to our whereabouts. The days spent dived, when one was supposed to snatch a few hours' sleep, were rendered hellish by fear of squashing the asdic dome on the bottom of the shallow North Sea—only ninety feet in these parts—and eventually this happened. We were almost due to return to England when in what appeared to be a world of frozen pea soup—sky, air, and sea all seeming of the same texture—we actually grounded on a sandbank. There we spent a pretty hour being nearly crashed to pieces and wondering when enemy air patrols might appear! We *did* get off, and after being dive-bombed by one of our own planes, we *did* reach Harwich—not exactly stimulated by all this glorious experience!

But throughout that freezing first winter of the war, while we chugged out on patrol after patrol into the shallow mine-filled North Sea, my own flickering spirits were kept up by three men in our flotilla, by Ruckers, our most understanding flotilla commander who reacted quickly to every emergency, by "Shrimp" Simpson,* his second-in-command who would eventually prove one of the very great war heroes, and by John Illingworth,† who as flotilla engineer officer used his drive and expertise to replace our submarines in piecemeal sections between each patrol so that we did not have to be taken out of action for a refit.

We four young CO's of the S-class were all bubbling with ideas, and we were encouraged to press them forward by Captain Ruck-Keene. Edward Bickford of *Salmon,* Ben Bryant of *Sealion,* and Pete Buckley of *Shark* never felt that what we learned in action and pressed for was ignored by those above us in submarine command.

Apart from being the perfect captain for overstrained

*Rear Admiral G. W. G. Simpson, C.B., C.B.E.
†Captain John Illingworth

men in perpetual danger of a disagreeable kind, Ruckers made us laugh. He was a "card." I seem to remember the stir his unorthodox methods created, when, after being sent to create a self-sufficient submarine base at Harwich, he received notification from the Admiralty Director of Dockyards that no skilled labor was available to man the workshops set up for damaged submarines. *"No manpower available! "* He gave one of his famous roars and a trembling secretary jotted down advertisements for "civilian workers ready for work of national importance." "Which newspapers have the biggest circulation?—Well, get it in." He assumed of course the right to employ whomever he could find. There were one thousand four hundred replies! A hundred and twenty with engineering experience were selected and the list of the others sent on to the Director of Dockyards "just in case you are short of labor." Such epistles did not always make Ruckers popular in high echelons.

He determined that all submariners should get VIP treatment while they were not at sea, and Shrimp devised an ingenious recall method whereby men could be summoned at one hour's notice from local cinemas and bars on an alert.

The gloom of our own heavy losses during fruitless scouring of the North Sea was splendidly shattered when Bickford returned from what the official report described as "a patrol unique in the annals of the submarine branch." He had been ordered to a patrol position about eighty miles west of Jutland, and on December 4, when he had been under water for half an hour, an object resembling a large box came into his periscope's vision. As the submarine crept nearer, engine noises revealed it to be a U-boat on the surface, outward bound.

He fired a spread of torpedoes and saw her blow up but refrained from wirelessing in case the enemy heard and diverted shipping from the area.

Then, a few days later, he sighted a huge ship proceeding southward from Murmansk and recognized the forty-thousand-ton *Bremen* on which he had once crossed the Atlantic as a passenger. So huge a prey, bang in the middle of the periscope sights, represented a submariner's dream, but, although sweating with excitement, he had to refrain from torpedoing her because at that time British submarines were still under orders to sink *warships* only. All that *Salmon* could do was surface and flash the letter X, which is the international signal for Stop. If she went on, he was permitted to open fire with his gun; if she fired back, he could torpedo her. Five times he flashed the letter X. No reply. The tiny submarine then fired a round ahead of the great bows, wildly hoping for the return shot which would permit the torpedoes to leave their tubes. But, at that instant, *Bremen*'s escorting aircraft appeared in the sky. The chance had been forfeited. Bickford had to slam down the hatch and dive. As Winston Churchill would write in *The Gathering Storm*, "*Bremen* reached Germany only because she was spared by the British submarine *Salmon* which observed rightly and punctiliously the conventions of International Law."

"Rightly and punctiliously" are fine words, not all that easy to remember in the strain of battle with huge casualties among one's own friends. Bickie told me afterward, "I nearly died of temptation—I guessed she must be carrying troops and I itched—I literally itched to torpedo her. I'd even traveled on her as a passenger. I knew every line of her. Will such a prize ever come into any of our periscopes again?"

It was hard to forgo that unique opportunity; it took far more self-control and discipline than any dashing attack—and not so long after the Admiralty gave orders that henceforth submarines were to sink all ships except those showing the Red Cross. Consolations came to Bickie, however. Before returning from this extraordinary patrol he had the luck of sighting three German cruisers and diving *Salmon* at full speed; he managed to torpedo the *Leipsig* and the *Nürnberg*. Then he had to dive deep and lie silent on the bottom while half the German Navy circled furiously around dropping depth charges. Twice he heard the hunters pass right over-head, but they did not know it, and although depth charges rocked and clanged around the hull, *Salmon* returned safely to Harwich where a great welcome awaited him from other ships.

Awarded the DSO and—much to his surprise—asked to go to London to lunch with Winston Churchill, First Lord of the Admiralty, on the following Sunday, Bickie found himself in the company of Anthony Eden and other VIP's, all eagerly hanging on his words. England needed a whiff of success in that dark terrifying month of December, 1939, and one little ship had produced the right stuff. Winston always wanted to hear and put to use the experience of front-line fighting—unlike many old dunderheads who clutter the higher command at the start of every war—and Bickie's exploits caught Winston's imagination. The courage, the luck, the for-bearance. So after the meal was over the young man, well-plied with food and drinks of kinds not usually found in the wardroom, was asked to remain behind for a chat. Bickie always recounted a story well, and he was superb on the subject of his afternoon with Winston. "Everyone else was sent away and the great man waved me to an armchair—brandy and cigars were placed nearby and Winston started to ply me with questions." It was understandably a moment at which a young officer might feel himself of enormous importance, and Bickie *was* important—he represented all the dash, the cool courage, and the chivalry of our civilization—but he couldn't tell the story without shaking with laughter. "You can imagine what I felt like—suddenly pulled up out of the squalor of submarine conditions and sat down

alone with Winston—large cigar, brandy and all, to be
pumped with questions for two hours. God, he was so
inquisitive. I told him how keen I was on the wolf-pack
attack, but he wanted to *know what it was like to be on patrol!* I couldn't quite see what he was getting at until
finally he asked me, "Is it a terrible strain? A bad strain?"
I had to answer truthfully, yes, worse, of course, when
you didn't find anything to torpedo, but even after
success it's not very pleasant being depth-charged—I did
tell him one gets tired. Then I went on—perhaps I wish I
hadn't—saying I'd heard the Germans had better submarines and far less pressure on the crews. He asked me
if a double crew for each submarine would make things
easier. It was thoughtless talk really; only I could see the
old man didn't really like us being worked so desperately.
He wanted me to think of a way out. He wanted to save
us."

There was no way out, of course. Our submarines were
sometimes used foolishly, but they *had* to continually go
to sea, and huge losses made the work more intensive for
the trained crews who survived. No one with experience
in submarines could be spared.

Winston was emotional and instinctive. The exploits of
the glamorous Bickie caught his imagination—he *felt* he
could not last long and tried to pull him out of action for
a time—devising some way of using him to teach attack
methods ashore. To the First Sea Lord he sent a
memorandum suggesting that *Salmon* be used for a time
as an extra practice submarine "after the severe and
distinguished service she had rendered. There would be
advantages in having Commander Bickford in the plans
division of the Admiralty for, say, six months in order to
bring them in close and direct contact with the very latest
conditions prevailing in Heligoland Bight. This officer
seems to me very able, and he had many things to say
about anti-U-boat warfare which, I trust, will be gathered
at the earliest opportunity."

But the submarine branch was desperately short-handed. No CO could be spared.

In January we lost three submarines in quick succession off Heligoland Bight, and in February *Salmon* did not return from patrol. Winston, uneasy that Bickford could not be given the "rest" he desired for him, had insisted that he and his men have their decorations presented to them "before they sail again." So they had their medals before they died.

CHAPTER 4

Bitter Battles

THE first winter of the war was unusually cold. When we were at sea, the spray turned us into crackling icicles moving stiffly on the bridge while the watch below lived in wet woolens, impossible to dry. I never undressed during the two or three weeks of a patrol. When I lay down in my bunk, I removed only my oilskin coat. My seaboots and oilskin trousers I kept on so that an instantaneous leap up to the hatch could be made in emergency. The captain of a submarine must be alert all the time, even in sleep.

From Harwich one could walk over the frozen marshes to shoot at starving wild fowl; one got fresh air and exercise, but I never really cared for shooting birds—I just liked walking. Ruckers longed for mountains to climb; he did not like destroying. Once in China he had shot a wild goose, and its mate came swooping out of the sky, calling to it again and again. He had terribly desired to give back its life, but that no man can do.

More pertinent to our needs than the diversion of "sport" or the desire to be *alone* for a few hours was the immediate overwhelming craving for women. There can be no contrast more perfectly balancing in a submariner's mind than the possession of a woman's body after the long torturous web of fear and hope in the hull of a haunted submarine. When I handed in my report after each patrol, to a certain extent I was tired of making decisions, but here was a decision that made itself. The beam which led one to London and forgetfulness did not need thought: one's feet walked, one's car sped, or the train ticket grew in one's hand—which led us all to relaxations of an intensity that one could only hope would allow one to totter back clear-minded for the next patrol. It was not a time for domesticity, and I pitied the officers who had young wives waiting for them around Harwich. It hurt *me* to look at their peaked, nervous faces, their haunted, frightened eyes; I heard sometimes the overshrill tones of welcome, never the soft good-byes. It was Ruck-Keene who had to break the news and answer questions when a submarine was overdue. How lucky I was not to have thought of marrying. I did not know love, nor did I want to. It could only have been a distraction from my job and a pain at every departure.

When spring came and the Norwegian campaign broke, submarines began to work full out on three to four week patrols at greater distances from base.

The German U-boats were now consistently disregarding the International Law forbidding the sinking of merchant ships, and thousands of tons of British merchantmen were being torpedoed in the Atlantic (Germany very nearly won the war this way). It was a relief when our Admiralty issued the order which allowed us to act in like manner.

A friend of mine, Jackie Slaughter, who commanded the submarine *Sunfish*, happened to be using an enemy merchant ship for practicing attack when the signal (for which Bickford had longed) came through. He remained glued to the periscope, running through the usual sequence of orders which would end without releasing torpedoes, when the radio officer whispered in his ear that a new Admiralty ruling was coming through—he would give it word by word as decoded. Jackie continued the dummy attack while the words were

read out to him one by one. "Sink all ships at sight in the
Skagerrak and Kattegat." The tubes were at the ready as
the message ended.

"Stand by," shouted Jackie. "Fire."

The practice attack had turned into a real one during
the full hour in which he never took his eyes from his
periscope. Within twenty minutes of an order radioed in
Whitehall, a German troopship blew up in the North
Sea!

I was at this time in Skagerrak. It was *Snapper*'s sixth
patrol, and I remember the calm gray sea blanketed in
fog that morning of April 10. Then the mists lifted and
Snapper traveled beneath the surface feeling terribly
vulnerable in that clear water. As the sun rose, I saw with
amazement that the sky was black with aircraft flying in
thick streams northward. Obviously they were supporting some extraordinary effort ashore. This was my first
inkling of the German campaign in Norway.

A large white Dornier flying boat, quartered by low-
flying Heinkel seaplanes, was covering the sea in search
of submarines. In the crystal-clear waters of the Norway
Deep I knew we could be seen moving as a dark shadow
down to ninety feet. It was most uncomfortable, but the
Junkers that attacked us had only surface impact bombs.
We had to remain deep-dived all through the first days
of the Norwegian invasion, but the new order gave us
incentive. Our orders were to attack capital ships, troop
transports, tankers, cruisers, and finally merchant ships
in that order; any attack would be broken off if a U-boat
came into one's periscope sights—to sink a U-boat was
the most important task of all, for at this stage every
German U-boat was sinking an average of nineteen ships
in the Atlantic before being itself destroyed. England
would die if her lifelines were completely cut.

Between April 10 and April 15 we sank five ships, but
the only submarine we saw was my old friend *Narwhal*
who would herself soon be sunk.

We were just south of Oslo when a small German tanker came into the periscope. We fired two torpedoes, but in the mirage-forming calm of that clear dawn I made a visual error and the torpedoes passed ahead and astern of her. She was nearer than I had estimated. Not wanting to expend more precious torpedoes on an only moderately important target, I decided to surface and signal the crew to abandon ship while we sank her by gunfire. She started, zig-zagged, and ran away. We gave chase and eventually halted her by a shot across the bows, but despite our order the crew made no attempt to take to the boats. Time was getting on, the dawn air patrols would soon be combing the sea, so there was nothing for it but to shoot a round from our three-inch gun into her forepeak. Up went a sheet of flame—she was carrying aviation petrol and it had been madness not to obey my shouted instruction. Figures now raced over the burning deck and hurled themselves into the icy-blue water which had just thawed and poured down from the frozen Baltic. As they swam toward us, I hesitated between desire to rescue and fear of endangering my ship by remaining a moment longer than necessary on the surface. A ship had appeared on the horizon, but I reckoned there was just time to pull the survivors aboard. Two men dragged them over the saddletank and lowerd them shaking with exhaustion and cold down the forehatch. I didn't like keeping my men out there twenty feet below the conning tower, a dangerous place in case of an emergency dive. They had the last sodden body on the casing when the first enemy plane appeared. "Clear the foredeck and dive," I ordered, but my third officer Geoffrey Carew Hunt begged me to let him drag this last man down the steep cluttered forehatch and shut it. I let him do it. It took perhaps fifteen seconds, but fifteen seconds count in the life of a submarine. Later I reprimanded myself.

Down we gurgled into the horribly clear sea, eager to steal away from the burning ship which must attract

attention for miles around. We were aware of many ships
making for that column of smoke and probably wondering how the crew had entirely disappeared. Now we were
to be hunted all through the daylight hours. Planes,
ships, torpedo boats, were looking for us. I remained at
the periscope, oblivious of the tender care which was
being lavished on the men we had pulled from the sea. It
was good for my crew to have something to take their
minds off the danger we were in. When dark fell and I
took a look at the prisoners, two had died from the shock
of their ten-minute immersion in icy waters, but four lay
huddled in dry blankets with mugs of hot tea in their
hands, being petted and pampered. The captain, a nice
old German, explained that he had thought we were a
Swedish submarine, which explained why he'd ignored
our signals. Our gun layer sewed up the dead in
hammocks, and I read out the burial service—or, rather,
I made as if reading it while inventing my own more
cheerful version. Then one of the younger survivors
jumped up and gave a short Nazi oration in German
while my men, who could not understand a word,
listened respectfully. It was all rather odd at ninety feet
below the waves. After dark we surfaced and dragged
the bodies up through the conning tower and hove them
overboard.

A new rather distressing order arrived—we were to
break the usual radio silence by reporting all enemy
vessels. This seemed terrifyingly revealing of our
presence, but now such was radio activity over the area
that the enemy could have imagined they were in a
hornets' nest. Our calls became impossible to trace in the
general buzzing.

Pushing on southward into the Kattegat, we found the
whole sea swarming with minesweepers and anti-
submarine craft. The mirrorlike calm continued and we
could but glide silently below the surface. Every hour of

light had to be spent at the periscope. I had been a long-distance runner, but my thigh muscles began to ache from ceaseless knee bends. When at the periscope, one pushes one's face against the eyepieces and rotates the brass tube with both hands, but the cylinder itself has to be constantly raised and lowered by hydraulic power to follow small changes in the submarine's depth and to heed the technical requirements of keeping the periscope's tip above the water. When the sea is calm, only the minimum tip of a few inches should show, and when we are attacking from close range the smallest possible slick should show.

It was about two in the morning and we were on the surface inhaling air for our battery charge when a fast ship appeared steering south. We chased after her at full speed but could not catch her. I let off one precious torpedo in her wake, turned north, and went below for a quick look at the chart. It was quicker than I expected. An alarm from the bridge brought me sprinting back into the night. As I climbed the conning tower ladder, the officer of the watch was pressing the diving hooter and I fought my way past the four bridge lookouts cascading down the hatch. As the water lapped up, I remained for a few seconds transfixed by the un-believable sight of two German destroyers, one on each side of us, encased in huge white bow waves; they were tearing along southward at high speed, so near that they could not try to ram us without ramming each other! Their captains must have been gnashing their teeth—a British submarine caught on the surface, slipping between them and nothing they could do! It could only happen once in a lifetime. "We're diving, sir, depth twenty-five feet, sir" came agonized shouts from below. I slipped back, slamming the hatch over my head as the sea slopped over. Perhaps I had enjoyed that astonishing spectacle a second too long.

The officer of the watch wrote in the log, "Surprised by two German destroyers." Later I read this and changed it to "*Very* surprised." But now came four long grim hours. We dropped to one hundred twenty feet which I was beginning to regard as the best depth for fleeing danger. If a submarine went deeper, the increasing noise of ballast pumps revealed her position. Finally, in the dawn, our hunters touched off the explosive sweep they were towing overhead and left us to a crowd of searching trawlers. I lay down to sleep—it had been a busy night and my crew was also weary. They called me late—late, that is, by about three minutes—on sighting a convoy of troop transports making for Norway, and I doubted if we were going to be able to steady up and loose off a salvo. My calculations had to be made in a flash: "Blow up all tubes. . . Stand by . . . Fire!" One bow cap jammed, so only five torpedoes left the tubes. But a tremendous explosion sounded at the correct interval. We had hit a ship.

Now again came hours of hanging silently in the depths, speaking in whispers, trying not to move, not to drop a spanner, not to notice the showers of depth charges reaching nearer and nearer. *Kerdowang* . . . *KerdoWANG* . . . they exploded in the water outside our hull, hammering our steel skin. Hot. Cold. Hot again. We waited, silent, wondering how the pressure hull could stand up to such sledgehammer blows. Day passed into night. We surfaced to charge our batteries and remained there until the faint gray of dawn lit up the sky. I was standing on the bridge with Geoffrey Carew-Hunt and it was nearly time to dive when one of the lookouts spoke. "Object bearing red five oh."

A dim shape showed on the sea a mile away. We would not dive. I stood on the bridge, binoculars glued to my eyes, seeking to identify the ship in that gray hull-light, while a stream of orders traveled down the voice pipe to the helmsman and messengers on duty who would transmit them by telephone and alarm-rattler through the submarine.

"Night alarm."

"Stand by all torpedo tubes."

"Slow both engines." (We were close.)

"Steer two hundred and sixty degrees."

The alarm-rattler sent men rolling out of their bunks, wide awake, ready for action, for the electric tension of a submarine attack galvanizes every nerve in a human. In swift, disciplined frenzy they reached their posts.

We always kept the tube bowcap open when on the surface so that they were ready to fire at immediate notice. Within sixty seconds of sighting this ship, *Snapper* was ready to strike.

From the bridge I then saw other darkened ships and realized we had run into a big convoy bound for Norway. There were escort ships all around us. My first instinct was to dive and attack from periscope depth according to the rules, but this would take thirty seconds and we were bound to be seen. I resolved to face the ships and attack directly. I ordered the lookouts to go below in case we came under close-range gunfire. Geoffrey and I remained alone on the bridge. There was no time to estimate the correct angle to fire, but I remembered an old rough rule and used it. *If the enemy ship is going slow, give nine degrees of lead which approximates the width of the human fist at full arm's length. If the ship is going fast, use two fists.*

In the mist the convoy had to be going slow. I steadied myself on the bridge, held out my arm extended over *Snapper's* bow, and used my knuckles as a gunsight. "Firing interval seven seconds." As the bows of the nearest ship came in line with my fist, I shouted *"Fire"* down the voice pipe.

We had only four torpedoes left, but as the forms of

other ships appeared in the mist, I used the same tech-
nique and shouted new helm orders intended to spray
the salvo.

Now for a few seconds the officer of the watch and I
stood alone on the bridge longing to see where the foam-
ing torpedo tracks led. But already the convoy's escort
vessels were tearing angrily toward us. There was a first
hit. A huge column of water shot up from our leading
target. "Dive! Dive! Dive!" I shouted down the voice-
pipe, and we both slid at lightning speed down the hatch.
Just as I clipped the hatch shut over my head and the sea
bubbled over us, there was a second thump which shook
the submarine. Two hits. As I reached the bottom of the
ladder into the control room, there was a third thump.
Seven seconds later at the correct torpedo running time
came a fourth. I looked at my hand almost in
surprise—that old adage had given us astonishing accuracy. Four knuckles. Four hits.

Now for the chase.

For an hour or more the escorts hunted us frantically,
racing about dropping depth charges, but I imagined
that there was great confusion on the surface and that
they were probably rescuing survivors.

We lay quietly at one hundred and twenty feet, listening to the clicks and explosions in the water around us.
By seven A.M. our hunters gave it up and we rose to
periscope depth for a quick look. As thick morning mists
still curled over the sea, I reckoned we could risk the
danger of springing to the surface to radio a report of the
convoy to other submarines that might be able to attack
it.

Then we sped away, keeping on the surface where we
could do thirteen knots (instead of the nine, which was
top speed when dived). I wanted to get as far as possible
from the spot where we had broken radio silence, for the
enemy would, of course, have heard my message and
would be able to pinpoint the position in which I had

made it. My keenness to get other submarines on the convoy's track resulted in a fleet of expert chasers setting out to track us and I soon regretted having taken the risk. All day long depth charges roared around us, clicking and exploding. *Snapper* rocked in the impact, and it seemed impossible that her steel hull should not cave in. Hour after hour we remained silent or whispering necessary orders. I knew how unnatural this agonizing suspense must seem to the ordinary sailors who were my crew; they had to wait motionless for death—there was no way of occupying them. And then my eyes lit on the four German prisoners we had plucked from the water; I had forgotten their existence, but in the long tense waiting their expressions suddenly intrigued me. Death had narrowly passed them by; now they sat wide-eyed and motionless, wondering if they were ever going to enjoy the pleasures of an English prison camp.

We made it.

At dusk the depth charges died away and we rose to the surface. E\ery man in the submarine was exhausted. Our twelve tcrpedoes were spent. It was time for the fastest run possible for home, and this meant keeping on the surface. Once only some enemy aircraft came into sight and we promptly dived, but explosions and excessive fatigue had numbed the crew and a stoker left the wrong valve open, ruining the trim so that *Snapper* crashed down too heavy for the density of water. We hit the shallow bottom, but we did not stick and I realized that had we been in deeper waters we would have descended until pressure crushed in our sides. There is no room for anyone to make a mistake in a submarine—the slightest inaccuracy spells disaster.

By the time we reached Harwich our successes were confirmable—a tanker sunk by gunfire and five ships by torpedo.

As *Snapper* entered Harwich, I stood, as always, on the bridge to con the submarine alongside and salute our awaiting depot ship. My crew stood at ease on the casing fore and aft, and I longed to overhear a few of their remarks as the long green shore grew near. We were awaited. Blue lines of sailors covered the deck of every ship in harbor, and suddenly all their caps came off and *Snapper* trembled a little as they gave her a "cheer ship."

CHAPTER 5

Desperate Odds

THE Germans now held Norway. Only spy-work by periscope around the shores could give advance warning of a possible invasion of England. May, June, July we patrolled in seas of glassy calm where a telltale feather showed the moment a tip broke surface. No submarine could be allowed more than a few days of rest between patrols. We worked in almost perpetual day-light—eighteen hours at a time I would remain almost ceaselessly glued to the big periscope, popping it up and down in quick flashes, trying to take in the whole seascape. Then we would run blind for perhaps five minutes with periscope lowered.

The psychic accord that exists between a submarine commander and the leading mechanics who work the periscope levers, responding to his hand and voice with delicacy, became brilliantly sensitive. If one sighted a ship nearer than three miles, it meant changing to the small periscope and trying for even quicker looks at close quarters.

In these conditions, we knew our dark steel hull showed like a shark in its depth of clear-blue glass and even two inches of small tip made a visible feather.

We had one extraordinary uneventful patrol which had a somewhat Alice in Wonderland quality. I had returned from a few hectic days in London to find the depot ship had departed to a new base near Edinburgh with all my uniforms on board. I had to board my sub-marine and drive her out of Harwich wearing my pinstripe town suit and take to old overalls for the next three weeks! Then we discovered that in the emergency *Snapper* had been revictualed with one kind of tinned food only. We ate the same soaplike meat for breakfast, lunch, and supper throughout the whole patrol. And we never sighted a ship, never had to hide from a plane. The seas and skies had grown suddenly empty. We returned to England to learn that our armies were on the Dunkirk beaches.

France fell. This inconvenienced us submariners by causing complete curtailment of shore night leave for the rest of the summer. We had to bring our ladies up from London and park them in hotels. I fear that I did not appreciate being kept on a split yarn in case of invasion, and I organized a method whereby I could leap from my bed, tumble into my sports car, and by driving at eighty mph reach the depot ship in six minutes. Unfortunately, the junior officers copied me, and their cars were not quite as fast.

Toward midsummer a sudden order sent us out to patrol the Norway coast, and my navigating officer failed to reach *Snapper* in time. *None* of us had been supposed to sleep ashore, and I realized what a bad example I had set. Geoffrey Carew Hunt, our torpedo officer, had to take his place and I saw him frantically searching through drawers for the right charts as I climbed up onto the bridge to con the submarine down the Firth of Forth.

Patrol work in the northern seas became a nightmare for submarines when the long white nights allowed us no respite in which to surface and charge our batteries. Now we had to keep submerged eighteen hours out of the twenty-four and then desperately try to recharge in between our patrols. At the end of these eighteen-hour dives air became so deficient in oxygen that our breath came in heavy gasps.

On June 24 we reached Skudeness fiord, and that afternoon the officer of the watch, sweating at the periscope, reported "Masts appearing from the fiord." A cold chill struck me because I thought this meant our end. My secret orders were that if we sighted invasion ships, we were to surface and radio the news, which meant virtual suicide. I took over the periscope and, with relief identified only four ships escorted by a trawler and three aircraft. It was no invasion force, just a group of ships to attack in the usual way. We fired three torpedoes at the largest ship and heard two terrific bangs. The other ships turned; we let off three more torpedoes only to hear them fall to the sea bottom—duds. The frustration was galling, although we were certain of the earlier hits.

On June 29, when we were on the surface in the half-light of the arctic midnight, we heard without warning the roar of attacking aircraft, and bombs crashed on our track as we dived. I realized that, in this silver twilight, planes could look down from on high and see us on the sea when we could not see them. We felt trapped. There was nothing for it but to change tactics and spend the day constantly surfacing and diving, trying to charge the batteries each time an air patrol had just gone over. On one occasion a lookout thought he saw two seabirds emerge from a cloud. Within seconds they turned into Messerschmitt 109's and a hail of bullets pattered on the hull as we dived.

The officer of the watch spends four hours on the bridge; the four lookouts, to keep their eyes fresh, do one-hour tricks. One day as we lay on the surface inhaling our lifeblood, oxygen for our lungs and power for the battery, a lookout called, "Periscope close to the starboard beam." I was below, but my standing orders were that in the event of sighting another submarine, *Snapper* would turn to ram. However, in this case the periscope appeared to be inside our turning circle and the diving hooters squalled their vibrant note as I dashed to the control room. I found it hard to accept the description of a periscope and wondered if the over-strained lookout might not have misjudged a floating stick. But he was right. As we got a trim, the asdic operator reported, "Loud engine noises," and a torpedo passed us and exploded in the distance.

A U-boat had been stalking us as we gulped in air and it had fired as we started to submerge.

Now it was that rare combat—submarine against submarine. Grimly we circled roundeach other like two great steel sharks, each trying to ascertain the moment when the other might turn broadside on and present a target. *Snapper* could only fire from her nose, so to speak. As we picked up the soft noises of underwater propellers, I turned *Snapper* end on to the other submarine and started tracking her. The weep-weep noise remained steady. I knew she was either bows on to us or she was stern to us and could be followed. When the asdic gave her range, we knew we were nose to tail. She had become the quarry and we the hunter. I kept the periscope up. If we got a glimpse of her we would be at the same depth, and I intended to fire our forward torpedoes, although the end-on target was narrow. Weep weep, weepity-weep. She was running from us. Even with the new German angled-torpedoes she could not fire backward. We had a chance. But, after two hours of this strange underwater pursuit, we lost her. I think she went deep.

Now the sea appeared oddly empty of big ships, although plenty of trawlers were combing our area. I reckoned the enemy knew we were there and were routing their convoys elsewhere, so I pushed seaward to investigate and found my guess to be right. Through the periscope I saw a dozen supply ships escorted by the same number of trawlers (*our* convoys had one escort to every thirty ships!). They were trying leap-frog tactics. Half the trawlers would steam ahead and then stop to listen with hydrophones while the others caught up with the convoy carefully surrounded. These boys were very nervous indeed about submarines.

I decided to wait until they looked bunched, then maneuver slowly inside the screen on to their quarter, where, at a certain moment, they might present a continuous target.

We crept cautiously inside the screen and then fired a full salvo of six torpedoes into the "brown" of them while swinging toward their bows. Three crashing explosions sounded at the end of our torpedoes' running time.

Now the escorts milled around, listening with hydrophones and dropping dozens of depth charges. Trawlers are slow compared with specialized antisubmarine craft. I decided to stay at periscope depth and dodge them by visual contact. While I was bobbing the periscope up and down, my crew had to remain silent at their posts, listening to the depth-charges clicking and exploding in the water around. *Snapper* withstood blow after blow as the shock waves clanged against the pressure hull. One wondered how long she could take it.

We spiraled downward when a flying boat bombed us, but then our ballast pump gave us away—its noise increases as a submarine goes deeper.

Then the attack ceased. I did not know until we had returned to base that Ben Bryant in *Sealion* had passed nearby and drawn off attention. We sat discussing the possibility of hunting in packs as Bickie had always wanted. But by now three-quarters of our flotilla had been sunk. We were told that so few of us remained that we could not cover the vital areas even when spread out singly.

About our greatest lack was any kind of snorkel. Before the war in Alexandria a Dutch submarine had shown me their invention . . . a tube which could be pushed up some thirty feet, *e.g.*, to around periscope depth, which was thirty-two feet, and through it the diesel engine could automatically draw in fresh air while expelling used air. This meant it was not always necessary to surface in order to charge the batteries and obtain enough oxygen to keep the crew alive.

(After the war the inventor wrote and told me how the idea first struck him. He was watching a herd of elephants crossing a river, which was out of their depth. They simply raised their trunks and breathed.)

I had described this gadget to senior officers at the Admiralty but failed to evoke interest. In point of fact, the German submarines had not thought of it at the time, but when they overran Holland and captured a Dutch submarine, they immediately saw the vital importance of this apparatus . . . so simple and so obvious to the ordinary submariner. Within a few months, all German U-boats were fitted with snorkels in the form of strong metal tubes which could be raised above the surface to draw in air. As a result, many German crews are alive today, and because the British refused to make any attempt to fit such a gadget, many British crews went to the bottom of the sea.

Eight months before, I had been the most junior lieutenant in command. Now, owing to losses, I found myself senior submarine officer in the flotilla. It was not a seniority I enjoyed.

Unknown to the crew, submarine captains now carried a large box of gold coins on board. If England was actually conquered, our orders were to refuel in Sweden and cross the Atlantic to continue the fight from Canada.

In the meantime we continued to operate from Rosyth, six miles from Edinburgh. I hoped my men got a good run ashore each time we returned for ten days' rest, but my sole effort to arrange decent living quarters for them resulted in a fiasco—one sailor got the landlady's daughter into trouble and another had to be disentangled from a singer too expensive for his pocket. There was a stalwart bridge telegraphist whose comments in a resounded West Country accent always amused me. I can remember returning from one horrible patrol that had been rendered a nightmare by the clear silver moonlight. We were a fairly exhausted, haggard-looking lot; none of us had been out of our clothes for three weeks and I was having to watch the men for signs of overstrain which might result in hallucinatory errors (I also had to watch myself). I could hardly focus my own mind. Once my report was in I intended to make for my cabin in the depot ship and sleep for many hours. But every man aboard was visualizing shore leave in his own way. As *Snapper* slid home up the lovely Firth of Forth, this sailor stood behind me on the bridge working the engine-room telegraphs and I heard him soliloquizing in his dialect, "Well, here *I* go ashore for a nice *invigorating* fornication."

July passed. August came. As the precious hours of dusk grew longer, we returned to surfacing at night and lying deep-dived by day. We grew cunning with experience, but so did our adversaries.

My tenth patrol in *Snapper* took us into a world of fantastic loveliness. We were ordered north of the Orkney Islands to waylay U-boats on their return from Atlantic forays.

Night after night the sky flamed into unbelievable beauty; the northern lights flamed and trembled for one bewitched little submarine tossing alone in the northern sea. I had decided to spend nights listening with the asdic on the surface, and the bridge lookouts stared dumbfounded at the splendor of that unearthly shimmering sky and could scarce attend to their job of concentrating on the enemy.

We only once heard sounds of a propeller, and this passed at such speed we could not possibly have caught her. Little did we dream that the new German submarines could travel at nineteen knots against our twelve and this must have been a U-boat.

This was my last patrol in *Snapper*. In the following winter she went for a refit and I became ill just before her return to the fray. A charming young man, Lieutenant Jimmy Prowse, took her to sea. It was his first patrol, and terrible storms blew at the time. *Snapper* did not return from patrol. We never knew what had happened.

CHAPTER 6

Mountain Courtship

WELL, that was the story of *Snapper* and it takes me a little way in explaining why, years later, I wanted to sail around the world alone. What happened next? I got another submarine—*Trusty*—and spent a year in her, having a few battles in the Mediterranean on our way out to the Far East. Ordered to Singapore in the guise of "naval reinforcements," I arrived a week before its fall and found the whole prospect unedifying. Given orders, *Trusty* made her way to Surabaja and then, leaking oil, returned crestfallen to Columbo. I was now covered with prickly heat and in a state described by the naval doctors as "run down like a clock." Sent back to England, I had a month's leave, and then because *no one* with submarine experience could be spared, they sent me out to Malta as officer in charge of operations, as a "rest."

This was the early spring of 1943. Malta was under siege and the submarine flotilla had for nearly two years been operating from its incessantly bombed base under the indomitable Captain "Shrimp" Simpson (who had been with us in Harwich). Admiral Sir Andrew Cunningham, C in C Mediterranean, had, when originally posting Shrimp to this most vital little island given him the directive, "If you don't get results and don't dispose your forces to suit me, I will soon let you know. Until then, you have a free hand to act as you think fit to achieve results." Shrimp achieved results as no other man could have.

When my plane touched down at Malta's airstrip, it

was like landing on an overused battlefield. I did not
know that the enemy finally had his chance of capturing
the island and that my aircraft carried the orders for
TORCH, the invasion of North Africa.

I drove to Manoel Island where Shrimp awaited me.
The jetties had received terrible pounding, and all sleeping accommodation was arranged in underground
shelters cut into the rock. They were very damp. The
sight of Shrimp, who had endured the hell of operational
responsibility in this vital rocky little fortress for nearly
two years, gave me an extraordinary emotion—how
could that man keep his zest and humor while raid after
raid of German bombers smashed up the island and his
submarines had to be sent out over and over again on
suicidal patrols? He gave me my orders and off I went in
a dghaisa, the local rowing boat, across the bay to naval
headquarters, a medieval flat-roofed building of honey-
colored stone giving a certain amount of protection from
bombers.

Fuel was desperately short in Malta; in the course of
one's duties one walked or hired rowboats. Food was also
extremely short; we finished our scarce meals with the
pain of hunger unassuaged.

I bedded down in my office in the old stone building,
making it my living quarters day and night for the next
two months while submarine patrols rose to a crescendo.
For a time we had to operate the new flotilla based in
Algiers as well as our own ships. I soon realized how
unfitted I was for a staff job. I was created to get inside a
submarine and fight it, not to send others out on patrol.
Crouching over the chart table, I got a sort of "fibrositis"
which prevented me from standing up properly.
Ruckers, who was the administrative commanding
officer in the Mediterranean, heard of my plight. He
didn't believe in fibrositis—"Rot—go bring him to
me—he's in the wrong job!"

I had worked eight weeks in the operations room. It

was enough. I determined to get through all medical tests and command another submarine.

Just before my orders came to leave Malta, the submarine depot ship, *Medway*, was sunk by a U-boat as she left Alexandria Harbor. The crew swam to safety, and Ruckers was pulled out of the sea, making a few choice remarks, for he was sad at losing his favorite Chinese porcelain goddess which he'd kept in his cabin. According to legend, he stood dripping on the deck of the rescuing destroyer and barked, "Beirut—I'll get my next base in Beirut near those wonderful mountains."

And so it was that the Second Submarine Flotilla arrived in Beirut, and I came back into the beneficent control of my former commanding officer.

To my delight, I found that I was to mess in the large peaceful house allotted to Ruckers. It stood in the flowering outskirts of the glamorous old port, and "glamorous" is the only adjective to describe Beirut during the war. After Malta, it was like stepping into a musical comedy setting into which uniforms had been poured to mingle with pretty women against the old historical background.

Ruckers welcomed me. "Just a little intelligence work for you and then plenty of skiing—nothing like exercise in the mountains. Don't worry, old boy, a few months of this, and then as you're set on it, a new submarine."

I perked up at the sight of a hall full of skis, ski-boots, and knapsacks, but before I could get going, I found myself dispatched to Cairo for that "little bit of intelligence work." This consisted of consorting with a group of toughs—nationalities unmentioned—names false—who were to waylay a German U-boat expected to land arms for an Arab rising in Syria. After so many years of operational action, I felt myself transported into an unbelievable thriller. No real people, I told myself, *could* behave like this!

Briefly, the plan was to meet this German submarine with a disguised fishing boat carrying a false keel of high explosives, which would be transferred by a limpet attachment to the hull of the U-boat.

The first boat, built in Beirut, shook to pieces in the lorry on its way down to Egypt. The second boat reached its secret base, which was a British "intelligence camp" where the anonymous commando chaps were waiting to be instructed, and the inmates had nothing whatever to do except haul my "secret boat" in and out of the water and consume alcohol. They were good at both. At intervals I had to fly back to Beirut to report on the general progress, and on one occasion bad weather grounded the plane at Jerusalem.

The high-ranking officers aboard sent their ADC's off to arrange transport, but I was merely a lieutenant commander. Eventually I was latched on to a French general who whistled up a car to take him on to Beirut. Dark fell as we bounced off toward the main coast road. The general and his ADC never stopped talking, and I fell asleep for an hour or so. When I woke and glanced out, I saw that we were driving *south*, back across the Sinai Desert! *"Mon général,"* I yelped in creaky French, "we are pointing *away* from our destination." *"Pas possible."* But we drew to a halt and all got out and stood staring around the empty landscape. *"Mais regardez!"* I pointed at the North Star constellation in the sky behind us. Three faces regarded me blankly. "But there was a signpost miles back that said. . . ." "I don't care what any signpost said—it's what the stars say. *Les étoiles disent. Non, c'est* là *il faut aller!"*

Half-convinced, the general ordered us back into the car, and his driver reversed the car indignantly. It was quite a long time before we sighted a village which confirmed my directions. Everything on earth can let you down, but not the stars, not the bright stars of heaven. And if one can but believe it, one's own star remains firm as long as one can steel the mind to follow the far-directing light which is for each man alone. So watch the stars above and not the stars on a general's epaulets.

The U-boat for which we were waiting never turned up. Either our intelligence had got the whisper wrong, or the enemy suspected interception. With relief I returned to Ruckers' house and started to join in his mountain campaign. He had superbly clear-cut ideas on how to "reconstitute" submariners. They had to fight deep down in the dark ocean and to suffer from lack of air, so he transported them on every possible occasion to the mountaintops of Lebanon, which provided the opposite conditions. Now as flotilla commander, he had these magnificent quarters and a fleet of cars allotted to him, and apart from his duties (always nerve-searing) of briefing operational skippers and sending submarines out on patrol, he could find time for the organization of frequent *all-night* skiing excursions! The hours of darkness were chosen not for reasons of debauchery but because in springtime the sun is so hot that it turns the deep snow of the Lebanon peaks to slush soon after dawn.

To reach the fantastic crisp snow, lit only by moonlight or starlight, necessitated unusual mealtimes, but Ruckers' naval stewards' cooks were quickly organized into new routines. Whenever a free twenty-four hours occurred, a party of exuberant submariners would arrive around five P.M. and be ordered straight to bed. Breakfast had to be served at ten P.M., and then came the "treat" which Ruckers reckoned would blow oxygen into their depleted systems. Stuffed with bacon and eggs, the sleepy mob would pile into several cars and drive off into the Bekaa Valley which stretched between the Lebanon Mountains and Syria. The local drivers (bleary-eyed but amused at British naval tactics ashore) would zigzag up to some village near the snowline. By midnight we would be trudging up the mountainside, skis on our shoulders; then as white diamonds started to crunch beneath our boots, we would don skis, strap on nonslip skins and start to climb into the looming whiteness. For two or three hours, hypnotized by the steady sliding of our skis as the seal-fur gripped the hard-frozen silver surface, we would mount ever higher. Every figure showed the hump of a knapsack crammed with spare sweaters, tins of sardines, sandwiches—every figure, that is, except one. Anita, the only girl in the party, carried no knapsack and looked different because she always wore a blue handkerchief tied around her head. How had she joined us? It was Ruckers, of course, who found her. One of the few girls who had worked as an ambulance driver in Egypt, she had reached Beirut to be placed in charge of the only English troops' newspaper, called *The Eastern Times*. It seemed quite easy to get her single sheet off to press in the afternoon and to ski all night.

To tell the truth, I was so worn out by submarining and so dazzled by the incredible beauties of dawn on that mountain range that for quite a time I took this girl for granted.

Our longest trek over the ten-thousand-foot summit of Jebel Sanin entailed twelve hours of climbing and skiing. We put on our skis at ten at night under the stars and took them off at ten next morning in the blazing sunshine just above orange blossom groves on the other side of the range. It was an expedition of incredible loveliness made at a slow steady pace. Soon after midnight when a huge copper-colored moon was beginning to set over the Mediterranean far below, and a faint dawn was lighting the eastern sky over the mountains that hide Damascus, we paused for a meal. It was cold but not icy on the mountaintop and we sat sideways on the hard snow without removing our skis. So bright was the moonlight that Ruckers could read his map by it. Then he gazed carefully at Anita, assessing her strength. Tall, thin, and frail—not at all the right build for a mountaineer—she was gulping down sardines with the rest. If she was not up to the final pull over the wide rounded white summit, there was a quicker, less spectacular way down a steep valley. "If she is not up to the summit, someone must accompany her down there." I stared somewhat apprehensively at a narrow ravine strewn with boulders, and hoped not to get the job. But when Anita announced that she was good for another five or six hours and we all skied slowly off together over the wide white summit of Jebel Sanin, I suddenly felt a little sorry that she did not need help—and puzzled at myself for so feeling. At this moment I did not realize that on a mountaintop in Lebanon, with a great moon sinking into the violet haze of the Mediterranean Sea to the west and the sun coming up over Syria to the east, the path of my life which would lead to Cape Horn was fixed.

On that morning, however, as we slid ever more carefully down the rapidly softening snow glistening in the sunlight to reach the highest valley, unfasten our skis, and march with the dawn to the flowering orange groves of the lower slopes on the other side of the range, I did not really think that I had any future at all. In fact, I suspected that my personal path on earth might end quite soon. The casualty rate of submariners being what it was, I could hardly allow myself the thought of a continuing relationship, let alone marriage, with Anita, despite the fact my heart had fallen. All I wanted was to get well and strong, fit to take command of another submarine. Ruckers knew this and desired to see me back in the right place. "I hate this bloody war. Let's finish it," he would say. "Let's finish it and get down to worthwhile things—like wood carving, that's all I want—a workshop with lots of tools." And angrily he would stomp off to give his submarine captains patrol orders, to pour his fighting spirit into them, to wait for them in a hundred gray dawns. And so often they did not return and one could never know why. So it was "Let's finish this bloody war by fighting it properly." And when he got his submariners on shore, they were treated like princes—taken up to the mountaintops and made to feel the world was theirs.

When the day came for me to fly away from Beirut, Anita came with Ruckers in the official car. She looked rather feminine in a skirt and trim khaki uniform and peaked cap with a bronze badge which said, oddly enough, Mechanised Transport Corps. I had never really seen her before except out of doors and in trousers. She was very proud of the badge. "But the MTC is famous," she explained. "We don't *just* drive ambulances. We can do the most extraordinary jobs—if you meet a girl called Kay Summersby in London, *she* is in the MTC and driving that American Colonel Eisenhower who is going to be so important. He is being made a general. We all paid for our own training in tanks and learnt how to change wheels right under those dogfights in the Battle of Britain days."

I said good-bye and climbed into the small plane which soared off over the sand dunes. For a time I could see the huge figure of Ruckers in his blue naval uniform and the slight khaki form beside him, waving. I never thought I would see her again. But I did not brood. I was too deeply immersed in the job to get het up on those lines. A new submarine was being built for me in England, and I could not wait to get there to supervise the last weeks of her construction. I had not the slightest intention of inspecting the lady drivers of the MTC especially if they were busy with American generals.

CHAPTER 7

VIP's

MY flight from Cairo to London in a bomber converted to transport VIP's was not particularly soothing. The VIP's were Dick Casey, Minister of State for the Middle East,* and Major General Sir Edward Spears, Minister Extraordinary and Plenipotentiary to Lebanon. The two nonimportant passengers were a wing commander returning from Burma and myself. For the Very Important, two seats with straps had been devised in the rear. Other chaps had to sit on the bomber's hard slippery metal floor. As we flew over the Mediterranean, the pilot noticed a convoy of British ships under escort and, for some reason, decided to investigate it. He circled down until white-cotton-wool puffs started to come out of the ship's guns. As a *naval* officer, I felt it incumbent on me to crawl forward and explain that ships did not in these days appreciate inspection by unidentified aircraft. Shortly after this, we found ourselves swooping low over Ceuta instead of Gibraltar and could almost see the Spanish antiaircraft guns lining up. On this occasion the RAF officer thought it incumbent on *him* to slither along and point out on which side of the straits Gibraltar lay. When, a day later with fresh crew aboard, we approached London, it was to enter such dense fog that one could not see the wing tips. The newly qualified pilot came down to land at so sharp an angle that we unimportant personages found ourselves sliding back and

*Later, Sir Richard Casey, Governor General of Australia.

forth down the full length of the bomber on our stomachs. Each time the pilot lost his nerve and deemed it wiser not to land, he rose sharply in the air so that we rolled back like eggs along the floor. Six times this happened, and we were becoming somewhat bruised when the navigator suggested flying away to an airfield in the West Country where visibility might be better.

A week later I was examining the great steel hull of what was to be my third submarine, and eight months later I sailed her out for the Far East. We had to pass through the Suez Canal, and here I made a tremendous effort to find Anita. Discreet telegrams and military signals designed to bring her to Suez without revealing the presence of a submarine were dispatched, but brought no reply, for she had left the Middle East and was now working in ambulance planes in Italy, where Cassino had fallen and General Alexander's advance to Rome had begun. The British Navy can pull quite a few strings, but it couldn't transport a Red Cross worker from Naples to Suez for a day. I would not see her until after the war had ended, and then it would be on a few days' leave from Londonderry in Northern Ireland. In fact, it was 1946. I had traveled over to Londonderry, testing a new type of submarine in deep dives. As there was much more to eat in the Irish Republic, all our chaps were busily slipping out of uniform to drive, bicycle, or even walk into Eire, the land of unrationed eggs and butter. Anita's home lay a mile over the border, and I reached it by a little train—the kind a child might rightly call a "puff-puff"—which halted in a small Victorian Gothic station. I walked through the gates of her father's demesne, and there, beside a lake which mirrored the big trees of an ancient forest, I saw her again—out of uniform, surrounded by dogs, horses, and family. We were married there—later—for she had many other interests, and I thought I could get *something* out of my system by ocean racing with John Illingworth, our flotilla engineer of North Sea days, now become a famous ocean racer and designer. Anita understood this; she knew exactly what she herself liked and disliked. I had the delight of crewing for John in his yacht of revolutionary design, *Myth of Malham*, in the Bermuda Race of 1948. Later I would make three Atlantic crossings in other yachts, and one in my own boat, *Galway Blazer*, built for me in Camper and Nicholson's yard. I have never suffered an hour of seasickness. This inbuilt immunity is a bonus for which I must always be grateful, in ocean racing as in the Navy.

At one stage during this getting-something-out-of-the-system business in 1949, Anita joined in, and to the horror of her family she stepped aboard in Antigua with a merry kicking baby in a basket. This was Tarka Dick, the cheerfulest little fellow ever to crow in a quarter berth. I had sailed *Galway Blazer*, an RNSA 24 designed by Laurent Giles, across the Atlantic in twenty-eight days from Gibraltar. She was my idea of the perfect small all-rounder. I intended to race her occasionally and enjoy her as a holiday family home as well. Ketch-rigged, she was easy for one man to handle, easier still for a man and his wife. We spent a blissful five months sailing down the Lesser Antilles—that chain of islands laid out to make a perfect sailing ground so that yachts can find a harbor every twenty miles, and a constant store of fresh fruits and vegetables can be purchased when babies are aboard.

We stayed for six weeks in English Harbour, where Nelson's ships had lain for refit. The buildings were in disrepair and ghostlike in the warm humid nights. Then we sailed on to Guadeloupe and Martinique, Dominica, St. Lucia, St. Vincent, Grenada—happy islands then with peaceful harbors. And Tarka Dick grew strong and brown and *extremely* lively. He was approaching a year old when we noticed with awe his ever more successful efforts to climb up the ladder into the cockpit. Once he could leave the cabin at will our peace of mind would be destroyed, and we felt that the time had come for a different environment. The green fields of Ireland would be better for a child who could scamper. I well remember how frightened he was the first time he sat down on a grassy lawn. Since he had never, in his small memory, been out of a boat, the wide green stretch terrified him and he bellowed and clung to his mother.

As I wanted to have a try in my own boat in the Bermuda Race, Anita decided to travel home by steamer. It had been an idyllic interlude. The days in turquoise-blue bays, the nights of quiet sailing with a train of jeweled phosphorescence in our wake, the fleets of tiny sparkling fish that would leap out of the water at night, the masts rocking against the sky, the baby's cry of delight watching them—all these unique moments swept through my mind like cool spray.

At the end of that year, 1950, when I returned from Bermuda leaving the yacht there, proud enough to have been fourth in her class, I was a new kind of person, a landsman I thought. From then on it was to be a rotation of cattle breeding, clearing rocks, reseeding the fields, lambing time, foaling time, and fox hunting with the Galway Blazer hounds all winter. A little daughter arrived, and life with two children, with farming and horses and hard work and many pleasures, made the years fly by. Occasionally we cruised with friends down the Brittany coast or through the Greek islands, and every winter I skied with Ruckers from his lovely home in Kitzbühel. Here the retired admiral had laid out the workshop of his dreams, and his skill in carpentry gave him the greatest pleasure. He came to stay in our Norman fortress on Galway Bay and himself made an oak door in a fourteenth-century stone arch which fitted more perfectly than any other door in the castle. "Much

more satisfying than commanding an aircraft carrier—one gets so tired of those kamikazes."*

It was a good life and full of variety. I seemed to have it
all ways. Sometimes I returned to ocean racing, though
not in my own boat. It was enough to share the thrill with
friends in one of the European races or in the Fastnet.
Occasionally, when in England, we went to stay at
Chartwell with Anita's cousin, the great Winston
Churchill (his American mother and Anita's
grandmother were sisters). He was warmhearted and
very human. During that terrible first winter of the war
when our flotilla losses were 75 percent, Winston, as First
Lord of the Admiralty, had closely watched over his little
submarines. He had time for us all—time and feeling.
When Bickford in *Salmon* achieved that fantastic patrol
in December, 1939, sinking the U-boat and cruisers,
none of us submariners ever forgot that it was Winston
who had insisted that the decorations won should be
published "both as to officers and men, before the
Salmon sails again." And we all knew that Winston had
pressed the First Sea Lord to try to use *Salmon* as "an
extra practice submarine for a few months after the
severe and distinguished service she has rendered."
Then Winston suggested that Bickford might be used in
the Plans Division of the Admiralty for six months to
bring his superiors into close direct contact with the
conditions prevailing in Heligoland Bight. "If the war
were general and everybody engaged to the hilt there
would be no need to consider variations of duty. But
considering that the particular brunt falls upon very few
at the present time, and that nothing is comparable to
submarine work amid the minefields and all its increasing dangers, I am strongly of the opinion that we should
keep a rotation, shifting boats and crews which have had

*During the last year of the war Ruckers had commanded the aircraft
carrier *Formidable* in the Pacific. Two Japanese suicide planes landed on her
decks.

a particularly hard time, or have distinguished themselves, to easier duties and letting others have a chance
of winning renown." Those were Winston's very own
words in the official minutes (published after the
war). At the time there had not been enough trained
submarine crews to allow any rotation and our huge
losses during that first bitter winter made the shortage
yet more acute. But we liked to know that Winston cared.
I had put the loss of Bickford from my mind for many a
long year. But one evening in the cozy, candle-lit dining
room at Chartwell, Winston wanted to run over the 1940
submarine campaign with me and it was as if the
enchanting Bickie rose up to sit with us. There were only
about eight for dinner, and I remember in this particular
instance what the first course consisted of—suddenly at
my left elbow a large silver basin of caviar appeared.
"Take all you can eat," encouraged Winston, "it's a gift
from Russia, we can't get through it!" I hadn't eaten
ladles of real caviar since 1936, when with a party of
young naval officers, I reached Harbin on leave. After
dinner, Winston, as was his wont, wanted to mull over
how things went when he was at the Admiralty and he
kept talking of Bickford. "I knew his luck had run out—
he'd drawn too deeply on reserves—I wanted him
rested."

"Sir, we couldn't be rested however tired—there was
no one to take a submarine captain's place."

"I *know* when a man's luck is running out—I know it by
instinct," insisted Winston. We argued for a time about
luck in warfare, and then I told him of happier carefree
days with Charles Bickford in the summer before the
war.

Our flotilla then lay in Alexandria under Ruckers'
command, and Bickie, the handsome, amusing Bickie to
whom above all the men I have ever known I would
attach the adjective "debonair," was obviously his most
brilliant submarine commander. Ruckers was very fond

of him. We all were. Bickie's efficiency at sea and his
charm ashore enabled him to get away with murder. The
submarine CO's lived in the depot ship and we had to go
to sea alternate mornings at five A.M. for practice. It was
as well to dine carefully the night before. I remembered
one morning when I woke to hear Bickie being called in
the next door cabin. Bang, bang on the door. "Four
thirty, sir. Your cup of tea." Absolute silence. It was not
my turn, so I tried to go back to sleep. Again, bang, bang.
"Four forty-five, sir. Harbor stations." (This meant the
crew were aboard at their allotted stations and the submarine ready to proceed to sea). Silence. Then came the
clear voice of his second-in-command issuing orders,
and loud thumping sounds. Lieutenant Commander
Bickford was being carried off by a stretcher party which
somehow lowered him down the forehatch into his bunk.
There he was left to recover while his adoring No. 2
climbed onto the bridge and took the ship out to sea.
Happily there was no top brass around at five in the
morning to witness these curious proceedings. Shortly
after this, Bickie very nearly got into quite bad trouble.
He was rather too attractive to be safe, and had a very
pretty girl in tow—the daughter of a high-ranking naval
officer ashore. Papa was stern and disapproving. Also he
knew our service hours. After the morning exercises at
sea or in harbor we were usually free in the afternoons
for polo, tennis, swimming, drinking, and dancing. But
at eleven P.M. sharp a curfew descended on the depot
ship and every submarine officer had to be aboard. This
particular senior officer began to grow anxious about the
hours his daughter was keeping, and eventually after
waiting up for her till after midnight, he telephoned the
depot ship's captain to ascertain if Lieutenant Commander Bickford was in his cabin. He was not. Absence
from the ship at that hour (not leading girls astray)
constituted a very serious offense, and Ruckers was hard
put to find excuses for his golden-haired boy. Furious

naval signals went back and forth. There were demands
for court-martial on one hand and demands that pretty
girls be locked up by suspicious parents on the other.
"What! Court-martial my best submarine captain!"
roared Ruckers. "Just as we're going to war! Bloody
likely!"

But Bickie was reprimanded or, at least, given serious
advice by his commanding officer.

We knew war was coming, of course. One did not have
to be a very clever junior officer to expect it, but all that
last year seemed full of gaiety and laughter. Most of it
was the sheer joyous laughter of youth—often at
someone else's expense. There was a rather dramatic
submarine exercise called *surface gun action from
submerged*, which consisted of suddenly surfacing from a
dive to fight a gun action. The whole point lay in the
element of surprise and necessitated gymnastic feats at
speed on the part of the gun crew. When practicing this
exercise at sea, a submarine would rise to the surface,
man the gun, shoot hard at what might be a ship with
bigger guns, and then submerge at speed. This
necessitated a fast but disciplined rush up the hatch,
hasty manning of the guns, shooting off of a shell and a
rush down the hatches before diving. All took place to a
stopwatch. Sometimes a version of the exercise took
place secured to the depot ship in harbor, naturally without submerging. The breaking surface would then be
simulated by whistle blasts. Dummy rounds made of
wood were usually issued, but on one occasion a very
keen young gunnery officer, wishing to accustom his
crew to the *feel* of a live cartridge used a shell which,
although it had a dummy head, carried a live propellant.
He explained all this to his men, adding foolishly, "But
when I say FIRE, DON'T FIRE." This order was beyond
the mental grasp of a sweating crew who had raced to
their stations, all het-up and anxious to execute their
duties at top speed. "Fire!" shouted the young officer,

meaning "Don't Fire!" The gun layer pressed his trigger. The shell sped out of the gun which happened to be aimed at the harem window of King Farouk's Palace of Ras el Tin overlooking the harbor. Bewildered faces peered from all sides, from the palace toward the harbor, from the naval base to the palace. Fortunately, the king and his ladies were away at their summer residence, for when a naval officer called to apologize, jibbering domestics insisted that a shell had ricocheted around the harem sitting room *forty-eight times!* This incident immensely amused those who were not responsible.

It was indeed curious to sit there in England years after, relating such stories to the man who had been First Lord of the Admiralty in our hardest hour. After all he had lived through, all he had to think of, Winston still had a place in his memory for that glorious character Edward Bickford. "I so much wanted to pluck him out of it—he couldn't go on like that—I *felt* his luck running out, but what could I do?"

One of the fascinating aspects of Winston Churchill was the extraordinary way he showed on his face how vividly he could imagine the adventure you were recounting. It is a trait natural in schoolboys—how often one becomes aware of a youngster, intent, big-eyed, holding his breath as you run over some tale. But such concentration, such power to live the story with you seemed quite amazing in a man who had led the whole nation in war. He could have wept, I think, for Bickford, all these years after.

And knowing that it had been a grim year for our flotilla, he would pry stories out of one. "Tell me what it was like to do the fighting out there in the North Sea."

I always found it hard to describe patrols of that first winter of war, but with Winston listening one's tongue was loosened. After all, one couldn't very well say to him, "Tell us about the Casablanca Conference" or "Let's hear *your* version of Stalin and Roosevelt at Yalta." But *he*

could say, "Come along now—what was your worst
experience in that winter of 1939-40?" And I would
comb through submarine memories—the moments of
delight when a twenty-eight-year-old, after obtaining
command of his own ship, finds himself piped aboard
great battleships along with the older captains; the tension of one's first wartime patrol; the responsibility and
terror of commanding a submarine in action. I would tell
him of the days spent dived at sixty feet in that North Sea
which is only ninety feet deep, and of the short white
nights when we struggled to stay on the surface long
enough to charge our batteries before being spotted by
aircraft.

When Winston asked for my *least* favorite experience,
I did not have to think long. It had occurred on a dark
winter's night in 1939 when *Snapper* was positioned off
the coast of Holland. A northwesterly gale had been
blowing for days, and with the navigator wedged on the
bridge beside me, I had been vainly struggling to obtain
star-sights out of the stormy cloud-filled sky. It was a
horrible area in which to be unsure of one's position. The
tidal stream forks in this area: One stream pours into
Heligoland Bight, the other south into the "Broad
Fourteens" off the Dutch coast. When bad weather
prevents the taking of sights, it is impossible to know
which stream you are in and errors accumulate. The
shore is sandy and featureless, most dangerous when a
full gale is blowing and visibility almost nil. Moving slowly along the coast, with a huge sea running behind us, I
could but *hope* we were in the right tidal stream.

The waves sloshed over the conning tower and poured
down the hatch, which always had to be kept open
because diesel engines need an eighty-mph wind blowing
down the conning-tower. We rigged up a kind of canvas
bathtub to catch the odd ton of seawater before it could
damage the electrical connections. A sailor remained on

continuous duty with a suction hose, tryung to pump out the tub before the next wave filled it. We'd had several nights of it and I had gone below to lie in my bunk in my wet oilskins for a half hour's sleep when a shout came from the bridge: "Light ahead. Looks like a shore light."

I wonder *how* fast one reacts in such conditions. I can't remember climbing up the hatch. I only know I was there on the bridge shouting, "Hard aport!" and realizing that we must have taken the wrong tidal stream and were driving straight into Holland with the wind and wave force behind us. The helmsman acted instantly and *Snapper*'s head started to swing away from the shoals and into the breaking waves. I thought we had turned safely out to sea and that her engines could carry her out against the storm. My blessings rained on that unknown Dutchman who had forgotten his blackout. But there came a fearful jarring shudder as *Snapper*'s keel hit a sandbank. "I'll take over," I shouted against the wind's roar to the officer of the watch who slid off the bridge, thankful to be relieved of further responsibility. There was nothing for it but to stop the powerful diesel engines; the submarine could not stand up to such crashing. I swung the telegraphs to "Stop engines" and change to the electric motors. At least we had succeeded in pointing out to sea, and as each great wave came surging in, it lifted us clean off the sandbank. By anticipating each wave lift I could order, "Full ahead together," and the power came on as we rose. Then as that wave receded, my submarine would be dropped back on the sand with a sickening crash. After a while I could better judge the rhythm of the waves and coordinate the burst of engine power, but the navigator informed me, "Tide falling. Depth of water getting less." and the engineer officer climbed up to the bridge to shout in my ear: "She'll fall apart soon, sir."

There was nothing for it, however, but to continue this

wild whirl of electric motors at every lift until she *did* fall apart. In the heaving engine room where the men had to wait at their stations with nothing to do, a frightened young stoker reached out for a Davis escape set. The chief engineer artificer snapped, "Drop that! You can *walk* ashore here."

But they would not walk. They would drown. And the broken wreck of *Snapper* might fall into enemy hands.

The helmsman could do little to steer, and I had to keep her pointed out by alternate burns on either propeller.

On and on it went in the storm. Up the submarine would go. "Full ahead" I would signal. Drop. Crash. "Stop both motors."

Eventually we noticed the half-light of early dawn. Enemy air patrols would be warming up their engines. I half remembered that this was almost the identical place where a British submarine got grounded in World War I—the crew had struggled ashore and been interned. In this storm my men could not make it, nor did I wish to live if I lost my submarine.

"Full ahead."

"Stop motors."

"Full ahead—"

Was it my imagination or were the bumps growing lighter? As they sky lightened I could see the shallows—long brown streaks with white breakers against the dark green water. This enabled me to pick our route out.

The crashes became less frequent. Then all the sandbank shadows lay behind us, the propellers bit into clear water, and *Snapper* knew release. She raced on into the open sea and slid beneath the turbulent waters like a child flinging herself into a mother's skirts.

"What happened when you got back and reported all this?" asked Winston. He was avid for detail. The Navy has a ruling that if any ship is grounded, there must be a

court of inquiry. I thought the former First Lord of the
Admiralty must know this, but went on.

"Well, I handed my report to Captain Ruck-Keene
who commanded the submarine flotilla—he was, you
know, famous for his fiery temperament and could blast
a man like none other, but he listened quietly while I
poured forth my tale. Then he looked me straight in the
face and announced, 'The grounding is a technicality. It
need not be mentioned. We're too busy fighting this war
to waste time with courts of inquiry—' "

This was the story of my first wartime patrol. It was my
least favorite memory. "And what did you enjoy most
that year?" asked Winston.

I told him about our strange spring patrol into the
Arctic with the sky ablaze with northern lights.

Sometime after this evening in which we chewed over
the submarine campaign, Anita asked Lady Churchill if
she might bring the eight-year-old Tarka Dick down to
the Churchill country home, Chartwell, for the day so
that our son could register permanent, unforgettable
impressions of his august elder cousin. We thought
Tarka was just the right age to absorb a lasting memory
and Clemmie agreed. We drove down on a Sunday
morning from London and found we were only eight for
lunch—mostly family—but Field Marshal Montgomery
happened to be there also, and Tarka Dick was placed by
Clemmie between Winston and Monty for a meal, which
was intended to be memorable, but in fact, became virtu-
ally intoxicating for the child. Well primed regarding the
privilege of meeting "the great," Tarka Dick behaved at
first with perfect decorum. Winston was wonderful with
children, and he deliberately talked to the small boy
whose face lit up on discovering that such a person could
have the same interests as himself. The field marshal was
also interested in the young, but it had become second
nature to him to stimulate and to inspire. Our eight-year-
old did not need inspiring—he needed sedation! In try-

ing to imprint the importance of absolute obedience during heroic endeavor Monty spoke to the child almost as if addressing troops on the eve of attack.

"What will I do if you don't obey my orders and win my battles?" asked the field marshal.

"What?" from his enthralled listener.

"I would *beat* you!"

Tarka squealed with delight and spilled his pudding. I saw Anita watching her offspring anxiously, but since he had been placed down the table away from her, Tarka could not hear parental pleas to "Pipe down!"

I remember the following conversation exactly. The field marshal had just finished his book of memoirs. "What does the publisher think of it?" asked Winston.

"The cat's pajamas," replied Monty.

"Cats in pajamas?" shrilled our son.

Winston patiently explained that this was a figure of speech, and then what a figure of speech was. "The field marshal's book can be considered as impressive as a cat in pajamas." Tarka's eyes rolled and Monty continued to stimulate him with admonitions on how to behave in desert battle.

That afternoon we spent deliciously strolling around the gardens, feeding the black swans, and hopping over stepping-stones in the lake (at least Tarka and Monty did so without breaking their necks and thus showed their agility). Then, as we had so hoped, Winston took Tarka off alone for a talk and to look at his studio and paintings and photo albums. "Here they have you *well* dressed up," remarked Tarka, examining Winston in the splendid uniform of the Cinque Ports. "Yes—that's a pretty good outfit—I liked it myself," murmured the old Prime Minister, with a glint of amusement. All seemed well, and Winston, after a strawberry tea, turned to us in his wonderfully innocent way. "He is so happy and full of mischief—keep him like that."

We left Chartwell at about six o'clock. As usual a small

crowd of sightseers had gathered at the gate, and having said good-bye, we were climbing into our open car, with Tarka racing around absolutely out of control after so many hours of statesmanlike behavior, when Monty came out to graciously bid us good-bye. "And what will I *do* to *you* if you don't obey orders?" he asked the little whirling dervish. Like a streak, Tarka raced up, gave the great field marshal a smack on the bottom, and dived into the back of the car—all this in front of policemen, detectives, and goggling tourists. Monty's jaw dropped and we drove away, too mortified to speak. When he sensed that he had done quite the wrong thing, a small voice quavered from the back: "Is that Monty a very *great* person too? Why didn't you tell me?" Thus on a summer's day our son unforgettably encountered the Victor of Alamein.

CHAPTER 8
Off

ONE night we could not resist reminding Winston of his icy bite at naval tradition: "Tradition ... there's no tradition in the Navy except gin, sodomy and the lash!" He could always floor one with a quiet summary of one's messily expressed projects. I tried to impress him with my own personal romantic view of sea life, but after listening to my account of the delights of keeping home in what my mother-in-law usually referred to as "that dreadful littly tippy boat," Winston just looked at me with his penetrating blue stare. "It's perilous, uncomfortable and unremunerative. SHTOP IT," he pronounced. And shtop it I did until the children were old enough to be merely amused if their father went off "doing his thing" as they called it.

After I had sold my little *Galway Blazer* in 1952, land life seemed to take over. I lived between the bare limestone hills of Clare and the purple peaks of Connemara on the inmost point of Galway Bay. I loved the magical Irish countryside, and yet its very magic shackled me. I never felt quite as alive on land as at sea. Certain fidgets affected me. Anita suggested keeping a bigger ocean racer so that I could occasionally get more out of my system, and she could amuse herself meeting the boat in ports. But ocean racing grew more expensive every year, and the thrill of competing had somehow died in me. What I really wanted, I did not dare say. It was to sail my own boat around the Horn alone.

Cape Horn has a strange attraction for sailors. It is

such a devil of a place, where the Pacific and Atlantic meet in furiously changing moods. One really can't go anywhere more violent. That is part of the challenge, part of the charm. In 1964 Tarka Dick was eighteen and Leonie, our daughter, sixteen when I told Anita that I wanted to have a bash. Two fantastic older men, Francis Chichester and Alec Rose, had sailed alone around the world, and I contemplated making a complete circumnavigation nonstop. I thought that the excitement and publicity concerning such exploits was over. I would simply embark on an adventure for which I had been aching during many years. I wanted to see if I could do it.

Reckoning that I had enough to pay for a boat to be designed and built specially for me, I traveled to England to confer with a young yacht designer, Angus Primrose. After I had explained exactly what I wanted Angus began excitedly to sketch out blueprints. Eventually he designed a special hull, whale-backed and able to endure endless buffeting. She would be a light-displacement boat only four and a half tons. The rig was to be very special—strong and easy to handle. For this I went to an old friend, the famous Colonel "Blondie" Hasler, who had invented what was, to my mind, the most perfect form of self-steering gear in existence, and who had sailed the Atlantic with a rig based on the Chinese, which, he thought, was the easiest in the world for a lone man to handle. Blondie's advice quickened the urge within me. We sat yarning about his own junk-rigged *Jester* in which he had challenged Francis Chichester when the two of them were trying to get the first Transatlantic Race going. Since then he had not been able to spare time for racing but had concentrated on his inventions. Apart from perfecting his vane self-steering, he was working on a large enterprise concerning "floating breakwaters" whereby temporary sheltered transportable harbors could be quickly erected. Blondie is one of those clear-minded inventors whose ideas always seem in advance of their time. He had been very pleased with *Jester*, and the grin on that delightful leathery countenance grew when I described my own baptism into a fleet of junks. This had occurred long ago on the first night on which I stood on the bridge of a submarine as officer of the watch. I was twenty-two, qualified but inexperienced. It was typical spring monsoon weather in the South China Sea, warm with a light wind, the sky overcast and the sea pitch-black. The engines throbbed as we clove the waters, pushing northward to our summer anchorage Weihaiwei. Being young, I was preening myself on the way I was keeping a lookout, when a muffled exclamation came from the signalman and a fizz of fireworks shot across our bow. Then dark shapes loomed up on every side and gradually coalesced into a huge array of fishing junks. I knew that the Chinese liked to shoot right in front of one's bow because that cuts off the line of following devils, but on this occasion they started to explode fireworks all around us, either as warning signals or to frighten off the devils who arrange collisions. Guessing that fishing trawls might be tied between some of the boats, I started to weave the submarine to and fro. She lost way, and all this tricky maneuvering was too much for a young fellow taking his first watch. My agonized cry rang down the voice-pipe to summon my captain, but at this very moment he sprang up behind me, for an alert sensitive captain automatically awakens if his ship alters tempo. "The Swatow fishing fleet," he said quietly. I handed over with relief.

Then in the pink dawn we passed close to another fleet, hundreds of up-curved vessels swanning along with their sails arched like angels' wings. I was much intrigued by these lovely-looking boats, and later when I took to small-boat night sails from Hong Kong alone with a Chinese hand, I sometimes drew near to a trading schooner just to watch the crew. Each ship was a home for a large family. Within these wooden walls they lived

and loved and bred. Babies slipped into the world and
the old passed quietly away. Children seemed to be
everywhere, clambering, playing, working at their
specific jobs, and grandma often sat cooking or gazing
silently out over the stern. Everyone knew the ropes, and
the sails themselves, being divided into separate panels
by full-length bamboo battens, could be shortened by
merely dropping a couple of panels of the sail into the
retaining ropes. Then the junk's great rudder would
swing over and she would turn easily into the other tack.
How simple it seemed—that rig, which has been used on
the stormy China seas for thousands of years, by generation after generation.

Blondie Hasler was of the same mind and I regarded
him as the most experienced and adventurous of men.
During the war he had led a famous raid up the Gironde
to blow up German ships, landing by canoe at night and
attaching explosives below the waterline. Only two of his
party survived. The other men were drowned or caught
by the Germans and shot.* After the war he turned his
inventive mind to the perfecting of self-steering gear on
sailing boats. He had thought out the first Solo Transatlantic Race, and with absolute tenacity Blondie spent
years trying to evoke an interest. Francis Chichester
joined in with him, and the two men swore that if no
yacht club would organize this "dangerous, eccentric
race," they would challenge each other to sail the Atlantic
for half a crown. Eventually five yachts participated.
Chichester won and Blondie was second. In the next
race, four years later, there were fifteen contestants!
This was the friend who would design my rig while
Angus Primrose designed a unique hull. What fun it
was—all that planning! After Blondie and Angus had
put their heads together, all we had to look for was a
first-class building yard.

*A film concerning this exploit was called *Cockleshell Heroes.*

Sitting beside the turf fire during the Christmas of 1967, with the blueprint for *Galway Blazer II* spread out under my wife's not overenthusiastic gaze, I felt my hands tremble with excitement. This would be a wonderfully easy boat to handle—and of great functional beauty. Her estimated cost was seven thousand pounds and I could manage that. My stores would not exceed three hundred pounds because at sea I prefer not to touch alcohol or tinned food. I had found in Atlantic crossings that nothing suited me so well as wholemeal biscuits, soaked raisins, and a special protein nut-oil. I did not want the bother of cooking and would only use the galley for an occasional hot coffee when it was necessary to keep awake.

Souter's of Cowes contracted for the building of this boat, and great interest was evoked in her design. The whale-backed hull with fin-keel and rudder-skeg aft was built of cold-molded plywood consisting of four strips of glued mahogany. Since she was four and a half tons, displacement meant, in nontechnical language, that she could be called extremely light for her size. She was, in fact, a boat that could bob like a cork in stormy weather, although, of course, the lines of her hull were designed for speed. When I stared up at her cradle in the builders' yard at Cowes, I rejoiced in her look—the look of a fish or a seal, of a true water creature. Unfortunately, during the six months that she took to build, the original estimate of seven thousand pounds escalated to fifteen thousand. I was therefore only too delighted when a newspaper, the *Daily Express,* offered to pay three thousand pounds in return for which I need only promise to "speak to no other paper." This seemed extremely simple, but a tremendous amount of publicity arose when the plans of *Galway Blazer II* were published on the front page in January, 1968. From then on I found myself photographed pickaxing rocks on my farm, jumping my horse over stone walls, drinking champagne with the children, and sewing patches on sails in Lucas' famous loft. Within the next two months the *Sunday Times* announced a Round-the-World Non-Stop Solo Race, and by the time *Galway Blazer II* had been launched, several other contestants were announcing their intention of participating. My lonely adventure, intended to unwind the springs of tension which had never quite been eased out of my deepest being since submarine days, was turning into a most unlonely scrimmage. As other newspapers took up the subject a snowball of publicity concerning this nonstop race started to roll and I was caught in it.

When launching day arrived in May, Sir Max Aitken threw a tremendous champagne party and my sixteen-year-old Leonie had to be rescued from a band of boys intent of plying her with bubbly while making her practice her launching speech. "I blame this goat *Galway Blazer.*" But she managed it all right, breaking the bottle on the third try, and *Galway Blazer II* slipped down with a splash in that always moving moment when a vessel ceases to be an *it* and becomes a *she.* We all, for a moment, held our breath at her functional grace. I believed that she could stand up to any seas, to knockdown or capsize, and that having no stays there would be little clutter on her deck in unlucky event of dismasting. The junk-rig made her impossible to sail close to the wind, but she moved well at an angle of sixty-five degrees off it, and with a following wind she could wave-ride at about double her theoretical maximum of seven and a half knots.

I did not like being rushed through trials and had intended to leave in leisurely fashion when I felt ready—in August or a year later—but having been caught up in the flurry of the race, and helped by the *Daily Express,* I could not contemplate postponement. As it turned out, before I was even ready, four boats had left England, and after I sailed, another four would depart, making nine contestants in all.

So there I was, in the summer of 1968, back in Plymouth waiting for the right breeze to blow before setting sail. Throughout this rather nerve-racking period, during which the press kept buzzing around like flies, trying to get some "dramatic human aspect" of the race with which to regale their readers, I had to try to keep pristine my verbal contract with the *Daily Express* and not speak to any other paper. But the *Express* could make what TV and radio arrangements they wished, and I often found myself being sort of psychoanalyzed by an eager interviewer while I hung head down trying to fix something in the bilges. Tarka and Leonie came to stay at intervals and worked away, or more accurately, watched me working away at those last-minute jobs which multiply into hundreds before every long voyage. I can remember Anita (who was under considerable emotional strain by now), on being asked by a reporter what she really felt about it all, answering crossly: "Well, I'll go mad if I have to trudge along Plymouth High Street again to buy another two yards of wire."

That was all one could talk about in the last hectic days—two yards of wire, a kind of glue, a pair of pincers. Everything faded into the fever of vital detailed preparations. Food was the least of my worries. I had never quite recovered from the nightmare smells of cooking on a submarine when some wretched untrained seamen had to be pressed to heat up greasy tinned meat over an electric stove in an icy corridor. I intended to cook nothing! I had once crossed the Atlantic in my own boat, eating soaked raisins, whole-wheat biscuits, almond nut paste for protein, and cress grown in jars for vitamin C. Never had I felt better than after twenty-three days of this carefully balanced diet, and I was sure it would suffice me for a year if necessary. Flying fish always add themselves to the menu in tropical waters. I would take no medicines and only one large tin of instant coffee to use as a stimulant when I must not sleep.

The submarine depot ship allowed me to tie up beside her, which allowed a certain blissful privacy. And when the family came to Plymouth, we all lodged in that wonderful pub, The Western, where Mrs. Chappel ran the coziest bar on the coast and cooked us superb breakfasts to "keep the strength up" and cheered us when the effort of the whole enterprise seemed to be getting out of hand.

So it was that on a day in August, 1968, when the silvery mist rose, I cast off from H.M.S. *Tyne*, and *Galway Blazer II* was towed smoothly out into the harbor, past a submarine—oh, the well-known outline of that grim steel structure—where a line of blue- and white-clad sailors gave me three cheers. Then I was past the break-water and threw off the towrope. It would be out through the Western Approaches and down past the Azores into the South Atlantic. I felt wonderfully free.

CHAPTER 9

Plymouth to the Equator

THE tonic effects of this self-prescribed medicine were slightly diminished by my having to communicate twice a week on the expensive Marconi Kestrel radio set installed in my little boat by the *Daily Express*. It was an excellent set, but owing to my junk-rig the aerial could only be attached to the foremast and this was not high enough for proper range. To contact me during the voyage, the *Express* laid on a top-class member of their staff, Michael Steemson, and I'm glad to say that our friendship never cooled throughout months of frantic effort to exchange messages at full shout across thousands of miles of ocean.

Mike's job was to jolly me up from Cape Town and to send descriptions of how I was faring and of distances covered by *Galway Blazer II* back to his paper in England. On Wednesdays and Saturdays we endeavored to communicate on a prearranged wavelength. How thankful I became that the congenial Mike knew Anita and was our contact. He would never rattle her. Nor would he forget her personal messages to me—messages which concerned foals and Connemara ponies as well as our son and daughter.

I had hoped that the Atlantic westerlies would push *Galway Blazer* quickly down to the Northeast Trade Winds and that once I got through the Doldrums, the Southeast Trades would bear me swiftly into the Southern Ocean where the Roaring Forties are supposed to rage ceaselessly from west to east around the Antarctic continent. Despite the hurry to get her off, I felt that *Galway Blazer* had all my requirements, and I grew ever more confident in Blondie Hasler's automatic vane-steering, which I reckoned was the most perfect ever devised to help the lone sailor. On dropping down through the hatch into a covered cockpit, I could sail the boat without getting soaked. The hull contained one long cabin with a bunk and a comfortable chair seat-belted as in a plane; the galley lay opposite the chart table, and the rest of the space was taken by stores, spare sails, and a jury rudder. Since the entire interior had been built without compartments, my quarters seemed light and spacious, almost empty, but then I always liked empty rooms. I kept a few photographs of my family and a carefully chosen library to entertain me through the Doldrums. The only decoration lay in a row of poems, prayers, and medals, sent by well-wishers, which my family glued onto the bulkhead. A bottle of water from the well of St. Brendan, the early Irish navigator, had been given me by Anne Rosse,* and this I tucked away and never could find. But whenever danger threatened, it would fall on my head as if from nowhere—a cheerful reminder of one whose tiny bark had explored the North Atlantic more than a thousand years ago.

With the long-awaited East Wind blowing behind me, I sailed away into the pearly mist of the Western Approaches intent, as every lone sailor must be, on swiftly getting my boat out of danger of collision with big ships. I knew that twenty-four hours without sleep awaited me, and after the strain of the last weeks of preparation, I was extremely tired. Once I got out of the shipping routes and found myself alone in the open Atlantic, a surge of joy assailed me.

This was, in a way, curious, for my emotional setup had changed intrinsically since those submarine days.

*The Countess of Rosse of Birr Castle.

Utterly dedicated to my career, I then cultivated no particular outside interests except sport, mountain climbing, and reading history. No photographs hung in my cabin (as they did in cabins of other officers); I really did not care for personal associations. I loved my family individually, but the last thing I wanted was to be reminded of them when at sea. That cold independent attitude had completely changed during the last twenty years. Now I could look back and laugh at myself, eagerly showing baby photos to all who would look—proudly explaining Leonie's puppy face as she first swam across a pool, nose just out of the water; or Tarka Dick on his pony grinning; or my wife surrounded by children and animals. All these happy memories now peopled the clean white solitude of my hull. No longer a tense commanding officer, I had metamorphosed into a doting father, a husband who winced at the pain of parting. Yet I had to go and the going was a delight.

On August 24 *Galway Blazer* left Plymouth and by October 1 she had reached the Equator. At first I found my peace of mind ruffled by having to remember that my boat had somehow got caught up in a race. Equanimity returned as I fell into the wonderful basic routine of living as a sea creature with nothing between me and the sky and the depths, with only the sun and stars to guide me, and nothing to think of except survival and the improvement of my mind. This latter goal, suggestive of prim study in enclosed spaces, was absolutely real to me on the ocean. I deliberately intended to *improve my mind* and can find no other words for it. I wanted to get my thoughts about the world I had been born into absolutely straight and to put my war memories into place. I wanted to get my perspectives right and eliminate the tedious resentments which had for so long afflicted me on account of technical flaws in our submarine construction and, what had seemed to me, indifference to my own "band of brothers." Before the war, submarines had been considered obsolete by certain factions in the British Admiralty. When war came, they were used full out without pouring the country's resources into design and improvement. No importance was attached to the fact that if a country has submarines at all no expense should be spared. I had really just *got* to stop chewing that bitter cud.

After all, my entry into submarines was partly my own fault! There had been a moment when I might have taken to the air instead. I was seventeen when we did a course with the Fleet Air Arm and we all went out for a day's flying off the carrier. I cunningly got myself assigned to the plane flown by the squadron leader. I thought he would be the most experienced, the most interesting to observe—and, incidentally, the most likely pilot to return his plane in one piece. Up we went in a very old-fashioned machine. The joystick had a wheel attached to it which, to my eyes, resembled the wheel of a boat. When ordered to take control, I could not forbear from automatically turning the wheel as though to alter course. It had a very different effect, however, for the wheel controlled the plane's banking and consequently, when I endeavored to steer, the aircraft turned on its side and started to fall out of the sky. My instructor quickly resumed control, and we then lined up with the other planes, each of which contained a pilot and a midshipman, and came in to land on the carrier, which from ten thousand feet looked like a postage stamp. Unbelievable as it may sound, in 1927 before arrester gear was invented, each plane would touch down on the deck, apply its brakes, and then be physically attacked by a team of strong sailors in gym shoes who somewhat in the manner of a rugby team manhandled the plane to a halt.

As we touched down, I myself—small, ignorant, and unimportant learner—thought the plane had far too much way. Sure enough the jolly jacks could not hold her wings and the plane trundled on toward the ever-narrowing bow of the carrier. My hair stood on end as we finally drew to a halt on the very farthest tip. I peered over the side of the open cockpit and saw below me the great ship's anchor outlined against the frothing bow wave.

Apparently my instructor did not give me better marks than I mentally gave him. Four years later I traveled out to China to join my first submarine as sublieutenant. One of my contemporaries, however, who did join the Fleet Air Arm, made an immediate reputation when he tried to buzz the huge French liner *Normandie* as she was leaving Southampton Water. He flew too close and crashed into a motorcar which was dangling on the end of one of the ship's cranes, being stowed into the hold. The car was written off, and the plane pancaked onto the deck and, incredibly, my chum bounced out unhurt and proceeded to the bridge where he saluted the very un-pleased French captain. Someone on the bridge had a camera and took a photograph of this extraordinary occasion; the photo appeared in the illustrated news-papers. We all saw it and were suitably impressed at the jaunty angle of our brother officer's cap while he "ex-plained."

I laughed to remember it all these years later, and far from feeling isolated in my little boat, as the full panorama of my life began to creep out of my memory, I found myself rather good company. There had been so many hilarious moments woven into the years.

Now my day consisted of many little days in the twenty-four hours, and "mind improvement" depended entirely on the weather! I discarded set mealtimes and ate when I was hungry (or, in rough weather, when there was time). The dawn I always saw, and the daylight hours were naturally those in which I kept most active because my tiny store of electric power had to be carefully hoarded for lights when I entered shipping lanes. Whenever I felt like it, I took a nap, and, of course, one never slept more than a couple of hours at night without waking for a "check"—listening to any wind change or warning note. And the sleep of a sailor is different from other sleep—one is always aware of the ship's rhythm and one's inner ear remains alert.

As the "fuss" of land life blew away from me, I started to feel wonderfully well and my food tasted delicious. Cooking and thinking out meals happens to bore me. Unless delicious meals are thought out and placed in front of me by somebody else, I would rather eat just what I need without having to plan. My diet of nut-oils, raisins, wheat biscuits, and cress, carefully worked out in advance, seemed to keep me in fine fettle. The only thing I ever had to consider cooking was a flying fish when one happened to land on deck. Then I had a variety of culinary ideas! I carried a few fishing lines but never used them because either we were sailing too fast or when the sea was becalmed I was never able to cease working on the rigging. One never seemed to travel at a speed which made it possible to troll.

As for books—I had badly miscalculated. My library proved inadequate for the unexpectedly prolonged calms of the Doldrums. When at sea, I only enjoy great literature. No thrillers of the type I read during train journeys could hold me for five minutes. I had brought with me a number of philosophical works and trans-lations of the Russian and French classics. Tolstoy and Balzac deeply involved me in their human dramas, but after a month, I could see that I was going to run right through them. Because my mind retained so clearly all I read at sea, I did not at all want to start rereading. These great novels which make you feel their drama with every nerve only bear reading once in five or six years.

What pleasure lies in being completely self-contained in constantly changing conditions. Every day seemed different; there was no monotony until I reached the

Doldrums, the zone of calms and sudden squalls which lies some hundreds of miles north of the Equator across the Atlantic. Then I had to realize that what *Galway Blazer II* did magnificently was to carry me along in a gale and what she did worse than I expected was to move in a slight wind—the weight of the top hamper swinging in the swell spilled the wind. There was no way round this fault of her rigging, but the design of her hull seemed absolute perfection. A whale-back presents no vertical surfaces against heavy breaking seas, while the buoyancy of her spoon bow prevented the boat pitch-poling end over end.

As well as keeping my log, I wrote an almost daily letter to my wife. These I intended to present to her in a bundle at the end of the voyage. On August 27 I wrote: "My darling. Early this morning in the pale half-dark, *Galway Blazer* jibed herself; this might be disastrous with a conventional mainsail, but the old Chinese rig does a wily soft jibe, as though to say 'white man no savvy.' I stood out more into the Atlantic on this jibe, taking a tack downwind to make it easier for the boat. I am reading Tolstoy's *Resurrection*, I think it is his best. His sense of dilemma here is unsurpassed, and so is the beautiful description of the Russian Easter." On August 30 I wrote: "How vastly different is the voyage on the surface to the years I spent darkly piercing the depths of this element in submarines; seeking to use it as a hiding place, whence to stalk my prey and in which to hide from enemy planes." Now the sea and sky horizon lay around me in a clear blue circle. The sight of an oil tanker seemed an intrusion into unbelievable loveliness. I took advantage of the perfect weather to climb the mast, inspect the masthead fittings, and try some photography. I had never been any good with a camera, but I felt I must try to get some interesting shots for the newspaper which had so generously helped me.

On September 1 I wrote with surprise:

It is a pleasure to get through at the allotted time to Mike Steemson on the *Daily Express* transmitting radio. At one time I thought the effort of keeping a radio in trim was going to be a nuisance; I wanted peace at sea. But I laughed like a drain when Mike, whose voice was as clear as if in the next room, regaled me with the story of Tarka Dick getting becalmed in Galway Bay for twelve hours without anything to eat or drink. Glad he finally landed his "guests" on a mud flat and that they managed to hire a car home. Mike found it very difficult to hear me. Instead of hating the link with land I enjoy it.

On September 2 I wrote:

This is a day I wish you could enjoy with me—smooth sailing over blue waters, riding down to Madeira in euphoric mood. At night we drove down a moonpath of burnished copper. . . . I care less for *Resurrection* and now don't think it is good as *War and Peace*. I suppose that the gloom of these great Russian writers came from their basic knowledge that their medieval society was doomed. . . . By now I eat happily my three meals a day, each cupful of soaked sultanas with two spoonfuls of nut-paste followed by nibbles of green shoots. I found at the start that I had lost my ability to do on very little water, as I could in the past during Atlantic crossings. Having got accustomed to a lot of liquid in Cowes, I suffered a raging thirst, but now the craving to drink more than a pint a day is fading. I feel like a creature completely adjusted to its element—like a horse on grass or, more aptly, a fish in the sea reaching for the same sustenance whenever hungry, unbothered by decisions about choice of food or cooking. All my mind can be put to the boat and her working. And I read with an avidity I have never known before. I can take in and enjoy the great classic writers to the full. This morning I took my first sun-sights for eighteen years. . . . I feel myself getting back into the world of seamanship, and my mind is adjusting to quick reactions with Chinese rig. This night was one of the loveliest for sailing I have ever known; enough wind to bowl us along, no squalls in the sky, and a world of unbelievable moonlit beauty around. The moonbeams came in through the skylight over my bunk and threw a little circle of moonlight into the cockpit over the tiller where the helmsman should have been. We were not traveling fast, but it was a night to remember for a lifetime. I could not try to describe it on the radio. I hope you will eventually read these lines.

On September 3 I wrote:

A hellish day after the sybaritic night. No wind and a long heavy swell. I hurry up to increase sail at each zephyr, but they just slat [flap noisily against each other]. I seem to be making a terribly slow passage—but at sea it's no use being a squealer there's no one to squeal to, blame, or ask for help. One just has to get on with the job, however unfairly the winds blow. And I think I will be able to get that terrible *thing* out of my system—the submarine summer of 1940. Groping about under water with no oxygen, no darkness to hide us when we had to surface to recharge batteries. The dice seemed so heavily loaded against survival.

I did not immediately know it, but being alone in the ocean had already started to erase the marks of that time. Being quite alone with the sparkling, thundering sea around me, I could analyze the past without rancor.

The searing iron for a submarine captain was incessant responsibility. From beginning to end of each patrol, one had to remain out of radio contact. Other fighting ships received their orders from headquarters ashore. Only the submarine skippers had to make every decision themselves and judge themselves afterward. I would accuse myself alternately of lethal rashness or of over-caution. Winston alone had seemed to understand what the summer of 1940 meant for submariners when short hours of darkness of the Scandinavian coast meant death. In seas lit by the midnight sun we had to surface gasping for oxygen to charge our batteries. And knowing this, German planes kept incessant watch through the long white nights, dive-bombing, torpedoing, and depth charging any submarine they spotted and directing surface ships toward our shadowy tracks in the deep. During the whole of this first summer of the war I sank ships, some six or seven, dragged half-drowned enemies from the sea, and tried to impose my will on a crew which knew that seventy-five percent of their flotilla had been wiped out. *Snapper* survived until, in the following winter, I had to go briefly into the hospital. The young officer who took over his first command in my submarine did not bring her back. The Admiralty never learned what happened. No enemy claim was made. Maybe she had been overpowered by stormy seas. I thought often of the crew I had known so well. The loss of that first submarine had preyed on my mind long after war ended.

But here I was, years later, sailing southward down the Atlantic for *fun!* Having been hunted underwater for six years wiped away the preliminary nervousness which some men might have felt at facing the elements alone.

After all, no one was *trying* to kill me on this jaunt. To battle against wind and wave was different from evasive action in the depths.

I wrote on September 5:

> Last night the sun went down in a low torrent of fire, while the moon emerged on the other beam out of a curtain of gold, blue and dark violet. It was so personal the moonpath —shimmering, silver, pointed straight at *me!* I drew in anew the fantastic beauty of a small nobly-proportioned boat sailing untrammeled through smooth warm seas over moon-burnished water.

All this was so absorbing that I forgot that such a thing as fear existed. Indeed I often forgot that I was supposed to be competing in a race until Mike Steemson's radio voice reminded me that I must press on as fast as *Galway Blazer*'s junk rig would allow.

Sometimes *Galway Blazer* covered one hundred and sixty miles a day, but when we entered the Doldrums, our speed dropped to one hundred and fifty miles in four days. As winds fell lighter, I realized for the first time the full disadvantage of a junk-rig. With no way of hoisting a ghosting sail, we hardly moved. To Anita I wrote:

> I cannot *drive Galway Blazer* against faster boats. I will plod on around the world, reveling in my boat's special poetic beauty, in her strength and her power. I will put disappointment from me, but I wish now I had no radio contact. Much as I like Mike, and value family news, I would rather be alone and immersed in the job.

Irritation at not being able to sail fast rankled me during long days of becalmed rolling. Tolstoy could not

The first submarine on which I served, *Orpheus,* off Hong Kong, 1932.

A German tanker blows up under fire off Norway, 1940, the victim of my submarine *Snapper*'s three-inch gun.

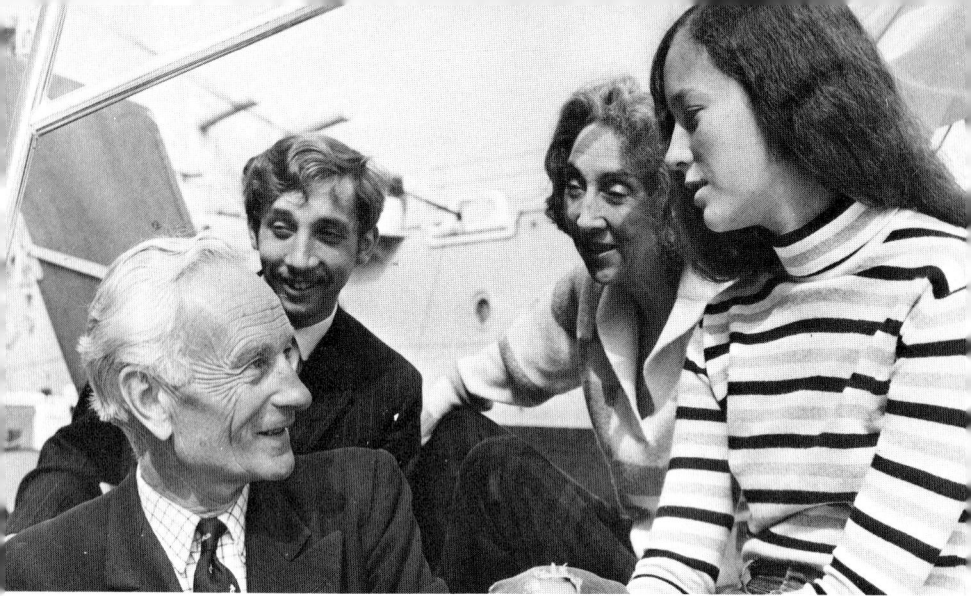

—Daily Express

Aboard *Galway Blazer II* just before setting sail from Plymouth Harbour, with son Tarka Dick, Anita (Mrs. King), and daughter Leonie.

Leaving Plymouth for the first leg around the world appropriately passing by a flotilla of British submarines.

—*Western Morning News Co. Ltd.*, Plymouth

Below deck in *Galway Blazer II*'s marvelously compact cabin, charting my course.

—David Baker

On route to Capetown after my capsize, with *Corsair II* in the background.

Underway in southern waters—the glorious world of wind, sun, and sea.

—*West Australian Newspapers Ltd.*

In a Fremantle boatyard repair work begins on the hull showing the damage inflicted by the killer whale.

This is how I covered the damaged hull with makeshift tarpaulin and sailcloth, inelegant but a lifesaver.

—*West Australian Newspapers Ltd.*

Almost home off Land's End in a Force 7 gale, a photo taken by an RAF plane that miraculously sighted me through the stormy overcast.

Home again in Plymouth Harbour with daughter Leonie and Anita at my side.

I receive the Alec Rose Trophy from the commodore of the Royal Naval Sailing Association.

entirely hold my attention. Then we slipped into the
Trade Winds and immediately everything changed.
With a beam wind she was even better than I expected.
Ecstatically she raced along. *Galway Blazer* proved fantas-
tically lively, bounding like a young horse. Tempests
elate, whatever the danger. Whenever we entered a
Doldrum, all my woes crowded in on me to be instantly
dispelled by a little breeze.

Petrels and shearwaters were my only companions
until, on September 14, I was joined by a flock of tropic
seabirds with delicate pointed tails. Then a swallow landed on deck, perched on the tiller. I thought he just
needed a little rest, but next morning he looked poorly
and would not feed. In the noise of a rainstorm he gave
up and died. I wondered what had gone wrong in the
delicate mechanism of his ordered life. Had he become
overtired or was it trauma due to losing his way?

We were sailing too fast to use a line, but I fried every
flying fish that landed on deck. After rain I would increase my water ration to just over a pint a day, but I have
always believed that a low liquid intake was healthy and
natural—the craving to drink a question of habit. On the
whole I prefer living dehydrated; I could write: "I feel
about ten years younger than when I left."

Then on September 23, winds dropped and I got very
sorry for myself.

> I have gone into a period of suspended anima-
> tion, a protective cocoon against this immobili-
> ty. This morning's sun-sight showed that we are
> in the Equatorial Counter Current, which sets
> fast to the eastwards. If we stop long enough
> without wind, we will finish by drifting to
> Africa!

Once I passed near a small tanker, but she did not see
me. Since the power of my batteries was not sufficient to

allow me to show lights at night, the possibility of being
run down constantly plagued me. Now the Suez Canal
has been closed a lot of ships cover the South Atlantic.

As we slipped at last out of the Doldrums into the
Southeast Trades, I was able to tack between the continents of Africa and South America, and how grateful I
felt for so much space.

Shearwaters and other birds increased in numbers
and, to my delight, another swallow—who alighted on
the top of the cabin door for one night and flew merrily
away in the morning. I wondered if his ability to do this
depended on the boat's lesser movement so that he did
not feel seasick or if he was a younger, stronger bird.

Fish as well as birds caught my imagination and I
wrote:

> I have been watching the high standard of
> airmanship amongst individual experienced
> flying fish. They are loners who fly separately
> from the coveys of small fish. These experts
> shoot out of the sea upwind, turn, and, taking
> advantage of the upcurrent of air in front of
> each wave, sail-plane down the length of the
> wave roll. I saw one "ace" as he swerved through
> a cleft in a wave, reversed course, and flew back
> along the following wave. Are they trying to
> evolve into birds?

All land creatures must have evolved through just
such experiments—and here was I, in a tiny fragment of
time, evolving so it seemed to me from the conventional
human being of early years, the conventional warrior in
fact, into fresh realizations. I was enchanted by these
thoughts.

One morning of hard wind I was putting in a second
reef when a large wave curled above me and a pack of
flying fish took off so that I was looking up at them as if at

birds flying out of a treetop. I was *underneath* a shoal of fish!

On September 27, I was able to record: "This southerly tack has proved a great success. Although going to windward all night in light winds, the sea was so smooth that we were sailing as though on a lake." But the next day I was pounding to windward and twice had to reef the mainsail. It was at those times that reefing became necessary that I blessed Blondie Hasler for encouraging me to adopt the junk rig; it was so easy to fold down the stiffly battened sail. But when winds grew light, I groaned at the impossibility of using a ghost sail to increase speed. During her trials in English waters I had never been able to assess the performance of junk-rig in absolutely windless conditions. One can't really do trials for sailing around the world without *sailing around the world!*

Now my moods of despondency or jubilation swung according to the winds. When becalmed, a lone sailor gets no more rest than when a full gale is blowing. He has to work incessantly to stop sails slatting, to catch any little airs which deign to skim his way. It is maddening. The noises just irritate, whereas a gale roar stimulates the adrenaline. The best wind for reading is the perfect sailing wind, when the boat is tearing along and you feel her loving it and you have looked at every rope and set her just right and have nothing more to do.

CHAPTER 10

South Atlantic

NOW some nine weeks out, we crossed the Equator and entered the Southern Atlantic, which was a new ocean for me. I was immensely well. The hectic struggle of preparations for departure had been fair hell. Now, despite *never* being able to sleep for more than a few hours without interruption, I grew marvelously refreshed. I heard the sounds of the boat in my dreams, as sailors do; my life depended on keeping a sixth sense awake so that changes of wind or waves against the bow were always registering. This sixth sense kept alert during sleep had been a necessity in submarine days, and now it was useful. The ocean's spaciousness overwhelmed me. Although working incessantly at the boat, a curious feeling of leisure, so illogical it is difficult to describe, pervaded every day. I began to ignore the "duty" of racing *Galway Blazer*. From Mike Steemson's radio communication I knew that the brilliant French yachtsman Bernard Moitessier in his superbly designed steel ketch *Joshua* was far ahead. I could not force speed out of my boat. She had not been designed to race. Anyway, Anita, who had made few but usually astute remarks concerning this venture, had insisted, "You've got caught up in this old race, but don't let it bother you. For heaven's sake enjoy yourself—that's what you *said* you wanted to do. That is what *your* venture is all about."

So, on October 2, without any feeling of guilt, I could write in my letter to her:

I awoke with a start at four A.M. to find that I had
had five hours' solid sleep. I realized the wind
had both eased and veered away from the old
sea; so no thumping and I went up to find we
were gliding peacefully along under clear sky
over a moonlit sea. I should have been up during the night shaking our reefs and driving her
to windward, but that sleep was without price
and so was the beauty of the dawn.

October third:

It was a very bumpy night and I was up and
down with a half decision to reef her in my mind
all the time. The Trade Wind is very puffy, and
as soon as one says to oneself, "reef," it sighs
down. . . . I think I would have reefed but for
the bulging South American continent under
my lee and the pull of the current nagging at
me. I felt I must drive on, but at dawn came a
real snorter, a thundery squall, most un-Trade-
Windy. I was up in a flash and again thankful
for the Chinese rig—reefing is so easy, like fold-
ing a Venetian blind.

On October fourth I wrote:

There is a period of full moon now; this is
comforting because I am passing the South
American ports of Recife and Montevideo, and
its brilliant light gives me security against being
run down in the night. At midnight I was thinking of this, and sitting in the cockpit admiring
the high clouds etched in sharp patterns against
the moonlight, when I felt a violent fluttering in
my right armpit; turning in amazement, I
found an equally surprised flying fish. I was too

slow to grab him and he skittered off into the
sea, little guessing how near he had been to
making breakfast. At four A.M. I watched a
scene of unforgettable splendor. In wild night
flight the boat tore over the wave crests under a
clear sky, the sea flashed like a bayonet charge,
and my white sails reflected the moonlight.
Smaller stars being muted, only Orion and
Sirius flamed overhead in the dark sector of the
sky. I considered reefing down, but somehow I
felt it would disappoint the boat, she was speeding so happily, showing her best points hard on
the wind; so I postponed reefing until dawn
when she really started to crash and pound.

Sometimes I would sleep heavily, lulled by a drop in
speed, then awake to the softer wave beat and dash up on
deck to shake out reefs. Sometimes the sudden change of
note brought me hurtling on deck to reduce sail for a
squall.

By October fifth I had covered four thousand miles.
This seemed rather a slow passage for forty days, but the
Doldrums had held the boat up more than I expected.
We had covered one thousand miles in the last week
while hard on the wind, making an average of
approximately one hundred and forty-three miles a day
—good going for a five-tonner. With the wind abaft the
beam she could reach nearly eight knots, and wave-
riding we might double that. I was looking forward to
those Roaring Forties blowing around the South Pole to
carry me along.

My special diet of biscuits, soaked raisins, and nut
paste never palled and never sickened me. The only
thing I added and felt worth the bother of cooking were
the flying fish which landed on deck, or in the sheet tail
boxes which proved perfect traps. I would clean the fish,
remove head and tail wings, bring to the boil in a little

seawater and rewarm in nut paste. This delicious dish I named *flying fish à l'Amande.*

I found that my navigating skill, allowed to lie dormant for several years, quickly returned with practice, and with smug satisfaction I noted that my calculated positions agreed exactly with the astronomical fixes. I started to write odes to the petrels that soared and dipped in the air currents above each wave. When not at my poetry, my reading, my eating, or my sleeping, I worked at carpentry, constructing more handholds with the set of tools given me by a friend, Jönne Lacon, whose home, Norris Castle, overlooked The Solent; she was often blessed by me in those southern "Variables," for although I have no flair as a handyman, first-rate tools can make carpenters of us all.

Many people had asked me what I would do about water. This was no problem. Having topped up with water in the Doldrum squalls, I made a ration test with a two-gallon jerrican and found it lasted nine days. I needed less than a quart a day for drinking, soaking raisins, and watering about one square foot of cress. As for food supplies, a check-over revealed nearly a year's supply! One might say I had not a care in the world.

The moods of the sea change like those of a primadonna. Off the southern parts of Brazil (where the distance was too great for radio contact with Cape Town), I wrote:

> The sea sparkles and is broken only by the flash of a flying fish; warm it is, but balmy-warm with a perfect breeze. One would like to sail on forever. When contemplating eternity, people often cry, "But how boring if *forever.*" But now I feel I could go on just peering at the sea and sky, transforming in light and color, never hostile! . . . The sea rewards as the land does. The sailor grumbles as the farmer does. But the rotating

earth and speeding clouds change his background. He is never stuck in a black mood like
city dwellers.

Anna Karenina became my companion in quiet hours.
How I understood her, out there—never had reading
given me such pleasure. Was I lonely? It never entered
my head to be so. Loneliness is a frame of mind; it is not
due to isolation from people. No, the lack of interruption
enabled me to understand my fellowmen far better than
before. I had the exciting feeling that my mind was
shedding scales, my vision clearing. Even the disintegra-
tion of the big, expensive movie camera fixed to the
foredeck by a television firm, ITV, in the hopes I might
bring back dramatic storm films did not fret me. I tried
everything I knew to make it work, but when I turned the
test switch it emitted a ghostly electrical groan which
faded into silence. Worse than letting down TV was the
disappointment of not being able to send my daughter a
message for her seventeenth birthday. Sometimes the
radio became very faint. We were now one thousand
miles from any land. Mike Steemson was only just au-
dible to me, while he could not hear a word I said.

On October sixteenth I nearly met disaster from sheer
carelessness. Later I wrote to Anita:

> I remember your fears that I would fall over the
> side! Yesterday I did just that. We were
> becalmed and I take advantage of these stops to
> refit the rigging and abate chafe. In order to
> give more mobility to myself and as we were not
> moving, I left off my safety harness. I was
> balancing on the foredeck in the heaving swells,
> rigging a lazy foresheet as an experiment to
> control the foresail when lowered. I was push-
> ing the foresail boom out to its limit for test
> when I found myself flying through the air and

into the Atlantic. I was able to resolve any doubts as to whether one could scramble back over the gunwale. Out of my dripping shorts I found the only damage was a bruised thigh, a scraped ankle, and lost sunglasses. Dividends gained were a smart lesson in caution.

Now *Galway Blazer II* always had an albatross in attendance, and when a flying fish landed on deck, I would snatch it up quickly—not his breakfast—*mine!* But how I marveled at that glorious bird gliding above the mast, wheeling in a quartering patrol. His wings hardly beat, for with wonderful economy of effort, he uses the upsurge of wind from the waves for his glide current. One tip of his huge wing is sometimes so close to the water that it looks as though it rests upon its surface. As we approached the Antarctic, my companions were *two* noble albatrosses. Now the antics of the sooty shearwater, which I had admired for weeks, appeared lacking in grace. My eye had grown as critical as a balletomane comparing ballerinas. I wondered about their guidelines. Little can be observed of albatross habits, and I rather suspect that, like land creatures, they cover definite territories, each bird keeping to certain sea zones while maintaining a homing beam to their breeding grounds on the Antarctic continent. Once I saw two seabirds fighting furiously. After squealing and circling each other for more than five minutes, the whiter bird flew off northward, leaving the dark rival, monarch of that zone.

On October twenty-fourth I wrote:

For the first time in my life I have been able to read Shakespeare's *Sonnets* with real enjoyment. During this voyage, when the requirements of life are simplified, my mind becomes uncluttered. Van Gogh said in a

moment of stress "It was as though a swarm of
bees flew into my nose." Well, my swarm is
flying out.

> Some glory in their birth, some in their
>   skill,
> Some in their wealth, some in their
>   body's force,
> Some in their garments though new-
>   fangled ills.
> Some in their hawks and hounds,
>   some in their horse;
> Wherein it finds a joy above the rest. . . .

How well I understand these lines. My hawk, my hound,
my horse is *Galway Blazer.*

By now I heard from Mike Steemson that Bernard
Moitessier in *Joshua* had worked out a tremendous lead.
My boat was not designed to race, only to carry me alive
around the world, so it was silly of me to feel bothered. I
wrote:

> The peace of the long sail, of the months away
> from mankind with only the sea and sky with
> whichto battle, and my beautiful boat as com-
> panion—this peace is wrecked by the nagging
> knowledge that I am in a race and reluctant to
> force the pace.

On the night of October twenty-sixth I received an
unexpected shock. *Galway Blazer II* was racing along on a
fast beam-reach, doing her maximum—a good seven
and a half knots when, as the wind rose, I went on deck to
put in a reef. There, about half a mile on my beam were
the lights of a steamship. My eyes must have popped in
horror, but I saw that I would pass clean ahead, so I
forbore to switch on lights. If a small boat suddenly

shows lights at the last minute, the other ship may get confused and alter course wrongly without time to take bearings. But it was an odd, frightening, jarring experience. How I disliked seeing another ship in *my sea!* I loved the seabirds and was able to watch their natural habits out here. A mass of exotic varieties which I had never seen before now surrounded us, and I cursed my thoughtlessness in not bringing a book to identify them. They must have come from the isles of Tristan da Cunha, for they vanished as storm clouds blew up. Only my constant friends, the two albatrosses, continued to circle around. Storms do not worry them; they sit contentedly on the water in high winds. In fact, I nearly ran one down at dawn. I think he *must* have been asleep.

I tried to catch rainwater in the squalls, but one catch landed a jellyfish and the others took in a lot of sea water in the swell. One can only catch rain when the sea is smooth.

At dawn on October twenty-eighth a gale hit us. Having reefed down, I went confidently to sleep. I always sleep well in a gale. My little boat rode it; these crashing seas suited her, and as I rocked to and fro against the wooden sides of my narrow bunk, I felt with every nerve in my body how bravely she reacted. Although we were just in 36 degrees south, we had picked up winds of Roaring Forties strength. We spent most of the night with reefed sail set, reaching happily along at a fair speed. The gale blew like playing scales through Force 6, 7, and 8. *Galway Blazer II* scooted over the big waves. I thought, "At last she is getting her proper trials, which we never had time or weather for at home." Everything seemed to be going right. I knew her to be a marvelous boat. At this point I began regretting not having brought an anemometer. I seemed to have lost the art of gauging wind force; I had possessed this knack in ocean-racing days twenty years before, but on the Irish farm I had only to assess when there was too much wind for carting hay!

On October twenty-ninth the gale started to abate, but I found myself darting around nervously attending to things which were doing perfectly all right. Then I made the mistake of trying to save time and wetness by not coming up into the wind. As a result, the sail did not set right and I was up all night wrestling with the results of my "time-saver." I ate a huge breakfast at five thirty A.M. next morning and scribbled a few lines to Anita. This was the last "voyage letter" I ever wrote her.

CHAPTER 11

Capsize

FOR three days I had no time to eat or sleep, much less take up my pen. *Anna Karenina* was forgotten as, on the afternoon of October thirtieth, the wind increased to hurricane force and the worst storm I have ever witnessed in a lifetime spent at sea broke over the Southern Ocean. I had seen terrible storms from the tiny platform of a submarine, and from sailing boats all over the world, but no seas that ever equaled the mammoth waves which battered *Galway Blazer*, now one thousand miles south southwest of Cape Town.

It was frightening in the way that an earthquake must be frightening. The entire ocean seemed to be erupting into black-pointing mountain peaks and vast valleys. The light grew gray-green. The wind shrieked insanely. For twenty-four hours I stood in the cockpit under the hatches, spellbound by these extraordinary sights and attempting to steer. I never grew hungry or thirsty. I never wanted to lie down. I was part of it.

The tumult came screaming from northward and my searoom lay toward the ice-bound polar landmass two thousand miles southward. At least there was no danger of being driven on a lee shore. Braced in the cockpit, I felt the hull lift and heave. Sometimes she pointed vertically downward; sometimes she was flung on her side. All through that long night and all through the next day *Galway Blazer* danced to the hurricane. I carried no sea anchor because, in a boat of such light displacement, I believed her safety lay in freedom to ride the waves unencumbered. Once the sky suddenly cleared and I saw a full moon cold and detached high above the chaos. Day and night hardly changed the light. I felt a sort of astonishment at what my world had turned into. We were out of the hurricane area, but hurricanes wander without permission. Once in thirty years they blow up out of season on some unexpected line as this one had.

On the whole, fate had always dealt me lucky hands. I thought she had done so again. As evening came on October thirty-first—and I laughed to remember this was Halloween, the witches' big night—the storm center moved on. Elated, I realized that *Galway Blazer* had ridden out the storm and suffered no damage. When the winds started to die down, I decided to remove the hurricane hatches and go out on deck to look at the vane-steering. The gale roar was over, although huge seas continued to rise and fall around us. I returned to the enclosed cockpit to fetch a piece of rope with which to secure the foresail before sailing on under bare poles, and I was sitting jammed into place under the two open hatches, coiling the rope, when the boat seemed to be hit by an explosion. I realized she was shivering right over on her side; knocked down by colliding mountains of water, she was sliding on her side as a surfer on his board. I had time to think. "She must go over, but she will come back again; the weight of the lead keel will swing her upright." I felt her nearly right herself—very, very nearly. But some new foam-lashed wave was tearing across the trough in which we lay as if resting before regaining balance. I felt her going and going and going, and then she was upside down. I was standing on my head, or, rather, on my shoulders, looking at the hatches through which green water poured upward. I knew the masts were pointing at the sea bottom and the keel at the sky. I felt no fear. There was nothing I could do except cling on in my wedged position. Had this rogue sea hit two minutes earlier or two minutes later, I would have been on deck and certainly drowned. As it was, I just had to wait for the two-ton keel to right her. There was a mighty flick, and back she came. The cockpit had shipped two or three tons of water. My eyes roamed over the mess in the cabin and focused on the gimbaled stove hanging upside down and stuck in this position as if to prove what an awful adventure it had known. I would never know if we had come up on the same side as we went down, or if we had done a complete roll over. But I did feel certain that she had taken a violent nose-dive at the same time and nearly pitch-poled end over end. Curiously I wanted to reconstruct in detail exactly what had happened.

There was no time for immediate surmise. The moment she had righted herself, I started to pump out water. After half an hour I pulled myself on deck to survey my lovely boat. The scene was one of utter devastation—the foremast had snapped off about twelve feet up; and the mainmast, although still standing, had obviously been cracked and bent over at a drunken angle; the vane-steering gear lay shattered in a tangle of twisted metal shaft. Had I carried the conventional stayed masts, I imagine the mess would have been worse. No masts could have supported the pressure of rising fast through the water.

Such is man's nature that, instead of feeling grateful that I had not been on deck during the capsize, I felt bitter that she who had ridden out the hurricane, had met defeat when the actual winds had died and only the phenomenal seas remained. There could now be no question of sailing on around the world. Cape Town, a thousand miles to the northeast, was my nearest port. I must rig the jury mast and get there somehow. Phase one of my "nerve cure" was over.

The memory of hours, nights, days after a complete capsize has broken the masts and steering, and thrown every object onto the cabin ceiling, is difficult to arrange into a clear picture afterward. First one has to deal with oneself, one's own sense of personal outrage that the sea had seen fit to render such a blow. Then comes frenzied action on deck and then a creeping, cursing tidying-up below, where Nescafé, wet clothes, nut paste, and raisins lie in jumbled heaps of compost. One stares at them, tries to salvage the most important things. After hours of work one tries to get a little sleep in a soaking padded bag.

Tremendous waves continued for three days after the high winds subsided. Never in my life before or since have I seen such colossal seas. (This hurricane, which Tristan da Cunha fishermen were to describe later as the worst in their memory, also caught Louis Fougernon some four hundred miles northwest of me. His thirty-foot cutter rode out the storm but was so badly smashed that he had to abandon the race and put in at St. Helena for repairs. No other race contestants were in the area.)

On November first, the day after the capsize, Mike Steemson tried in vain to contact me by radio, but on the following day I managed to get the aerial fixed up to the broken mainmast. Since this gave it more height than its previous place on the foremast, it enabled Mike, who was trying like hell to get through from Cape Town transmitting station, to suddenly hear me with surprising clearness. We were still tossing on and over vast valleys and mountain ridges of water. "How are you, Bill?" Mike's voice sounded as if it came from the next room, and apparently my shouts boomed in his radio room where the operators listened transfixed. "Rolled right over . . . dismasted . . . foremast gone completely . . . mainmast bent over at a big angle . . . don't yet know if it will carry a sail . . . vane gone but I think I can fix up some self-steering . . . I am uninjured except for bruises where I stood on my head on the roof. I'll rig a jury if it ever gets calm enough . . . there's a huge sea running after the gale and it's blowing up again now, but somehow I'll get the jury mast up amidships if I can cut the mainmast away. . . ."

Mike telephoned this news back to London within the hour and John Coote, managing director of the *Daily Express* who had been a submariner, considerately got the news through to my wife through a friend in Ireland. She was just off on her horse with the Galway Blazers and could not make out if she ought to be appalled at the disaster or thankful I was alive. She told me afterward that, when she dropped in for the usual Wednesday message, a friend met her at the door. "Johnnie Coote came through early. He says Bill is *all right* but has capsized and broken a mast."

"*All right!* " she said. "What kind of 'all right'? But one must be thankful for any kind." Then she asked for a drink.

After hacking off the broken foremast with a machete, I worked at repairing the vane-steering, and when the wind fell sufficiently, I got up the mainsail, with trepidation, for this increased the mast's bend and I wondered if it might fall on me. Then, while the sea roared itself out, I lay down on my bunk surrounded by the shambles—jars of soaked raisins and wheat had burst all over the cabin. The chart table was deep in cress and wet biscuits. I had omitted to hook up a few rubber holding cords, but no precautions could have prevented bilge water from deluging clothes and bedding.

Hardly had I fallen asleep when a lightning storm started—I awoke pressing my eyeballs in disbelief at the incessant electric flashes. In the dawn, gargantuan thunderclaps rumbled. I took down the three panels of sail I had dared to raise and switched my aerial seaward. The moment she was down to bare poles (or pole in this case), *Galway Blazer* revealed she was unable to run downwind without her foremast. I had to lie hulling throughout a violent Force 10 to 12 storm; but these seas were as nothing compared to the hurricane. Although high, steep, and with breaking crests, the waves kept arriving in orderly rolls one after another. Even in such a moment I had to register admiration for *Galway Blazer*'s design and construction. Once she was laid sideways on her beam ends an in such a way that any coach roof or deck house would have been broken had it existed. By now I felt *Galway Blazer*'s trembling hull like part of my body, and in this moment when she was lying flat on the surface, I could sense her going over, but *not going farther*—just as an acrobat must feel himself approaching a somersault, then balancing back into a half-somersault. Luckily the bent mainmast did not dip deep into the water and came up as before. The fact that it did not snap in this flick roll gave me confidence in its power to hold a sail, and on the next morning, November fifth, I tried out a little sail with the wind against the bend of the mast. Would it hold? It did. I saw with relief that wind pressure on the sail was decreasing the bend instead of increasing it. For a moment I wondered if I could risk sailing on to the Horn without a foremast, but this wild hope soon faded. I might creep to Cape Town without cracking that bent pole, but obviously it *could* snap at any sudden pressure. So I retired gloomily below to shake wheat out of navigational charts and water out of chronometers. Human beings throw out prayers for help in danger and then forget to be grateful. The elation of having survived my capsize lasted about twenty-four hours. Had we pitched over sixty seconds later, I would certainly have been on deck under the water and under the broken foremast. This nasty fate had been averted through outside forces of time and destiny. I tried to be suitably grateful, but as we wallowed slowly northward, I began to feel extremely sorry for myself.

Angus Primrose had once asked me for a list of faults in the boat's design. I had thought, during the colossal seas of the hurricane, "There's not a fault in this boat if she can run and lie a-hull so smoothly in this." Then she had been caught in a caldron of breaking crests which I honestly had to believe no other boat could have resisted without hull damage. Her rounded lines without any straight surface had enabled her to turn like a fish or a seal when submerged, and she had swung up again uninjured. Had she possessed stayed masts, I believe that they certainly would have snapped and that the stays might have broken parts of the hull, creating a far worse situation. Therefore, I ought to have been grateful. And indeed, had it been possible for me to mend my masts and voyage on toward the Horn, I should have been so.

As it was, I knew that after several weeks remasting in Cape Town it would be very late in the season. We could never be ready to sail until after Christmas, and that would mean rounding the Horn in the icy autumn, instead of in the Antarctic summer, which is cold enough.

It took me twenty-two days of creeping along under short canvas at about fifty miles a day to reach Cape Town. Bored and resentful, I found myself eating double what I had before the capsize—compulsive eating is, I believe, a well known symptom in jilted females. Males take to the bottle. I had no bottle, so now that this particular "love affair" had gone wrong I took to surfeits of raisins and almond paste.

Eventually I managed to get the jury mast up. This was a wonderfully designed affair of two tubular metal legs bolted together at the top. Each leg had a sliding base which moved along a track to be screwed in position. Easy to handle in harbor, it proved extremely difficult to raise in a jumpy sea, and while working on the foredeck, I kept making mental notes of gadgets which would help one not to fall off the whaleback—a low bulwark to get my feet against and holes in all the deck stringers to lash myself down. For this boat was an experimental design and there *would* be a next time—there lay my luck—unlike most men who take an ocean holiday I had time at my disposal. I could wait to try again with certain small alterations, and the sooner we reached Cape Town the sooner I could get these in hand. Sometimes when I was becalmed I felt about as cheerful as Napoleon returning from Moscow, but the moment a breeze blew I would crawl out along the foredeck and loose the storm jib and off we would bound and my spirits flickered up.

The Royal Cape Town Yacht Club was taking enormous interest in my plight. After a fortnight of listening to my plaintive radio messages Colonel Jeffery, owner of a powerfully engined yacht, asked if he could meet me two hundred miles out to give a fast tow back. We made a rendezvous by radio and on November seventeenth I saw a large ketch, *Corsair II*, to starboard. She circled, floated a line down, and Mike Steemson came on board by dinghy, bringing champagne and steaks, which we cooked in my almond paste. He also carried an advance copy of *South African Yachting* with my picture on the cover. I did not feel like anyone's pinup boy at the time, but I had to be proud, later, when I read an article written on *Corsair II*: "When I first saw *Galway Blazer II* after her Roaring Forties capsize I could not believe how trim she looked."

As I had no ship's papers whatsoever, complications could have arisen but the port authorities smilingly glanced at my passport and Bible as sufficient testimony of good intentions.

Back on dry land after nearly three months alone at sea, I found no strangeness or difficulty in adjusting to the world of people. Perhaps I talked more than usual; certainly I drank more, because the local wine was so delicious. For a few nights I would wake with a start, thinking myself still at sea, leap from my bed and stagger toward where the cockpit should have been. On one such occasion the noise and lights of a car outside caused me to jump into the middle of the room—I thought that a merchant ship had come close to running us down and that I could hear her engine noises and see her lights illuminating the cabin.

Tarka Dick, preparing for A-level examinations, flew out laden with lesson books which he kept intending to open. I reminded him occasionally of the importance of his A levels. But, to tell the truth, such exhaustion swept over me *after* the long slug to Cape Town amid the debris of my masts that I was only too glad to have him here working cheerfully at clearing up smashed gear. And I was hardly in form for the lavish hospitality which Cape Town offered, but Tarka, aged eighteen, was of course ready—only too ready—to go ashore for dinners, cocktail parties, and picnics. The only occasion when I saw the smile fade from his face was when he had offered to stay working on board through the lunch hour. "Come on," I said, "there's plenty to eat, my usual sea diet." "Oh, yes, let's try it." After a couple of spoonfuls of nut oil and raisins he began to look thoughtful. "I think actually I *will* go to the Club House."

After some little cogitation, I decided to ship *Galway Blazer* home on the deck of a cargo ship. Had we remasted in Cape Town, it should have been an easy sail back with the winds mostly free, and Tarka Dick was longing to come with me—he talked of the "stimulus" the trip would have on his studies. But several things weighed against it. As this initial effort to sail around the world had ended late in the season and I could not have belted straight on, I thought it better to take my dismasted boat back to Souter's yard where Blondie could discuss possible modifications in her rig to increase speed in the Doldrums. And if I was not sailing, there was the farm to attend to. And, above all, the lure of Christmas at home.

While in Cape Town, Mike Steemson and I climbed Table Mountain together. He had been a splendid link with home during the past months of hectic exertions and strain, and apart from my own knock, I was genuinely sorry that his paper, the *Daily Express*, which had backed my boat to get nonstop around the world, had been let down by our dismasting. But I could not blame the boat which had survived in unbelievable seas. We climbed for two hours in the keen winelike sunshine and sat down on Table Mountain's rocky summit, looking out over the Atlantic and discussing the four boats still in the race. We did not yet know that Louis Fougernon was heading for St. Helena, badly damaged in the aftermath of the hurricane that had broken my masts. And we *could* not know that Bernard Moitessier, the likely winner, who was at that moment approaching Cape Horn, would decide to opt out of it all and sail on into the Pacific to settle in the South Seas, or that Nigel Tetley's trimaran *Victress* would sink when overcanvased off the Azores, leaving him to be rescued after forty-eight hours in a rubber dinghy, or that his supposed opponent, the tragic Donald Crowhurst, who never actually left the Atlantic, would die, leaving his trimaran abandoned in the silent ocean. Of the nine boats which had participated in this solo race only Robin Knox Johnson's *Suhaili* would sail from England to England. His boat damaged by Pacific storms was at this moment anchored on a sandbank off New Zealand while he himself did repairs.

To Anita, I wrote: "I am longing to get home to refit and sail again next August. I hope there will be no race, but just me against the sea."

Part II

CHAPTER 12

Plymouth, England, to Western Australia

DURING the following spring, 1969, while Souter's yard made two new masts, Blondie Hasler and I spent our time trying to devise a method of altering the junk-rig so that I could sail closer to the wind. In the hope of obtaining a better set for the sails, we peaked up both mainsail and mizzen. This new layout certainly improved speed when we met head winds during trials, but it is difficult to find storm conditions just when you want them, especially during the summer. I was moderately hopeful of finding *Galway Blazer* able to make much faster progress when I again set forth to sail around the world. But I would have to discover just what could happen with this new experimental rig later on, after I got into the open Atlantic.

Anita again saw me off from Plymouth, and while waiting for an easterly wind, we stayed with a submariner friend in Admiralty House. John and Philippa Roxburgh* showed immense understanding during this rather nerve-racking period of waiting. Tarka Dick did not join us because he was busy traveling around the world, "keeping to the *land*, Daddy, and seeing things my way, not yours." But Leonie came to stay, and I had to realize for the first time that she was no longer a little girl

---

*Vice Admiral Sir John Roxburgh, V.C.B., D.S.O., D.S.C., and Lady Roxburgh.

but a young lady of the long-haired, blue-jeaned variety—a very serious art student. "Don't worry about *me*—I know how to look after myself—*you* look after *yourself.*"

But the boat was ready, and when one day the wind blew from the northeast, I set out for the second time from Plymouth. As soon as I reached the Atlantic and had experienced a week of rough open ocean, it became obvious that the new rig was simply not going to work. When fully reefed, the yard fouled the topping lifts so that the sail became inextricably jammed and would go neither up nor down. I battled angrily with this tangle all through the turbulent Bay of Biscay, and then accepted the bitter fact. This experiment was an absolute failure, but only stormy ocean conditions could prove it so. I'd found my gales too late in the season. It was no good struggling on. The sensible thing was to pack it up immediately and turn into Gibraltar. The "race" was over and no press were covering me. What a relief it was to be completely my own master and able to take such action without feeling that anybody would be "let down." An ex-naval officer sailing his own boat around the world can be certain of a warm reception in any naval base, and I knew it foolish to let myself become downhearted at having to make this decision. There was really no alternative, and it is *indecision* about possible lines of action that wears one down. However, this was a very unexpected change of plan.

As I sailed toward the Strait of Gibraltar, into an ever-thickening stream of traffic, I realized that with no local charts I must keep my wits about me. I sat back and refreshed my memory of the topography by recalling the many occasions when I had operated in, over, and under these waters. The winding, narrow strait with mountains on either side seems more like a river than a part of the sea. A cold Atlantic current pours in through the narrow strait, and ninety feet down a countercurrent flows back out of the Mediterranean. This two-way current was the greatest help to German U-boats during the wars, enabling them to drift in or out at the required depth. And it must be the reason that tunny fish can be netted on their way into the Mediterranean but never on their way out. Presumably they "go deep" and ride along in the current for their run westward. The winds which blow back and forth through this funnel between Spain and Morocco attain such force that they can govern the surface current. A sail through the Pillars of Hercules always needs hard concentration. In a blow it can become very difficult indeed to beat through to windward, and the old square-riggers could not manage it. An anecdote of the last century was passed on to me by a very old sailor. In his day there was a certain irascible admiral in a sailing battleship who, finding himself immobilized, ordered one of his squadron, fitted with "auxiliary steam," to tow him through. The towrope was passed with precision, and great effort was made by the captain of the ship who carried "that innovation, a steam engine." After some hours of thrashing into the wind without making progress, the captain of the towing ship made a signal to his superior. "Unless the wind and tide abate, I cannot tow you through the strait." The admiral, nettled by failure and the apparent levity of the unpremeditated rhyme, instantly retaliated in kind: "While in your bunker you have coal—you'll go ahead, god damn your soul."

I had no auxiliary engine, but I hoped for and got a favorable wind. *Galway Blazer* sailed in fast through the Pillars of Hercules, while I raced around on deck, and the great Rock seemed to be looking down on me in friendly fashion—after all, we'd known each other for forty years. Of course no one expected me at the naval base, but what a welcome I got! After a few days in the mess, it seemed best to leave the boat there for the winter and fetch her back to England in the spring. I traveled home on a destroyer which boasted the best food in the navy and the largest cook. It was all very different from my youthful memories of bully and biscuit.

Winter slides by quickly in the Irish countryside. A late northern dawn opens up hours in the saddle; early sunset brings the long night of reading and talk by the turf fire. Then suddenly the feel of the air changes and the sounds in the woods are not the same; a first snowdrop has hardly looked through the grass when some much-too-early violets show in sheltered hollows. For me it was soon time to return to Gibraltar and bring my boat home to be rerigged in her original fashion.

On reaching the Rock, I made the unfortunate discovery that an acquaintance had taken it upon himself to sail my boat out uninsured and do expensive damage, breaking off her foremast. I had to sail her back to Cowes alone in this state, and it was a very exhausting voyage because not only did I have this difficult broken rig, but winds blew against me all the way. *Galway Blazer* was unbalanced by the loss of her foremast. I could hardly believe it could take so long to beat through the Bay of Biscay. As a result of the broken mast, I reached the Western Approaches so late that I had to slave as if in an ocean race in order to reach a certain wedding in time. It is strange how such motives can drive one. Alexandra Jellicoe was Anita's goddaughter, and I had known her since childhood. As I beat up the channel, struggling against those consistently adverse winds, I kept visualizing her as a little girl, golden hair flying, as she rode a pony around our land, and I grew ever more determined to see that particular bride walk up to the altar. I nearly hit a buoy in my haste to find a mooring, get off the boat, take a train to London, plunge into a bath, and find a suit! But I managed to reach the church with half an hour to spare.

During the summer Blondie came down to Cowes and *Galway Blazer II* went back to her original rig. After being so horridly fouled up in Atlantic gales, I was only too ready to creep through the Doldrums. Apart from adding a few handholds in useful places, I could not suggest a single alteration which might improve my boat. She had shown that her light, buoyant hull gave the greatest possible safety in ultimate sea conditions, and the more I thought it over, the surer I felt that no other boat could have taken that hurricane capsize with so little damage. When the men of Souter's yard, who had fashioned *Galway Blazer's* complex hull, examined her after the disaster, they reported *no sign of strain or movement.* She had emerged from her capsize in that caldron of violent, seething, cliff-high waves in perfect condition. It takes time to really know a boat and what she will stand up to, and I certainly knew *Galway Blazer II* by now! In fact, by this September of 1970 I had far more confidence in my little craft than when I had set sail the first time. And as well as this, I had accumulated a big reassuring bank of experience on which to draw. Sailing experience is real wealth; you can stuff it in every crevice of your mind, it doesn't weigh you down; it keeps you buoyant. In submarine combat I had gained more experience than most, but this kind wears out one's mental reserve and the elasticity of one's nerves becomes overstretched. Now, despite two disappointments, I was moving off into the healthiest, if hardest, of routine. The sea always suited me. I used to say that once I got away from land I *could not* feel ill. But one exception always proves the rule.

On this occasion, pounding out into the Atlantic, I ran straight into a northwest gale and got a migraine! It was, I am sure, the result of last-minute shopping in Plymouth, but whatever the cause, I felt immensely sorry for myself. Tottering around the cabin or resting briefly in my bunk, literally groaning with self-pity, I wondered what my temperature could be. Miserably I watched Ushant lighthouse slide by in the distance—the famous landmark meant nothing to me. Even after a few hours' sleep I still had a headache and kept muffing my tasks.

Once, in the dusk, I looked out on deck to find we were about to run into a fishing trawler. I tacked quickly away and then again had to change course to avoid a merchant ship. When the wind fell light, and I rehoisted the sails, shaking out all the reefs, I was trembling with weakness. "So, you're never sick at sea!" I muttered to myself crossly. But we were only three days out, and I knew this migraine would fade as I shed the nervous tension of setting off. The seemingly unavoidable last-minute rush, combined with dependence on the wind and visibility which necessitates perpetual telephoning for weather reports, wears down all lone sailors before departure.

As the sun rose on the fourth day out, I knew myself cured, and when the wind freed, I made my point around the next mark on the course—the northwest corner of Spain. But I still remained in a crowded shipping area and was horridly aware of a gaggle of six ships, including a vast oil tanker southbound. I was scared that one of these might alter course and come on top of me. Because the wind had fallen so light, I could not tack away from them and I thanked the moon for lighting dark shapes. All around me the sea seemed full of gliding ships, and I longed for the open ocean and empty horizons.

Slamming into a tumbled sea that seemed as hard as concrete used to make me wonder if the thin laminated hull would break up; but *Galway Blazer* had stood up to so much of this treatment that by now I felt she could thrust along forever.

We had two days of crashing seas, and then suddenly the roar died away and *Galway Blazer* sat becalmed in the Bay of Biscay. The sun came out to give me the luxury of a warm convalescence, and gratefully I used its free heat to liquefy the tallow to make it easy to smear all the parrel ropes around the masts twice. Tallow makes the sails easier to raise; it also silences creaking noises and prevents chafe.

In the Bay of Biscay I really had to concentrate entirely on tacking out of the shipping lanes. It was not easy because, while I was trying to avoid traffic and fishing banks, vast new Jumbo tankers were doing the same thing. One of these monsters throbbed so close to me in the calm sea that the officer of the watch could give me a cheerful wave. This tanker looked not like a ship, but as if a skyscraper had toppled on its side and butted off across the ocean.

As my boat danced along in sunlight and moonlight through the Finisterre area, an ancient fishing trawler passed close to me on a northerly course with a small gun in her bows. For whales, maybe?

I no longer wrote daily letters to my wife (although she had enjoyed reading the first bundle), but I kept a detailed log. On September nineteenth I wrote:

> All night I cruised silently southwards in a light north wind with only the foresail reflecting the moonlight curved like a porchway in a Greek island hilltop village. A velvet night with little movement. By dawn and perhaps before, while I slept, the wind increased and I hoisted the mainsail. She sped south like one of those angry swans charging a rival across Galway Bay. But it's a poor run for the first week—less than six hundred miles.

CHAPTER 13

Dolphin Migration

IN the stretches where I had always known rowdy conditions, the sea now remained a sheet of polished metal. Soon I felt the normal fretting of sailormen, a longing beyond reason for wind, any wind—a typhoon if need be—anything to bring movement to one's vessel. At last a little flock of clouds heralded a breeze and my spirits lifted with the sails as we surged slowly forward with noises at bow and quarter like a small babbling brook.

In immense lighthearted happiness, *Galway Blazer* crossed the fortieth parallel toward the Trade Wind belt. But on September twenty-sixth I knew sudden panic, for when I switched on my shortwave converter to get a time check on my chronometer, complete deadness on every wave band. So I tried my Kestrel transceiver (the big one kept for reporting my position at special intervals), and that seemed stone dead also. I groaned. I hated fiddling with radio and kept consoling myself with the thought our ancestors sailed the seas without accurate chronometers. But, of course, they never quite knew were they were and whenever they encountered another ship, both would heave to and compare notes on the time! Then I remembered purchasing a small electric test-set from Brookes and Gatehouse—in fact, I had nearly refused to be persuaded by their Plymouth agent, but he kept on praising it, saying, "You may find it invaluable." Now I blessed that ardent salesman, for the electric tester enabled me to iron out the faults in both radio sets.

122

Soon I had to decide whether or not to pass inside Madeira. I could see there were many ships about and *Galway Blazer* was now crossing the shipping lanes which run out of the Mediterranean for the Americas. At night I switched on a light. By day, with her sails billowing against the sun, my boat made a dignified dreamlike progress disturbed only by soft susurrus and splashlets at the bow.

Then, to a series of gold-pink sunsets I had to settle philosophically down and relax. This had often happened to me before, and I laughed, remembering a windless week in the middle of the Atlantic when I was crewing in Bobby Somerset's *Iolaire*. On saying good-bye to Anita, I had told her, "We expect the voyage to take about twenty-eight days—" She thought I said thirty-eight and, when *Iolaire* did not reach Bermuda in the expected time, was alone among the wives who did not worry. In fact, she was puzzled when congratulatory telegrams reached her rejoicing that *Iolaire* was safe, having been spotted by a plane.

At night a faint easterly breeze might rise, but it was not the Trade Winds, only Africa breathing out. Once a yellow butterfly flew past and once a dragonfly landed on deck to groom himself. I watched his exquisitely articulated neck turning his head in complete reverse. On land I had never had time to study such minuscule performance. We were the only living creatures on top of the ocean for a hundred miles.

It was October first when a Trade Wind at last elected to blow, and *Galway Blazer* ran smartly past Madeira. I aimed to pass sixty miles west of the Canary Islands to miss their wind shadow. Now the sails filled in their silvery beauty and we started to cover one hundred and fifty miles a day and sometimes one hundred and seventy-five.

By October eighth we were bearing down on the Cape Verde Islands, and I could hear their air beacon on my radio. Flying fish began to jump prettily onto the deck; when I found one dead, I fried it, but those that were skittering about alive I dropped back into the ocean, they being doubtless much astonished by their peculiarly uncomfortable adventure. Some petrels flicked close overhead, and a band of porpoises played around the bows making their soft "chunk" noise on breaking surface to breathe.

In a dawn of violet lightning flashes I reached the Doldrums, and they proved even more deadly than before. But now I had learned a lesson and carried a larger and more varied library. Thomas Hardy and Anthony Trollope helped me to endure day after moveless day, and a friend had presented me with a superbly illustrated book on ocean birds.

As the Doldrums marched in, piling up a design of baroque white cloud, I devised a new plan for using fresh water. I had purposely trained myself to drink very little, so I thought I had enough to risk sailing with the large higher tank empty. When *Galway Blazer* had capsized in that incredible hurricane, I had felt, in the split second of her roll, that she very *nearly* righted herself before turning upside down. I had a feeling that had she carried less weight high up, she might have been rolled on her side without capsizing. So I decided *not* to let rain fill the upper water-tank from the deck catch, which is always rather brackish anyway, but just to fill the jerricans each time we had a downpour and drink from them.

With no steadying wind and a lumpish sea, I found it tricky going up to the masthead on a rope ladder. The cord lanyards which lashed the rungs to the mast firmly when in harbor would not stand up to the swell, and I had to improvise a lot of new fittings. Yet no matter what I worked out, I always returned from the masthead bruised and pouring with sweat. Exasperated, I took to lowering the rope ladder and using it as a bathing ladder. Owing to her high freeboard and bulging sides, *Galway*

Blazer is a very difficult hull to climb aboard without scraping one's shins. This ladder made all the difference. Now I washed my hair in "Fairy Green" and plunged down into the water to examine my log fitting and to scrub loose barnacles off the bottom. Little clouds of frightened fish swam off, and I hoped their presence meant that no sharks were around. One day three big fish followed the boat, doing porpoiselike surfacing movement, but they were bigger than porpoises and a light gray in color. I reckoned they must be the kind known as Risso's dolphin.

Much of my time was spent gazing longingly at the sky for any alteration of cloud formation which could presage wind. The clear blue of the Doldrums frequently carries a great amorphous mass of bulging black thundercloud which will produce a brief rainsquall, but what one prays for are those little white cottonwool puffs which accompany the Trade Winds. When not staring upward, I spent long hours scanning the flat, metallic, ever-heaving sea in case there should be a sign of approaching waves.

One day while I stood on deck hopefully straining my eyes, a most wonderful and astonishing sight was vouchsafed me. In fact, I have to wonder if I am the only man in the world who has ever witnessed this fantastic spectacle.

My eyes were, as usual, fixed on the glassy blue eastern horizon when a wide line of white ruffles, at least a mile across, appeared in the water. Waves! I trembled with the usual feverish excitement which fills a becalmed sailor at the slightest touch of wind. Hurrying around, I got ready to hoist sails and catch every whisper of a breeze. But this was not the froth of waves. As the long white wall rolled nearer, I saw to my amazement that thousands and thousands of porpoises were advancing together at full speed in a rectangular formation. Never having heard of their mass migrations, I could hardly believe this strange phalanx was true. As a rule porpoises are full of curiosity about a boat, and they sport around, playing a game that looks like last-across-the-bows. But this advance gave no time for playful inspection or games. Not one creature broke away from the massive formation. They passed me by with the deliberation of an army on the move. When the lines of foam disappeared from sight toward the west, I dropped below to plot their course on the chart. With absolute accuracy these creatures were moving across the South Atlantic at its narrowest point—from the bulge of Africa to the bulge of South America. I sat back to wonder—do they often migrate in a mass from one continental shelf to another? And, without charts, how do they know with exactitude where the narrowest part lies? For days I found myself overwhelmed by speculations on the mind of a porpoise—within each shining head must lie a chart table, compass, and the memory of feeding grounds and topography. All this wisdom must pass from one generation to another—the inheritance of their ages in the sea.

Toward the end of October we got enough wind to fill our ghoster, and a little lapping music sounded at the bow as *Galway Blazer* moved forward. Overhead, the clouds turned into fleets of galleons instead of the white headless serpents of the true Doldrums. I tried to calm my fretfulness with occupational therapy—splicing, carpentry, and battery charging, as well as Trollope. The Doldrums seemed to be moving south at just about my speed. I must have hit off the end of the African monsoon. The old ship masters probably knew of this timing and avoided it.

Then a teasing wind started. I had the sail up and down a dozen times each day for little fitful breezes, but moved nowhere. The sea has a very uncomfortable movement in this Doldrum area—the North Atlantic sends down its accumulated swell and the Southern

Trades push up their foretelling waves. These swells run opposite and through one another. The result of colliding waves looks like a series of mounds made of polished basalt.

When it rained, I washed out my sleeping bag sheets by just leaving them on deck for the drumming raindrops. I watched this process smugly, for the result was as good as if a strong peasant laundress had beaten them in a mountain stream. I found that rain caught by the sails tasted cleaner than off the deck and arranged for my drinking requirements in this way.

When, after three weeks of rolling in jolting seas, a real wind came blowing Force 4 from the south southwest, I had almost forgotten what sailing could be like—oh, the joy of clipping along at six to seven knots on a tack toward Africa. A long period in the Doldrums humbles a man, and now I grew jubilant at covering even sixteen miles in a day—when, a month earlier, I had been doing nearly two hundred!

On October twenty-sixth, just as I had got the foresail up and we were moving off nicely, I heard a loud crash on the vane steering-blade. I rushed aft to see a shark attacking the blade inquisitively. Frightened that he might break it, I beat his nose with a boat hook and drove him away. As soon as the mainsail went up and we increased speed, he ceased to follow me. I had the sensation of driving fast to discourage a barking dog.

On October twenty-ninth I made a short tack of about twenty-four hours to the eastward to give me a more comfortable slant to clear the bulge of South America—better, I thought, to try it here than farther south where the track is against the fast westbound equatorial current.

Not until November did I really get out of the Doldrums, and as the first Trade Winds started and it was up sails and properly away, a large blue-green fish, a dorade, joined me. With his small escorts, he darted around all day showing off his jumping. As we hurried faster, *they* attacked the vane-steering till it juddered—I tried to beat them off with hard blows, but, unlike the shark, they seemed to enjoy the challenge and swam faster and faster as if for Olympic medals.

Now the scurrying wind clouds were like vast herds of wild animals in migration. The fat elephant clouds blew Force 6 and the buffaloes Force 5 and the prancing deer Force 4. I could set my reefs by zoological display.

After Trollope and Thomas Hardy I enjoyed several long novels by Balzac, and then in the increasing heat I turned to my translations of the old classics—Socrates, Plato, Seneca, Julius Caesar, and the Greek anthology. I had a few technical books also.

One day I sat down to put together some ropes with long splices. This particular job had to be done perfectly so that the ropes would not be too thick at the joins to run through blocks. I had kept an excellent little handbook on rope-work to refresh my memory, but when I looked up the page about long splices, I discovered that some kind person in Plymouth had scissored it out for his own use.

In November the Trades blew southward and we shot along dancing from one wave top to the next at maximum speed. I could not call it making up for lost time because one would need wings rather than sails to make up for three weeks of becalming, but it was intoxicating to be released at last from that mid-Atlantic glue pot.

On November eleventh we reached the equator and passed under the ecliptic where the sun stands bang overhead at noon, leaving no shadow except a little round pool at my feet. I was becoming quite a dab hand at taking sun-sights in these conditions, but one has to work fast. There is something rather amusing in the way the sun behaves in the sextant down near the equator. A few seconds before noon you check him on an easterly

bearing and get his approximate altitude set. He appears
to be rising unusually fast, and then bang, right on noon
he runs around to south or north, according to which
side of the ecliptic one is on; in the sextant he appears to
roll right around the horizon like a golden cartwheel.
You have to be quick to snap the fix accurately. I always
had to obtain my latitude from the sun because, owing to
an eye injury, or, rather, an eye burn, I cannot take
star-sights. During submarine patrols one had to be constantly on the lookout for enemy aircraft, which always
attack *out of the sun*. I had years of this in the North Sea,
Mediterranean, and the Pacific. Eventually the strained
peering into brightness affected something in my eyes
which made them refract starlight so that I cannot get a
point of light. When peace came, the dazzling rays of the
sun no longer hid sudden dangers, but a certain bit of my
eyesight had gone and I had to turn to the golden globe
in a different way. At sea now, the sun had become my
guide and friend.

As we fled southward from the equator I rechecked all
stores. Perhaps I had overstruggled to reduce top weight
in the boat. I noted:

> *Clothes*: Plenty, but wish I'd brought more
> bedsheets. Laundry fine but drying slow.
> *Food*: Much less than last time. Only just enough
> for six months.
> *Water*: Much less owing to new policy of post-
> poning the time when I began to catch rainwa-
> ter. Must economize and live from one
> rainstorm to the next.
> *General stores*: Satisfactory.
> *Rope*: Not nearly enough, but this shortage
> turns me into a handy seaman. I am forever
> forestalling chafe and inventing devices to
> prevent it. Every spare bit of rope must be used
> up or spliced into another. I constantly change

> ropes round end for end to work into the idle
> parts or "freshen the nip" (alter the length of
> rope to put the chafing point on a different
> spot.)

At least I had plenty of tallow and could slosh it into rope leads and on parrels around the masts. I went around the boat fashioning little anti-chafe pads of slippery plastic hose liberally smeared with tallow.

On November fifteenth I obtained my first radio contact with Cape Town. I could just hear the operator, but we could not establish communication. In my log I wrote: "This seems quite natural as I am way back on my time schedule owing to the unexpected length of my becalming. I expected bad communication. At least the operator can let the family know that he got a few peeps on my wavelength, and that *Galway Blazer* is sailing along somewhere in the Southern Ocean. Anyway, how could I transmit the scenes that now held me riveted—the brilliant skies feathered by streaks of high cloud that turn to pink and gold at dawn and to scarlet at sunset. This is my personal world? While its beauty lasts, I own it." And the first albatross arrived just as I finished trying to talk to Cape Town, as if to say, "Pack it up. Forget the human world for a bit. Join us." He was of the gray-headed variety which is smaller than the great wandering albatross, and shyer. He didn't like to come close at all, but kept circling like a lookout. Meanwhile, a pair of South American terns, very shrill and assertive and not at all nervous, kept darting around the masts. They seemed mad about the boat, like children who had made an exciting discovery.

I had by now lived so long without any clothes, save short pants, that it was quite a surprise to find that I had to pull a sweater over my mahogany-colored skin. As we plugged down into the Forties, an adverse wind met us, but the current ran against it, which was a nice bonus. I

began studying the various albatrosses following my
boat—as well as defining their species, I could pick out
individuals. There was one splendid big fellow of the
wandering variety, with peculiar wing markings;
another smaller bird; and a sooty albatross which wore
the most peculiar expression on its face. I am rotten at
remembering people's faces at a cocktail party, but out
here one could see an individual creature with absolute
clarity. The same bird never followed my boat for more
than three or four days. They must divide up the ocean
into sectors; each male bird is probably as jealous of his
rights as land birds are of their territories. One day an
enormous wandering albatross came to watch me. He
was so big that when I noticed a white blob moving just
under him I wondered if he was choosing to drop a mess
on my deck. Then I perceived the blob to be a tiny petrel
who seemed to enjoy flying beneath him. There was a
very rough sea at the time, but this magnificent bird
calmly alighted on the water only a few feet from the
boat. His flight stirred old memories of Messerschmitt
fighters when they would turn in to attack low, fast, from
upsun. In a steep bank the lower wing tip would dip
down toward the sea at just the angle used by a wheeling
albatross. But then, instead of observing with delight, I
would have to reach for the button which sounded the
strident scream of the diving hooters and the air would
splutter out of the vent tanks as the submarine dived for
safety. As I slammed the hatch shut over my head, sometimes I saw flames blossom or heard the stutter of
machine guns or the throb of cannon fire while bullets
landed on the flooded bridgehead, disappearing under
the waves. Would I never forget those patrols when we
were ceaselessly hunted, with no darkness in which to
hide. Each attack we made on an enemy convoy brought
deluges of depth charges from escorting ships and
aircraft. I remembered one uncomfortable occasion
when a U-boat and a seaplane were both trying to

torpedo us at the same minute while their supporting fighters closed in and banked steeply, revealing their backs just as this great albatross did. The outlines of planes in close attack were scored deeply in my memory.

How different were the delightful problems of this voyage. Now I sat peacefully in my lovely boat, driving eastward in the track of the old sailing clippers, and the perspex cabin window might darken briefly in the shadow of a giant bird who was my friend. For hours I would remain on deck admiring the graceful powerful sweeps of each wandering albatross that took to inspecting me. In my log I recorded each new watcher, with his Latin name *Diomedea exulans*. All through that vast sweep around the South Pole, all through the world-girdling Roaring Forties, one *Diomedea exulans* after another came to be my companion.

Mariners have loaded the wandering albatross with lore and superstition How can a bird so immense sustain himself out of sight of land for all his life, save the breeding seasons? My follower always seemed to be a mature male, perfectly white except for a black border on the wings. Without wingbeat he would glide on the current of air pushed up by each advancing swell; effortlessly he used his momentum to turn on the opposite course and glide along the next wave. Each great bird would follow my track, but not for more than a day or two. How, I wondered, did each maintain his position? If pelagic birds are territorial, they must inhabit a section of ocean with a pineal beam to their breeding grounds. But out there alone with them, I began to wonder if albatrosses do something quite different—circle the entire globe in a westerly wind between each breeding cycle and then beam back on to the route home?

Now that the old clipper ships no longer go around the Horn few sailors have the chance to study the ways of the great albatrosses, and the most enthusiastic bird watchers cannot make their way to the Antarctic to note breeding habits and chick raising. They only know that the single egg is laid on a sub-Antarctic island or on the Antarctic ice cap in surroundings of appalling bleakness and amid terrible snowstorms. When hatched, the little creature is stuffed with fish until it is almost spherical and then left all on its own to feed on its own fat and sit out the ferociously cold winter. How many die in the blizzards? How often do the chicks have to wriggle upward through a snowfall? Naturalists cannot wait in igloos to see what occurs. They have to surmise. Around the South Pole, nature ensures that only the fittest survive and the superb shining bird which emerges from this Antarctic chickdom holds one in admiring awe of the system!

When we passed near Gough Island, a deserted mountainous paradise which lies south of the Tristan da Cunha group, my aerial attendants became a dozen thin-billed prions who breed there in absolute privacy. My boat obviously filled them with curiosity and amazement and delight.

On I went, studying every bird with reciprocal interest. Now there always seemed to be a pair of albatrosses wheeling overhead, and every time I threw any gash overboard they would solemnly land to inspect it. I wrote in the log: "It would be interesting to discover up to what windforce an albatross can sit on the water, but whenever it blows over Force 8, I am too busy with the sails to do bird watching."

One glittering morning, when running fast downwind, I looked up to see a glide of eight albatrosses soaring around my masts. I felt immensely important at the magnificence of such an escort and could almost imagine the expressions on their faces and their thoughts—what large bird is this nosing through our territory and why does it never rise to fly. A magical scene was revealed one moonlit night when I slid up through the hatch and saw two wandering albatrosses alight side by side, to go through a charming courting dance, kissing with their beaks, face to face. Beautiful feathered lovers in the lonely ocean.

CHAPTER 14

Indian Ocean

BALZAC's *La Cousine Bette* remained my companion through a week of the Roaring Forties; then I started to read the New Testament. It was the first time I had ever applied all my intelligence to assimilating the Gospels. I found that the words I had heard so often in school or church presented quite a different meaning out here in the ocean. An extraordinary tranquil clarity filled my mind and I found myself putting down the book and saying, "How curious—I never understood *that* before!"

After the New Testament, I read a translation of the Koran from end to end. The poetic metaphor of the original Arabic was, of course, lost to me, but I certainly became impressed by the variety of *unending* tortures described for those who do not conform. The grimmest pages of the Old Testament hardly equal in horror the scenes evoked by Muhammad in which unbelievers grew unending skins to be burned or flayed throughout eternity—a picture hardly enhanced by the promise of unending virility and ceaseless ardent virgins for the good boys! After these theological excursions I turned to Pascal, and like him, I started to have my *pensées*, though on less elevated spheres.

As we sped around the South Pole and the days grew wilder, I found myself carping at Pascal's insistence that man should hate himself—unless he meant that man must hate his own cruelty. Now I knew that the factor which induced me personally to accept religious faith was contemplation of nature. Alone in the Southern

Ocean, I felt the whole world stretching around me, and I believed that none of the beauty, the violence, the albatrosses' markings, or my own restless mind, came into this tremendous pattern by chance. Perhaps that was what Pascal postulated in the seventeenth century, and his scientific arguments appear to show insight into the existence of the then-undiscovered molecules. How far in advance of his time he was when preaching on the hopelessness of trying to instill religion by terror—terror remains, religion flees. My own basic instinct that nothing happens by chance became fanned and fortified by the vastness of these turbulent seas and my own curious mental affiliation with the albatrosses overhead. The very perfection of their design made my mind reach out to their designer—my designer, too.

By now I was long past the area in which that freak, rather unfair hurricane had capsized me. As we tore on, I began to log over one hundred and fifty miles a day, but I discovered that the Roaring Forties do not always blow around the pole from west to east as the sailing manuals promise. They blow hard, but from every possible direction. You can't just sit and let your boat bound along in a following gale. You *work!* We were getting pretty far south and the cold increased daily, but the storms we encountered seemed trivial in comparison to the three-day hurricane which preceded my capsize. Those unforgettable cliff-high waves had made me slightly blasé about bad weather. Occasionally I had wondered if I had imagined the size of those seas, but down here in the Roaring Forties I could see that my memory did not exaggerate. The challenge of the Southern Ocean was child's play after surviving *that.* And I grew ever more infatuated with my lovely craft. *Galway Blazer II* would be the first boat under five tons ever to attempt this particular voyage through the Roaring Forties, but I would not have wished for any other.

Now, in these ever-changing seas, gray and green and

deep cobalt blue, I felt again exalted and triumphant.
This was a world of fantastic beauties which only a man in
a small boat could grasp. The tremendous influences of
sky and wave once more held me in their grasp. I became
aware of my own mind changing and expanding, and the
sense of kinship with nature and all her creatures made
me lighthearted. I could not really carry this sense with
me in that busy noisy other world of telephones and
traffic holdups. All I knew was that something happened
to me out here away from mankind—something that, far
from cutting me off from the human race, helped me to
understand it.

On December sixth I obtained a firm radio connection
with Cape Town and was able to give my position. Going
to bed complacent at having sent messages which would,
within twenty-four hours, reach Anita in Ireland, I went
happily off to sleep and awoke furious when at three A.M.
it started to blow hard. Yet lying rolling to and fro in my
bunk, I noticed with pleasure how steady *Galway
Blazer* kept with a gale blowing at consistent force. The
most unpleasant cause of commotion is gusting up and
down so that you are left with a Force 8 sea and a Force 6
wind, but now we looked like getting a Force 9 wind with
a Force 8 sea which is good—for a bit anyway. By four
A.M. it was blowing Force 9, and as the barometer had
fallen steadily from 1027 to 1010 during the last twenty-
four hours, I thought we must be in for a terrific storm
and decided to fill my two stainless-steel thermos-flasks
with boiling water so that if I had to keep steering or had
to remain on watch for twenty-four hours I could keep
myself awake on hot coffee. The disadvantage of never
using a sea anchor or towing warps is revealed when one
has to steer in rough weather for hour after hour, but the
point is debatable. With my light-displacement boat I still
felt it better to be free to roll with the punches. If I were
sailing a heavy-displacement boat, I might alter this
opinion.

Getting the stove to light in a gale always presents drama. Sudden thumps can cause burning methylated spirit to cascade around the galley, like a river of fire. I managed to brew up a kettle successfully and only suffered a slight scald while filling the flasks. Then I stuffed a good breakfast inside me, and, as so often happens, when I was completely ready for the gale, it lessened, and the mercury dropped down from 1010 to 1005. Although seas became calmer, my next radio transmission proved a failure. I think that Cape Town could just hear me across one thousand miles of ocean, certainly they got a "bleep, bleep," but then my set went dead. Choking down oaths, I tried to detect the fault—it was in the power input, a shaky connection to an almost inaccessible device at the far back of the set. Wedging myself upside down, half in a bend, from for'ard to aft, I stripped down the parts and made good the connection. I reckoned this fault must have always existed but never showed up in harbor, only when the boat was busting into the waves. After doing this repair I could hear far more clearly than before, but my precious scheduled meeting time was over. No message could reach home for another fortnight.

As the gale died away into a Force 6 with squalls and a big sea running, the steering became difficult and the vane gear started to fail. I moved aft to inspect and found the worm and vane-shaft were not engaging fully in the worm wheel, the teeth slipping when a severe load came on. But with the right tools I was able to repair it. Blondie's wonderful vane-steering gear would last me to the end of my voyage.

The bewildering extremes of exhilarating, fast sailing days, interspersed with sudden gales, which necessitated a hasty scramble into oilskins and much racing around the deck, continued. I think the extraordinary characteristic of the Southern Ocean is its sudden change of mood. The close proximity of tropical and polar air causes the temperature to rise and fall fantastically. When one is sailing in these parts, the wind will alter direction completely in a few minutes and the change in wind strength can be unbelievable.

My irritable efforts to diagnose our radio fault were well repaid. On Sunday, December thirteenth, I established a clear call to Cape Town some thousand miles due north, and next day the Antarctic air began to bite. Caught in this ocean between southwesters and northwesters, I felt rather like a slice of ice cream occasionally dolloped with hot chocolate sauce. Usually I was extremely cold. Sometimes I awoke in my bunk sweating.

Just after I had finished the New Testament and was deep in theological speculations, I wrenched an old injury in my back. It bothered me immensely, and just at this time I wanted to get up the mast to examine and repair some chafe on ropes. This wretched strain made it absolutely impossible to get aloft while big seas were running. There seemed no reason to expect calm weather for months, so eventually in a full gale I lay on the cabin floor comically trying to do physiotherapeutic exercises to unwrench myself, but all my kicks and writhings were of no avail. The possibility of having to again turn back on a voyage because of a wrenched back was so bitter that I realigned my principles concerning prayer. I read St. Mark, Chapter eleven, Verse twenty-four. "Therefore I say unto you, what things soever ye desire, when ye pray, believe that ye receive them and ye shall have them."

I was brought up in the lingering Victorian tradition of the English public schools, varnished over with the crackling ferocity of the Royal Naval Training College. The result of my long-drawn-out, expensive education had been a stultifying of certain sections of my mind. Perhaps this had been useful in war. But now I wished to break through the shell which all my years in the Navy had formed. We could talk about sex unblushingly, but the hereafter formed an embarrassing subject to our crisp factual minds. Looking back coldly on my own sense of duty and muddled theology, I realized that I had always regarded it as *bad form* to consider possible indulgence from heaven. All during the years of combat I had felt that no *gentleman* would ask for divine intervention on his behalf. Yet while recoiling from the idea of personal prayer, I rather liked other people to light candles for me.

Now was the time to cease being that old me—the fellow I was tired of. In the ocean my beliefs and opinions and habits of mind were changing. I was glad I could change. I had a sense of inner power. I was learning almost more than I could comprehend. I could see myself with all my faults—tearing along in this frail craft—a speck on the world's surface, but what an interesting speck! No, I did not grow humble in this immensity, I became part of it. I loved it. And thus it was that when disappointment smote and for the third time I had to abandon my effort to sail around the world, I was able to accept it philosophically, like a bird who is dashed down to earth but who knows that his wings are still unbroken.

Trouble came to me in two ways. The first, which was my back injury, I overcame in a curious way. After all those ineffectual struggles and exercises to twist some muscle back in place and get up the mast, I sat and contemplated the situation. Here I was and no one in the world knew my plight. I had *got* to get up that mast, and I couldn't do it. So what? I tried to put my back on a direct line of communication with those who cared for me and at the same time turned the boat northward out of her tight polar circle, to find calmer waters in which even a hobbling invalid might get up the mast. After making this change of course, I had to work out my navigational problems. As a full gale had been blowing for several days and I had been unable to obtain a good sun-sight, this was not an easy task. My log was out of action, and the currents of the Southern Ocean are very strong and not fully predictable. Having taken a row of sun-sights, I lowered myself carefully down the hatch and got to work at the chart table to determine my position. The boat was pounding along, rising and falling like a horse in the Grand National. It was impossible to relinquish one's hold for one minute without getting roughly knocked about. I wanted to remain fixed firmly in place while I worked out navigation at the chart table, and to do this I had to lock my body against the angle of the keel with my back arched backward to balance me. When I had finished and sought to rise from perhaps an hour of this cramped, uncomfortable position, my agonizing back muscles had unlocked! No osteopath could have worked a better miracle. I returned on deck astounded that all pain had vanished and within hours we reached calmer waters. I was up the mast and attending to the chafe with a grin on my face—it did not seem to me to be a coincidence.

The next trouble started around this time. It was to force me to abandon the Horn and turn to Australia, but at the start I could not have gauged the seriousness. I always developed thick protective calluses when at sea but whenever we reached icy Antarctic waters and my hands were perpetually wet, I noticed the hard callused skin on each fingertip beginning to wrinkle and peel off. As soon as we moved into a more temperate zone, as for this mast inspection, the skin hardened again. I was puzzled but thought that after it happened once or twice, the skin would grow even harder and stay put. On we went.

On December twentieth, I hoisted sail by the light of the moon in a steady wind and could write:

> As well as adding to my theology and meteorology, I have established the wind force limit for a wandering albatross to alight on the

sea—Force 8 he will, Force 9 he won't, *i.e.,* about
forty knots. . . . A tiny petrel has now joined my
feathered companions. I identified him as a
British petrel (these frequent the Cape of Good
Hope, *not* Britain). While the wandering
albatrosses and the great winged petrels glide
effortlessly and often sit on the water, this tiny
bird, no bigger than a swallow, is always fluttering its wings. How can it sustain perpetual mo-
tion a thousand miles from land? How can this
little throbbing leaf of life never tire?

Toward Christmas Day we got caught in two cross seas
which made me feel that *Galway Blazer* was being tossed
in a blanket, but our fast progress continued. We kept
steadily running eastward and I tried to keep a path just
out of the iceberg region, between 40 degrees and 42
degrees south.

Christmas Day brought a flat calm and I spent twelve
hours attending to defects and patching sails which were
beginning to wear. Strange it was to be down there near
the South Pole, having endured eight severe gales in
succession, and then suddenly to find myself able to rest
for a day in zephyrs which might have graced the
Mediterranean. These winds I renamed the Purring
Forties. The gales had filled all my tanks with sweet-
tasting well-aerated water. I started using the top tank
first in order to reduce top weight before we sailed
through what is supposed to be the world's stormiest
quarter, but nothing approaching the gales south of the
Cape of Good Hope ever hit me again.

My reading for Christmas week included the epistles
of St. Paul—they struck me as disconnected notes hard to
form into a lucid rhythm, yet every now and again,
through the translation of King James' Bible, a poetic
simile would ring out for me like a cathedral bell. That is

the charm of reading at sea—the sudden comprehension.

In January, the Roaring Forties, which are supposed to roar incessantly around the Antarctic continent from west to east, felt contradictory and did just the opposite. They bellowed out of the east at *Galway Blazer*'s nose and headed off southward toward the iceberg line, which I was so anxious to skirt. A collision with a floating island of ice would certainly end this spree.

I sailed under a delicious canopy of smaller birds. My albatrosses seldom left me long unattended, and now I had flights of prions swooping around the boat as well. I recorded: "No day resembles another—never for one moment am I bored or lonely—only sometimes cold and a little afraid."

As the air grew ever more icy, I began to worry slightly about the new skin on my fingertips. The hard skin had peeled off and grown again, but there was a constant soreness around my nails which I thought must be due to scrabbling with the Terylene mainsail when it blew out. But still the skin kept peeling away, making it almost impossible to handle hard rope or effect repairs efficiently. A horrid suspicion crept into my mind. Supposing this soreness was due not to injury but to constant immersion in icy seawater? I had never thought of wearing gloves. The best method of improving my own circulation had always proved to be cold baths and cold water on the wrists, but maybe seawater might have a different effect. With consternation I watched my hands getting gradually worse. If this peeling continued, I would not be able to do any repairs whatever. After storm damage this could mean death. I had one pair of gloves aboard, and these I started to wear for rope handling. At first I felt incredibly clumsy, but practice overcame this. Soon I was able to accomplish quite neat work. It simply needed hard concentration and a kind of belief

in one's own ability—I felt, however, as odd as a bear
darning a sock.

Then those extraordinary and most annoying Roaring
Forties died away completely, leaving *Galway Blazer* rocking on a strange flat sea covered by an oily scum that must
have been plankton—the ultimate source of all marine
life. When churned by our rolling in the swell, the
plankton formed into long white threads. Once a small
purplish crab moved around beneath the surface, and
once a long slim shark nudged the boat hungrily. In the
log I wrote:

> When becalmed, I tend to get headaches and
> these I cure by sitting down and rolling my head
> around several hundred times in each
> direction—an occupation too tedious to do in
> normal conditions, but out here one has
> nothing to do but keep oneself and one's boat in
> condition.

CHAPTER 15

Submarine Flashback

DAYS passed, the incredible calms continued, the new skin kept peeling off my fingers, my interest in the albatrosses sitting around my boat cackling at each other waned. I began to wonder if we would reach the Horn this year or next. Then I turned to my library, chose *Letters from a Stoic*, and Seneca brought me up with a jolt. "Though you cross the boundless ocean, though, to use the words of our poet Virgil, 'Lands and towns are left far astern,' whatever your destination you will be followed by your failings." I knew these now—my failing was to chew over past failings! Had I not got out here over a thousand miles from any other man with a paperback classical library, I might not have turned self-detective. I had never become completely adjusted to the long year which I had skippered my second submarine, *Trusty*. She was larger than *Snapper* and carried more torpedoes, but she had no snorkel as the German U-boats did. Nor did she, like them, keep the captain perched high in the conning tower, making it possible to shoot at an advancing ship, then lower periscope and allow the target to pass right overhead. *Snapper* had been able to fire only six torpedoes forward. *Trusty* possessed three stern tubes as well, and I had in my mind worked out a special tactic for retaliation against escort vessels after attacking. My plan was this—to attack, firing the forward torpedoes, then to do a high-speed turn as the enemy moved in to retaliate, and to fire off the stern torpedoes while racing away. As torpedo tracks always revealed their point of origin, submarines would be depth-charged around that area. I had my new tactics clearly worked out. All I had to do was find the foe.

In the spring of 1941 *Trusty* sailed to Gibraltar. Our passage on to Malta was beset by Italian minefields. We had to dive to one hundred feet where the seaweed kelp, which must have grown to extraordinary lengths, made a weird susurrus against the hull, as if fingernails were scratching us. Malta was about to receive her terrible battering. Already many submarines and their crews lay dead at the harbor bottom because a prewar scheme to create submarine shelters had been considered too expensive, and, rather late in the day, shelters were being hand-dug in the sandstone rock. The submarine flotilla was commanded by my old friend, Captain "Shrimp" Simpson, of iron resolve and golden spirit. How can I describe him—the man who of all brave men, we submariners salute with most respect and most affection? The one whom we who served beneath the water would most wish to decorate. His country seemed to ignore the fundamental burning courage with which he kept his submarines working throughout Malta's two-year siege when the whole base was under continuous attack, but for us who patrolled those waters, he was the fighter of all time.

I thought of him now in this queer-acting Southern Ocean, and a sort of fury filled me all these years after, that his huge contribution to the victory in Africa should have been disregarded. At last I was old enough to say what I felt about Shrimp—to the South Pole!

Then I mulled over *Trusty*'s outings in the Mediterranean, where I had planned to use my new firing power in new ways, but on the first patrol we never sighted an enemy ship until on the return journey we met a lighted Vichy French hospital ship. I was watching her through the periscope, when, to my amazement, a U-boat rose to the surface signaling furiously to the hospital ship and closing her to opposite courses. I had lined up with all our torpedoes ready for a shot at the U-boat when I realized that, by an unbelievable, maddening coincidence, our torpedoes, the U-boat, and the hospital ship must all converge. I could not let go a shot without hitting the inviolate hospital ship. The Ace of Targets had been presented, and I must not fire!

Since one of Rommel's supply lines ran down the coast of Greece, *Trusty*'s next patrol was spent off the island of Cephalonia. North of the island of Cephalonia I sighted a small convoy with only one escort. *Trusty* was lined up to fire the first shots she had ever let go in anger. A captain at such a moment becomes metamorphosed into part of his submarine. My voice spoke the longed-for orders. "Blow up numbers one, two, three, and four tubes. Enemy speed nine knots, bearing red fifty, I am forty degrees on the starboard bow. I am going to fire two salvos. Two torpedoes at each ship. Firing interval five seconds. Down periscope. Full ahead. Group up."

"Numbers one, two, three, and four tubes flooded," came from the torpedo room.

"Up periscope."

"Stand by."

"Range three thousand."

"Fire."

I split the salvo between the two ships, but only one blew up. The escort turned to attack and we spiraled downward amid the din of depth charges in the water around us. One ship sunk was a disappointing bag.

A few nights later we encountered some ships in the moonlight and tried to work up into a position ahead of them for a submerged attack. A flying boat buzzed high in the dark-blue sky, but he did not spot us. I reckon these ships were making for Africa, but just as I was trying to intercept them against the setting moon, they turned for Greece and we missed them. I returned to Malta in a sour, disgruntled mood.

By the autumn of 1941 the torpedo supplies in Malta were running low. *Trusty* was ordered to Alexandria when her next patrol ended. Since we would not be returning to the island, we had to scrape the bottom of the barrel. It was no good complaining that the torpedoes allotted to us were over twenty years old, so old that their engines could hardly be trusted (the explosive warhead of course *had* to be new).

We glided out toward Cephalonia, whence Rommel was running fuel in fast destroyers to his desperate African armies. As we crept up to our position from the south, we sighted a tanker lightly guarded. Rejoicing at the easy target, I passed orders to get the torpedo tubes ready. We couldn't miss.

The tubes were ready when in the tense silent moment just before my voice would call "Fire," a buzzing started. "Torpedo running hot in the tube." With horror, I realized that one of those torpedo engines had started prematurely in the tube. Its noise was enough to awake the dead. I hesitated. Either I could fire it out in the few remaining seconds before getting the tanker into my sights, thus betraying our position without getting a shot, or I could hold on. The decision was then taken from me. The torpedo-tubes crew collapsed, unconscious from exhaust fumes. The enemy never even noticed us and roared quickly out of sight. Sick with frustration and carrying three empty stern tubes, we tried wildly to devise some new stratagem. When a single destroyer emerged, signaling from Argostoli Bay, we reached close range, set our torpedoes to shallow depths for his light draft, and fired three careful shots, one at his bow and one bang in the middle and one at his stern. It was the easiest target that had ever come my way.

"Down periscope."

We sped away under the water to escape retaliation. But instead of hearing one or two explosions as our torpedoes reached their objective, we heard a strange angry whine approaching *us!* It shot over *Trusty* while my crew stood transfixed, wondering if we were to be hit by our own torpedo. My first lieutenant gasped: "Our own fish! It's had gyro failure and it's circling us like a hornet—the other two must have dropped to the bottom."

There was nothing for it but to try to slink away, hoping not to encounter this lunatic whirring cylinder of explosive. The effect on the destroyer was electrifying. Seeing three torpedo tracks, the captain must have assumed that two had missed and that this circling object was some new secret weapon. After dropping sixty depth charges at random, the destroyer made off at top speed. So did we.

How can one describe the feelings of fighting men who have been attacked in great peril, using all their training and ability, only to be let down by their own weapons? Earlier men than we, whose swords broke in combat, may have experienced the same anger and probably murdered their armorers on return. I felt even sorrier for my crew than for myself.

By this time I was tired to the bone, I knew that I hated killing, and after two years of incessant undersea action, I thought that I personally had been depth-charged quite enough! I wanted to cease hunting ships and I also wanted to cease being hunted. The feelings were entwined.

Only the conscience of my conscience pinched. If killing had to be done, better that I should do it—I who knew how, rather than inexperienced CO's who would take my place and more easily lose submarines. I resisted the temptation to apply for a surface ship.

Noble thoughts bored me, but during this period of inner conflict in which I realized that my revulsion to killing was not that of an ordinary conscientious objector—because I still wanted desperately to destroy the cruel Nazi power, and that entailed killing. My real desire was to escape from submarine command. I had had enough.

Then I discovered deep within me what I really cared about—the simple seamen who had endured two years of war like myself and were going on to the bitter end, sweating, grease-covered, the unsung heroes.

From Alexandria *Trusty* was ordered to Singapore carrying vast quantities of gear and a spare crew so that we could set up a submarine base there. Knowing that the British Navy had recently lost six capital ships and that the Far East was going up in flames, we chugged at twelve knots down the sweltering Red Sea. At Colombo both crews, who had been living like hot sardines, went ashore for a carousal, and I reported to the C in C for orders. He sat tapping his pencil.

"Singapore is bound to fall, but I can't refuse these desperate pleas for reinforcements."

"Where are the enemy now, sir?"

"I put ten miles a day on my dividers and usually find that is the extent of our retreat."

"Do I take on the spare crew and land them there to wait for a submarine?"

"Yes."

I returned on board somewhat deflated to find that two of my men had got drunk ashore and were now involved in a quarrel with some locals. They were staggering around the casing trying to cut loose and man the anti-aircraft machine gun. I put them under arrest and we set sail next day. I would administer justice at sea, where every moment was hell in this overcrowding.

When we reached the naval base at Singapore, a huge pall of smoke covered the island . . . the sunset of the British Empire. I set about refitting my ship amid a torrent of bomb crumps. Since all intelligence reports had just been burned, I could only try to disentangle the overall strategic situation from hearsay. There were no air-raid shelters in Singapore, though an old native woman was trying to dig one in the road outside Raffles Hotel. All the families of service personnel were being evacuated in troopships. I wanted to get my two wretched crews ashore because here the hatches had to be kept shut so that splashes from bomb salvos would not swamp us. The heat and humidity inside the submarine became hellish, but the shore accommodation allotted to us had been destroyed that afternoon by a bomb!

There was a dreamlike quality in the deserted dockyard. Exploring the ruins of the bombed officers' club, we found six small bottles of champagne in the rubble. We opened them and drank them tepid. Then we signed the chit book and placed it carefully in the debris and walked away laughing. Our only laugh.

Back in *Trusty* I decided I must gather the men and explain our predicament. At that moment Admiral Spooner arrived and heartened both crews. "It will be the best lodging we can find in Singapore for all of you. Find what you can in any hotel and I will be responsible." We commandeered a damaged lorry and the off-duty men were bounced along the much-bombed ten-mile stretch to Singapore city, where the feather beds and nightclubs had not yet gone up in flames. I was for a week the houseguest of Admiral Spooner, who was to die when the small boat in which he finally escaped was stranded on a jungle island.

After a fantastic fortnight trying to refit and revictual amid this shambles, *Trusty* was ordered to go out on patrol and report in three weeks to Java. I had to make the decision whether I would leave the extra crew, which we had transported for a new base, or carry them on with me. I lined them up and said they were to come with us, but kitbags and hammocks must be left behind to give us a little more space in the submarine. They looked relieved. Everyone could see there was no chance of a new base forming.

Just before we left, a convoy of ships came into harbor

which contained the ill-fated Eighteenth Division, immediately captured by the Japanese. Japanese planes
appeared and dropped a vast pattern of bombs which
enveloped the whole area in smoke but never hit a single
ship, although the bombs landed right in the center of
them.

Having no information or detailed patrol orders I had
to guess where we would be most likely to find Japanese
ships and made for Cam Ranh Bay in Indochina. As we
slid away from Singapore, a pall of black smoke from the
burning oil and rubber dumps arose. *Trusty* crept sadly
away into the hot China Sea and our hearts were
troubled for we feared what was to come, although we
could not quite believe that Singapore would fall. A lone
raider, we wondered where to turn to find the enemy.
Our torpedo tubes were full, but once discharged, God
knew where we could get replacements, so I would not
waste them unless we found a big ship. When we sighted
a ship carrying a deck cargo of mechanical transport, I
thought it better to go in for a surface fight. We rose out
of the water and opened fire on the deck cargo and her
one long gun. Evidently she carried petrol as well, for the
whole ship blew up like a torch. No crew appeared on
deck, and although we remained for a few minutes in
case swimming heads appeared, it seemed that they had
all been killed in the explosion. The blaze lit up the sea
for miles, so we made off at speed into the Gulf of Siam.

The burning days. The cool beautiful nights. The
knowledge of England's loss. The queer horrible fantasy
of this patrol where one fought undirected, not knowing
if *Trusty* would ever be able to find more torpedoes when
she had expended her store. We were fighting quite
alone it seemed, on the edge of a doomed world. I sensed
my crew's impatience and their longing for action. At last
a little tanker appeared. Without diving, I maneuvered
to get her against the moon. Once again I did not want to
waste a torpedo on such small fry and went into a close

attack on the surface. At eight hundred yards we opened
fire with our gun at the base of her funnel and hit it.
Bang! A great soot cloud rose up from it and obscured
the view. We turned to get upwind and, for a short time,
lay broadside to broadside as did the old sailing ships,
pouring shot at each other. Our fast-diminishing supply
of shells kept scoring hits, but they were not sufficiently
powerful to sink her. Her stern gun was silenced, but
another gun amidships continued to fire, riddling our
bridge and gun platform with splinters. As wounded
gunbreech-workers were dragged down, I felt for the
first time thankful for that eager spare crew.

In a flash the situation turned against us. Almost any
ship can ram a submarine if it gets near enough, and this
one knew it. I saw the bow swing toward us. We were too
close to let off a torpedo and possessed no stern gun with
which to shoot backwards. Then we saw the ship was
losing speed due to our first hit, and once again we had
her in our power. I knew my men were praying for the
order to use one of our precious torpedoes. Dare I?
There were no replacements, and we might meet a battle
fleet or convoy. *Trusty* was the only British submarine in
the China Sea. I must keep her ready for big sinkings. It
was hard to decide I could not spare a torpedo to finish
off this paltry target.

"Close up the guns and clear decks." This meant
"Dive."

A sort of sigh went up from my ship at this order to
leave the enemy. It was clearly the wisest thing to do.
Even now I am sorry for the lost chance.

When we got below, our shell loader's hand was
pouring blood. He had been hit by an enemy shell splin-
ter, and when what we called battle tension wore off, the
pain became intense. A ship's captain is supposed to act
as doctor in time of need, but I really was hopeless at this.
All I could do was turn the wardroom into an operating
theater and send for the medical book from my cabin.

Our valiant loader gazed up with pathetic trust while I flipped through the pages, "Mustn't get gangrene," I read, but this didn't cheer him up much. "Morphine," murmured the coxswain, and that was more to the point. He produced a couple of phials and a syringe. Now I turned hopefully to our first lieutenant, "Flash" Gordon, a doctor's son who might be able to pick out some of the shrapnel. The gun crew stood around sympathetically until the coxswain, practicing his syringe in the air while reading aloud from the instruction leaflet, sprayed them all in the face with morphine.

"Where do we stick it?" was the next question.

I turned my head away and hoped that Flash Gordon had watched his father "find a vein."

When he did get the needle in, the coxswain was somewhat overgenerous with the morphine phials, and his patient relapsed into unconsciousness for twenty-four hours. However, we nursed him carefully in the officers' mess and he reached Surabaja alive.

My policy of hoarding precious torpedoes paid no dividend. The capital ships for which I longed never loomed on the horizon, and my men minded. I thought in terms of eventual tonnage destroyed. They thought in terms of immediate, hotblooded success.

Grumpily *Trusty* sailed through the dirty-looking waters of the South China Sea. Our natural prey, the big Japanese invasion fleets, had already left for Sumatra. We ended our patrol in Surabaja where nothing was discussed but the fall of Singapore and America's entry into the war. Then our oil fuel tank sprang a leak. There was nothing for it but to reembark the wretched spare crew and make a run for it to Colombo's workshops. For three thousand miles my overcrowded ship chugged along under hot skies, leaking oil, unable to attack. An injured shark looking for a hospital. I had never before been in a submarine incapable of fighting. It was an unpleasant sensation. Knowing the mood of my men, as a captain must, I felt their devotion still, but they were flat—apathetic with repeated disappointment. The extra men we had carried with us during six months of intolerable discomfort could at last disembark. "Funny sort of trip, sir," said one. I thought it a superb understatement!

We had sunk only four ships since leaving England. Could I have done better? I chewed it over and over.

I was chewing it still, rehearsing in my mind different decisions I could have made, when on January 17, 1971, I awoke to see that my hands had become worse in the polar air. My single pair of gloves could not sufficiently protect them from icy seawater; the new skin, which had hardened around my fingernails as soon as we had driven up northward into a warmer clime, was again peeling off, and if we ran into storms—and we certainly would—I would not be able to effect essential repairs. It seemed utterly ridiculous that tender fingertips should make a voyage around the Horn impossible, but I had to face the maddening fact. I must turn northward toward warmer waters, and in Western Australia I could heal and reharden my hands and devise some method of protection.

Seneca helped me to make the decision to alter course without bitterness . . . "whatever your destination you will be followed by your failings. . . ." Now I knew full well what mine were and I was tired of them, tired of chewing over the might-have-beens. To sail around the world accepting disaster as interesting experience must be my own personal fulfillment. *Whatever* happened, I must stay grateful at remaining alive and sustained by the wonders of this world. After all, I was having a pretty good time of it for a sixty-year-old. In a philosophical state of mind, which would have been impossible to me prior to the chastening invigoration of this last voyage, I altered course.

And passing some one hundred miles from deserted

Amsterdam Island—the single peak which shows above the ocean in these parts—I felt myself lucky. Had my hands been *very* much worse, I would have been forced to land and wait while healing up. A hut with tinned food exists there for stranded mariners, and I believe a ship pays a six-monthly visit. Had such an excursion been necessary, I fear that more than Seneca's admonitions would have been needed to keep me sane!

I had no charts of Australia, but I knew, of course, that Fremantle must be my nearest port. My third submarine, *Telemachus*, had been based there during 1944, and as I approached, I thought it would be some sort of amusement to see how well I remembered the landfall.

In a light wind and brilliant sunshine I sailed up through the Thirties—Blissful Thirties one might call them—and on February seventh, nearly three weeks after I had made my fateful decision to abandon the Horn for a year, I sighted the coast of Western Australia. As we drew nearer, I could discern the outline of Rottnest Island, which guards the enclosed waters of Fremantle Harbor, and I felt rather pleased with myself —I had made a spot-on landfall.

A brief message, which I knew would reach the newspapers *and* be transmitted to Ireland, got through to Perth by radio. *Galway Blazer* started to lollop along in a heat haze, and I hung over the bows, seeking to identify the harbor entrance which I had known so well. Suddenly I saw a huge tower sticking up out of the water on the very line where *Telemachus* had been wont to glide in from patrol. Panic! If I was out of the channel, then sharp reefs lay hidden in all directions. *Galway Blazer* might feel her keel crunch at any moment. Then I perceived that the tower was a new oil-rig, and the outline of Rottnest Island lay etched exactly as it had twenty-five years before.

I was reliving thankful returns from wartime patrols when a motor cruiser tore up in a cloud of spray. This was *Hiawatha*, a press launch, sent to guide me through the small boat channel which wound between the reefs. It was kind of them to surmise how puzzled I might be without charts. I followed gratefully into the wide sound where there was room for *Galway Blazer* to beat up against the wind. The launch directed me into the fishing harbor, which had not even been built when I left those waters, and after brief formalities I accepted the offer of John Plunket, commodore of the Royal Freshwater Bay Yacht Club, to enjoy the magnificent facilities of a mooring. To get *Galway Blazer's* mast under the low bridge of the Swan River, we had to heel her over 45 degrees with weights, and haul down the mastheads to an accompanying boat alongside by using the sail halyards. As the tops of the wind-vane brushed the supporting girders of the low-plow-span bridge, each click caused me to throw a near heart attack, but my helpers knew their job. *Galway Blazer II*, lying almost on her side with a somewhat indignant expression, was towed under the bridge and then stood up to sail gently on to a tremendous welcome at the Royal Freshwater Bay Yacht Club. It was a curious, nostalgic, unexpected return to Western Australia, and my old friends started to appear from all parts of the country. *Galway Blazer II* was the first boat under five tons to sail from England to Australia in one hop, and a thousand questions awaited me. I tried to answer carefully and in detail, even when invited to the bar of a neighboring club where a crowd of two hundred male sailing enthusiasts popped the questions. I did not know at the time, but was told afterward, that having spent nearly five months alone at sea, I was now talking like a gramophone adjusted to "Fast."

The overwhelming kindness shown, the touching interest, and the delicious meals (not to mention alcoholic sustenance) absolutely dazed me. I slept and ate and drank and talked—yes, I fear, talked and talked—in rotation.

My hands now looked absolutely normal, but I knew that it would take some weeks to toughen them up in the sunshine. Already I had made my plan. I would return home for the Irish summer and try for the Horn next year.

A few days after my arrival, the correspondent of the *Western Australian* told me that Anita was flying out. She had apparently been on her horse, just going out with the Blazers in County Galway, when the news that I was putting into Perth reached her. She had a good gallop while thinking out what *she* would do in the new circumstances, and then drove to Shannon Airport and bought a ticket to Perth. "Any old plane will do," she decreed, "as long as they are going the right way and I can get off and rest occasionally."

"*Which* is the right way?" asked the Irish travel agent with impeccable logic.

"That way out and the other way back." She placed a finger on the office map.

And so it was that after two nights with her brother in Rome and another stopoff in Singapore, she reached Western Australia. "Whatever's happened now?" she asked when a friend drove me out to meet her. "You've had masts—you've had rig—what now?"

"Hands."

"Not possible!"

But a sailor is as helpless without strong hands as without masts.

She came to live for ten days on *Galway Blazer*, sleeping in my bunk while I borrowed a lilo. We made a good use of the luxurious club facilities, and the only meal we ever had aboard was breakfast—a cup of tea and some fruit. Then came a swim and maybe a stroll on the lawn, and our hosts and hostesses would start to arrive. "The one thing I never thought of bringing was an engagement book," muttered my wife.

"Well," I replied, "neither did I!"

I was still talking much too fast; the rhythm of normal social habits had to creep slowly back. "I won't ask you anything for a while," said Anita. "It's so difficult when the answer comes like a burst of staccato machine-gun fire."

Having entrusted *Galway Blazer II*, my pet, to the care of kind friends, we spent two months traveling home together, leaving Perth by air-conditioned train in order to see how *big* Australia was, and then staying with Geoff Gellie, a submariner friend in Melbourne, and then staying with Anita's school friend Betsan Coats near Brisbane. Everyone understood. Everyone was amused. Everyone showed kindness and suggested protection for my hands—turtle-oil cream was snatched from beauty parlors, waterproof gloves from the operating table, Arctic gauntlets from explorers' lockers. Come back and next time you will make it, they said. Just what I wanted to hear. Next time I *must* be all right—how lucky I was to have a next time.

Part III

CHAPTER 16

Holed by a Killer Whale

IT was 1971. I had done a lot and learned a lot during the past three years. I had capsized, broken my masts, and sailed from England to Australia in the first four-and-a-half-ton boat ever to face this nonstop voyage through the Roaring Forties. I knew how good *Galway Blazer* was. I could master my hand trouble. I had profited from each hard lesson. And I still hankered for the Horn—I had always wanted to get around that rocky island on my own, and a string of setbacks in no way lessened the desire. Most men have known the urge to break away at some time and do something which may have caught their imagination as schoolboys. Very few are lucky enough to be able to try. Submarining had taught me that life is an incredible mixture of good luck and bad luck; if your destiny involves danger and action, you are bound to occasionally feel rather like a tennis ball being batted back and forth across some monstrous court by those twin-gods Bad Luck and Good Luck. You have to lump the former, but until one actually gets killed, a man can help Good Luck by taking immense pains and concentrating on possible disasters.

I reckoned that I'd had good luck throughout the war, but seeing so many others miss it had twisted something in me. Then I'd also had good luck in romantic and domestic issues, and again it was luck to find a paper eager to back me when I ran short of funds. My bad luck came from running into an out-of-season hurricane of unbelievable force. The breaking of my masts could not be called bad luck; that was inevitable in the violence of the capsize. But the actual hurricane could not have been expected, and its force had astounded me after a lifetime at sea. I couldn't call the unsuccessful experiment with the rig bad luck. I had simply wanted to try sailing faster in light winds and the sails would not adapt. Nor could I call my hand trouble bad luck; I had to get into Antarctic waters to discover the effect that prolonged cold wetness could have on me. I couldn't have guessed it.

So now, having met with what seemed fairly equal doses of good and bad luck over the years, I was jaunty enough at the prospect of a seventeen-thousand-mile sail home. Each time I looked at *Galway Blazer's* hull when she was out of the water I admired her lines. Anita had said almost crossly, "You're in love with that old boat." In fact, I just enjoyed reflecting on that whaleback which presented no vertical surfaces against a heavy breaking sea, while the buoyancy of her spoon bow could prevent pitch-poling end over end. If you sail a lot, the mere look of a boat can give a sense of artistic pleasure. You can stand in dry dock and feel how she will respond in high seas.

My final preparations took place in the fishing boat harbor where all repair work was rendered fascinating by the presence of Marko, the Yugoslav owner of the slipway. I spent many hours here, scraping and painting *Galway Blazer.* Marko was a man one could never forget: a cheerful giant, with a booming voice, shouting orders in Italian, Serbo-Croatian and Australian alternately. He had suffered some fearful accident which caused him to limp around his yard, but he could climb with agility up the wobbly ships' cradles to inspect and instruct. Such was his zest that few people realized that he was seldom out of pain, and when he remarked, "All the Horn needs is know-how and courage," I only wished I could borrow his.

December 12, 1971, was the date on which I sailed, and

as might be expected off the southern tip of Australia, I immediately met hard, adverse winds. The first three days out of Fremantle are always spent beating hard to windward. In this part of the Indian Ocean gales seem to enjoy playing cat and mouse with a boat, matching each turn you take to get first west and then south, and then southeast to get round stormy Cape Leeuwin.

For three days I battled along, and then, having covered four hundred miles, I was freed by the wind and could point south of Tasmania. Once again I reflected on what misery it must be for a lone sailor who knew seasickness at the start of a voyage to have to force himself to work a boat day and night. Whatever winds blew, I felt well in them! Now that she could point gaily toward Cape Horn, *Galway Blazer* sped along with full sail, and my spirits rose at the renewal of our relationship—just us two in the ocean.

The morning of December nineteenth was sunny and sparkling. I had been so busy while winds headed us that I hardly had time to think about the kindnesses shown on my departure. Now in the exhilaration of the open sea I realized that the cheers of friends were still ringing in my ears. It was all set fair for a fast bash across the Pacific.

No land, no rocks to worry me—until we reached the Horn a couple of months away. The old exhilarating sense of freedom returned. Again I was alone with my lovely boat in the ocean.

Midmorning passed and I relaxed, rejoicing in the speed of our passage and the excitement of wind and sunlight which only a sailor—or perhaps a skier—can know. Eventually I tore myself from contemplation of this vast panorama which gave me personally such delight and went below to attend to a few chores. Everything was going so well. I felt in a tidy mood and set about rearranging things in a locker. What strange instinct made me turn suddenly toward the side of my boat! I was for some reason staring at the woodwork when, above the slap-slap of the waves, there came a horrifying sound—a strange sound that did not belong to the boat, and I was facing whatever made that sound. In front of my unbelieving eyes a large mushroom of splintered wood had been stove in. It was as if a terrific fist had hit the hull. I could see blue ocean through the bulge and water started to pour in.

My immediate reaction was to rush to the cockpit to see what had hit me—ice? an uncharted reef? a whale? Nothing was visible except a green swirl astern where a huge dark form was making off fast. I thought I could see blood. I could not be sure. Whatever it was hardly mattered. I had to stop the boat from sinking. My brain began to race. I tried to keep my thoughts clear. *Galway Blazer* was going down in the water, but she was still moving in a strong wind. The blow had come on the leeside, which meant that the splintered hull lay pressed down beneath the waves. If I threw her onto the other tack, the aperture might be lifted right out of the water. Suddenly I turned into a human dynamo; frenzied action was needed to keep her on the surface—action as fast as thought. Within seconds I had gone about onto the other tack and was sailing in a direction I did not wish—away from Australia, but with the hole raised above the waterline. I could only keep her thus while a strong wind blew; if the wind dropped, the boat would sink within minutes. But this eventuality I did not envisage. I worked with things *as they were*.

Having turned *Galway Blazer*, I looked below and saw that, although waves kept spurting in through a big bulge of broken woodwork, the steady gush had ceased. Perhaps a ton of water was slushing around, but she could sail herself while I leaped to the hand-pump and started to work it. Gradually I realized that as long as this wind held I could beat the inflow. If a storm blew up or if we met a dead calm, the boat would sink, but at this angle she was only shipping water by the bucketful, not as if a hose pipe had been laid on. In the back of my mind I registered that from now on I would be struggling for my life, and I must not get too tired to struggle, for it would be pump—pump—pump for days on end. I determined to work calmly. At last there sounded a coughing gurgle and the bilge had emptied. I waited a few minutes, resting, deliberately allowing my own physical resources to adjust, than as water sloshed back in, I pumped her out again while carefully trying to gauge how much time I could grab for examination and repair in between each pumping session. While she kept on this tack with her injured patch nearly out of the water, I reckoned it was possible to steal ten minutes at a time for repair work in between each period of pumping out.

Ordering myself to keep cool, I tried to examine the damage and assess what could be done as if I were strolling through a carpentry shop. My heart sank a bit when I looked under the lockers to the hull itself. Two or three feet of laminated wood hull had been smashed inward. Much of the fibers still held, but it was impossible to guess how long they would last, and if they gave way, the hole* would be big enough for a man to crawl through! After this inspection, it was back to the pump. Pump and pump again. Next time the bilges emptied I must go out on deck to see how the damage appeared from outside. Head down, I hung miserably over the side and viewed

---

*Later examination of the hole caused naturalists to suspect a great white shark had been following the boat and attacked from astern. The possibility of a single killer whale is less likely. They usually move in packs.

Within twelve months of this episode, the Robertson family had their yacht sunk by a pack of killer whales and the Baileys by a wounded sperm whale. Both these boats were sunk in calmer seas, which meant they could not change on to a tack to lift the damage above the surface. However, these disasters took place in warm, fish-filled waters so that with immense fortitude both parties managed to survive in dinghies or rafts. See *Survive the Savage Sea* by Douglas Robertson (New York, Praeger, 1973, and *Staying Alive*, by Maurice and Marilyn Bailey (New York, McKay, 1974).

The great white shark is the most aggressive creature in the ocean and measures between twenty and thirty-six feet in length.

the smashed area. It looked even worse than from the cabin. Then back to the pump. Each time the bilges gurgled dry I left the pump to search for tools and materials. Every possible method of stopping up that hole had to be used.

It had been day—golden sunlit day. Now it became dusk and I could not count the hours, touch the log, eat, or drink. All that mattered was keeping on the surface. Think. Think. Think. Pump. Pump. Pump. While I collected tools and stuff to ram into the hole, I wondered what would be best to do if the wind dropped or a storm blew and she *did* sink. My alternatives were to go down with the boat or to take to the little one-man dinghy in which I might survive the cold for a couple of days. There is no chance of keeping alive by fishing in these icy waters, and certainly I could not expect to sight a ship. This part of the ocean is empty.

It was a dismal prospect, but then something strengthened my resolve. It was almost as if a hand patted me on the back and I assessed the more cheerful facts. I was uninjured. The boat was driving along. I would fight it out carefully. Take each action in order of importance. Go down fighting if it had to be.

Although no shipping routes used this area, I decided to send out a Mayday* distress signal on the radio. Some operator might possibly be listening, might catch it and my position. And I comforted myself with the reminder that Fremantle lay only three days away, although we were lengthening, not decreasing the distance by this enforced tack out toward the South Pole and away from her harbor.

All through that long night of frenzied endeavor I raced between repair work and the pump. The first thing I tried was according to classic instructions—I

---

*The international distress signal taken from the French word *M'aidez* and spelled *Mayday* in all languages.

would tie a sail over the damaged area on the outside. This ploy often works when the top sides of a boat are stove in, but I doubted if sailcloth could hold in rough seas *below* the waterline. However, I resolved to see what happened. Leaving the pump for nearly fifteen minutes, I dragged the triangular storm-jib up on deck and prepared it with fore and aft lowering lines at each end of its foot and apex ready to pass down the side. Then I returned to the pump. Then I got a line under the boat for a downhaul by sitting up in the bows, throwing a loop over, and wriggling aft while continually letting out rope and hauling it aft to the damaged area. Every ten minutes I would leave it all and dart below to pump. Meanwhile the boat sailed on at full speed; and I saw that mercifully the wind was just sufficient to keep her well heeled-over on the port tack, leaving the gaping rent mostly in the air. It took hours, but by degrees I hove the sail down taut over the damage and slipped below to inspect the effect it had. To my dismay the sail tied on over the hole caused more water than ever to pour in. I could see why—the sail was too big and clumsy to adapt itself to the shape of the wineglass hull; the edges of the canvas sagged and acted not as a collision mat but as a water scoop. Laboriously I gathered the jib in and stowed the soggy mass below. Then I sat down and tried to pump serenely while thinking out new tactics.

There was plenty of toweling and foam rubber aboard. These I stuffed into the worst rents from the outside. Then I cut a piece of Terylene cloth to nail over the whole area. To do this, I had to hang myself upside down over the side with my head in the waves, suspended by ropes around my ankles. I possessed only long serrated builder's nails, and these proved extremely difficult to hammer in straight while the boat was being buffeted about. Seawater poured up my inverted nose and I kept gulping it into my stomach. It acted as an emetic, but I saw with relief that this large Terylene patch was holding firm. It made quite an improvement to the water intake.

Then, purple in the face and coughing up seawater, I returned to the cabin to sit down, let the blood drain out of my head, and consider what could be done to the inside. I ripped away lockers which half hid the damage and stared at the great bulge with its ever-spouting cracks—if only I could find some really strong puttylike material to insert into them.

Just before leaving Fremantle, Marko had been doing a small job aboard, which involved using lengths of rubber strips about a quarter of an inch thick. There was a mass of this stuff left over. "You keep it," he said. "Oh, God, no; I've nowhere to put it—I hate unnecessary junk. . . ." But he insisted. "You may need it." And I did—right now! I cut up short lengths and stuffed each one into a leaking rent, gently so as not to increase the damage, but firmly enough to exclude the sea. The rubber strips, which had seemed useless rubbish, might have been specially manufactured for the job. If a laminated hull gets stove in, stuff it with little bits of rubber! Staring at the hole, I could see that my life depended on one of the boat's ribs which lay vertically across the center of the bulge. Although sprung inward from a concave to a convex form, its fibers remained firm and it held the whole delicate fabric in place. I touched it reverently; at all costs this vital supporting rib must be kept in place. With immense care, I measured off the length of the requisite shore from the center of the rib to a strength member on the other side of the boat. Then I cut the necessary length from a spare main boom. I lashed the shore delicately in place and wedged it home with prayers. Should a storm arrive, it might hold. Then, after an arduous pumping session, I quietly searched the boat for any stuff which might be used to stop smaller cracks under the rubber. Like a bride in a trousseau shop, I fingered everything in the boat—how strong—how soft—how resistant. An unexpected source provided the perfect material. To save laundering, I had carried a large quantity of disposable underpants; these were the best quality pants made of stuff that resembled washing-up cloths. Cutting up my underwear, I inserted pieces into each small crack with a knife point.

By the time I completed this curious job, it had become clear that unless a flat calm prevented me from keeping the boat heeled over at an angle, or a gale arose that would beat waves into the aperture, the leak was containable. But I must not sleep. All night I must remain watchful and awake, pumping out at regular intervals. All through the darkness I worked away, quietly intent on keeping the boat afloat. I had time to send a few more unheeded distress calls on the radio—and time for another sort of distress call, a kind of thoughtful prayer which took away fatigue. So the first night passed.

On the morning of December sixteenth, dawn broke in a bright clear sky. After twenty-four sleepless hours of hard physical effort, my muscles ached, but I knew I could keep going for a very long time indeed without lying down. I worked out a timetable for the next twenty-four hours, giving priority to improvement of the nailing down of the Terylene cover. I spent a few more hours hanging head downward over the side. My ankles started to get very sore from their suspended ropes, so I tried to evolve into a better working position by putting my mastheading rope ladder over the side and swarming down it. But it seemed impossible to work from it. Eventually I managed to hang the bosun's chair over the side, perch in it, and lean over at a right angle reaching to the damaged area.

It was mighty cold, so while I was at these capers, I wore my Antarctic flock-filled oversuit. Although it got soaked by seawater, it kept the wind off and retained heat around my rather tired, shivery body. Sleeplessness and disagreeable surprise—I won't use the word "shock"—can make one very cold. Meanwhile, I was using my wits to devise a form of collision mat which would be more effective than the triangular sail which had scooped up water. The immediate placing of a collision mat over damage is old naval practice. Usually the mat consists of a pad specially designed for the purpose, held in place by a lowering line and downhaul, and fore and aft hauling lines. The placing of such a mat was quite simple in a slab-sided ship, but *Galway Blazer's* hull was wineglass in cross section and torpedo-shaped longitudinally. I tried a waterproof locker-cover with one rope at each corner pulling slightly outward. I managed to get this into position and drop two downhauls into the water down under the boat and up the other side. Since all the ropes I got around the boat to tie her up had to be pulled taut, I found the force needed for the job was more than my muscles could give. But eventually I discovered that I could lie on the deck, using all the strength of my legs, and using my arms as links and thus tighten the ropes sufficiently. I did not notice at the time that my shoulders were being badly wrenched by this mode of using myself as a pulley—one shoulder would never quite recover.

It was all to little avail. The locker-cover consisted of stiff plastic material, and when I finally tied it in place, it would not adapt to the curve of the hull. Horrible wrinkles kept appearing. To flatten these, I undergirt the boat with two more ropes and hove them taut with a supreme physical effort. But *Galway Blazer* was not made to be tied up like a parcel.

Now a fever of improvisation beset me. Every article in the boat could perhaps be used for a purpose for which it had not been designed. I went through the lockers and fetched up a pair of waterproof trousers—yellow, shiny, strong. I ran ropes through the legs and reckoned that by nailing them along the bottom of the damage and using hauling lines up to the deck I could fix them securely. They were not large enough to cover the whole damaged area but they kept a lot of water out. I crouched on deck, surveying my boat—there she was sailing along quite nicely with nearly a dozen lines hauled tight around her and a pair of upside-down trousers tacked to her side. Those waterproof trousers proved just the right consistency to stop a leak. They must have been made of the most marvelous material. I tried to recall where I had bought them. One might have said to the salesman, "Are these really waterproof?" "Oh, yes, sir, this quality keeps out *anything*." Anything? The ocean? I tried to see a comic side to it—my lovely boat in oilskin trousers! It was ludicrous, but it worked. Because the material held, I could now reduce sail, allow the boat to come more upright, and occasionally turn her in the direction of Australia. At intervals I swallowed small amounts of nut paste and raisins. I was too tired to chew biscuits. That would use up saliva, take energy. Now I could reduce pumping out the bilges from ten-minute to hourly routines. I was getting on top of the job. Now I could think of brief sleep—but only think of it, not take it.

It seemed as if the wind would never veer from the east. It kept cruelly forcing me to sail *away* from Australia. When the great fish had attacked me, *Galway Blazer* had been four hundred miles from Australia. When the sun rose three days later, she was six hundred miles. What I needed so desperately was a southwester so that I could sail back to Fremantle on the port tack, keeping the damaged side out of the water. I tried not to fuss. West winds were supposed to prevail in these parts. We were moving ever farther from land, but I had to discipline my mind not to waste itself with worry. I had to concentrate on stopping the leak.

During the first two days I sent out several Mayday signals, but my cry for help was unheard, and I did not wish to waste time in futile calling. Nor could I spare the time to take safety precautions on deck. All during my lone sailing I had made it a strict rule that whenever I

moved around the unguarded deck I would always hook
my lifeline to the jack stay, because if you fall over the
side of a boat with vane steering you have to watch her
sailing away out of your ken forever. But now there
could be no fiddling around with clip hooks. It was
steady action—pumping and repairing in rotation.

The time came when I was right to discipline myself to
snatch an occasional half hour's sleep every so often.
Curiously, I found it difficult to adjust myself to pumping at intervals of an hour. Every fifteen minutes a kind
of pumping hysteria filled me and I would awake feeling
that I must get going and I would hear the reassuring
gurgle of the emptying bilge. My mind had become so
concentrated on methods of stemming the leak that it
was almost impossible to rest. Despite the more upright
position of the boat I still did not dare let her sail in the
right direction and we continued to move out into the
Indian Ocean. Not only did the wrong wind blow, but a
new trouble assailed me when it veered suddenly and
hard. *Galway Blazer* jibed, and, in so doing, the peak of
the mainsail got foul of the topping lifts. It took all my
strength, supplementing the use of my muscles with the
use of rigging tackles to get it clear and to lower the
damned thing into its slot. I felt the winds were
deliberately behaving badly, tricking me when I was
down.

Bruised and aching after this battle, I lay down and
ordered myself, "Sleep for an hour." But I couldn't.
Every fifteen minutes I woke with a jump and rushed to
the pump. The idea of gurgling down into the deep was
beginning to prey on my mind. I could force myself
through physical labors, but to control one's own subconscious fear is more difficult. However, I persevered in
trying to obey my own orders and gradually the rhythm
of my sleep snatches lengthened. I could switch off completely for fifteen minutes and then for twenty minutes.

When dawn came to light my fourth day in this

horrible predicament, I was able to close my mind to the drama and rest in real unconsciousness every few hours. And my usual healthy hunger returned. Whenever I felt like it, I consumed a mugful of nut paste mixed with raisins. It was absolutely the right digestible protein for such an emergency. For something happens to a man when he is pitching about in a sinking boat; it is as if he himself had received a terrible blow on his own body —his vital organs feel bruised. To start eating again with enjoyment alone on the sea, alone with disaster, is quite a curious sensation. At first I had thought to myself, "Now I must eat," just as I thought, "Now I must stuff something into the leak." Now that I was damn hungry I felt it extraordinary to have such an appetite.

Having done all I could to the outside of the hull, I decided to devote most of this fourth day to the interior. Much of the damage was hidden from view by strips of copper sheeting. These had been fixed with the intention of firing radio waves along the forepeak and then projecting them up into the aerial. Other strips were intended to earth my set to the keel bolts. I had not much hope of getting a radio message through but after hacking away most of the metal so that I could expose and deal with the seeping dented hull more carefully, I decided to leave a little ridge of metal along the top edge—just in case it might be possible to transmit later. I gave a lot of thought to this decision, and as it turned out, I made the wrong one.

If I could stay afloat, in seven days' time, on December twenty-fourth, the day before Christmas, I had a rendezvous with Perth radio station. I longed desperately to speak to a human being, so I chose to leave a metal strip to make contact more likely. I thought it more important than increasing watertight precautions. For this decision I would nearly pay with my life.

In an attempt to cover the whole damaged area with some kind of inner lining, I wove a sort of plaster of wedges which supported one another while a starfish of shores held them in place. I had no bent for carpentry, but my mind was growing inventive and my fingers sensitive. When I had placed this great cap of wedges over the hole and softly lashed the shores in place, it looked as if the new strengthening would hold the cracked fibers of wood in place through untimely pressure without splintering them. If no storm arose and I did not sail hard to windward, I thought the whole structure would hold. My fingers kept running over the copper band which prevented firm fixing at the top. I longed to chip it away, and yet I could not bear to reduce my chances of getting through by radio when the time came. This task of inner construction occupied the whole of the fourth day, and when it was completed, I sat back admiring the job. A wonderful conceit began to keep me alive. I had never thought myself capable of such neat invention. The tiny triumph cheered me. With the realization that no preparations for abandoning *Galway Blazer* need be made, there came a philosophical calm. I had subconsciously dreaded this eventuality. I knew my ordeal in the dinghy could not have lasted more than two days and that really was the only ray of comfort! In these cold seas no man could survive for long in an open boat and starvation would hasten death, for there were no fish or turtles to catch in icy waters—only the great fierce creatures of the deep.

Now I had time to wonder about the animal which had holed my hull. I had recently heard of killer whales attacking and sinking small boats as if it were a new fishy fashion, but in all the great literature of the sea I could not recall such a happening ever having been described. Killer whales usually traveled in packs. I wondered if the monster had been killed or severely hurt. I wished I had seen more in that green swirl. I tried to remember how much blood there had seemed to be in the water; in the agonizing second in which I realized my boat was about to sink, such detail had not been imprinted with exactitude in my memory. Now that I had time to think, curiosity filled me concerning things I could never know.

The dawn of the fifth day, December nineteenth, brought a feeling of increased security. I was getting stronger. As the ocean flooded with golden light, I felt the beat of life in my ears. I moved around, diligently tightening the leads of my lashings, improving each rope as it stretched, and gently urging the supporting wedges into positions which would counter possible increased rush of water. And every hour I pumped and heard that final gurgle which meant safety. Pumping had become a sort of hourly tranquilizer.

By the sixth day I was keeping the log as usual and had grown strong enough to hate the wind. Once my spirits leaped when it veered slightly to the south, and with only the foresail up, I could nudge around toward Australia. But then it again turned sour, and when it slipped back into the east, I felt it had ceased to be a wild roistering companion carelessly bearing me along and had become a personal enemy. Why should the usual westerly winds have changed to blow from the east? What was the wind trying to do to me? Why drive my injured boat out toward Africa? Any increase in wind force, of course, meant that fresh rivulets would enter the boat, but I worked on countering these. If only it would let up a little, I could head in the right direction. Then, as the wind remained contrary I hove to and began to think up new methods of doing repairs. I tried to keep my mind intelligently concentrated. If only I could get some putty or seaming material into the cracks, but every tube I picked up had a label demanding a "clean dry surface" and all *my* surfaces lay under a permanent waterfall! I searched on through every locker till, groping at the back of one, my fingers closed on something reassuringly sticky and malleable. It felt right. I pulled out a roll of cotton tape impregnated with yellowish goo, which a

cotton tape impregnated with yellowish goo, which a
half-washed-off label proclaimed to be zinc chromate. I
was not sure what it was meant for but it looked useful. I
began to cut it into short lengths, roll it up, and stuff it
with my fingertips into all the cracks. I couldn't
remember the uses of zinc chromate, but whatever its
raison d'être, this substance behaved gloriously—it stuck,
it worked. What treasures my boat contained. Perhaps
one should always stock up with a few things you don't
really know what to do with—the opposite of my
philosophy when previously listing stores! In vain I tried
to read the tube's trade name. It was indecipherable. If I
got back, I wanted to thank the makers of my sticky roll,
but the source of supply remained a mystery and I never
even knew who had left it aboard. In my log for that
afternoon I wrote:

Plans: (1)   Make another PAN tonight. (This is
                 a distress call but without the
                 urgency of *Mayday*.)
           (2)   Hope for westerly wind.
           (3)   Try to *remain afloat* until the
                 December twenty-fourth radio
                 meeting.

As I look back at this page now, the three points seem
silly, but at the time, I found it pulled me together to list
priorities. After number (1), I later scrawled "NBG"
standing for "No bloody good."

And still the wind kept blowing hard from the east.
Thank God I had not guessed this could happen. It
would have disheartened me during the early stages
when there was real likelihood of the boat going down.
Thank God I couldn't know that the winds would keep
against me. All day long, as I worked on the collision mats
and leak stoppers, I remained hove-to, drifting away
from Australia. At one moment I wondered if instead of

making back to Fremantle, I might more easily work the
boat toward India.

Day seven, December twenty-first: No wind change.
No new ideas. As I stumbled through my routine of
pumping, brief sleeps, and improvised leak stopping I
felt my mind drifting like the boat. This was dangerous. I
kept telling myself, as if speaking to a dotty stranger, how
important it was to remain intelligent, alert, active.

Day eight came on December twenty-second. This
proved to be the big day in my own rehabilitation, the day
in which I ceased to suffer from shock and became a
normal human being again. Suddenly my body stopped
aching and my brain began to work properly. Slowly and
carefully I looked around for a triangular collision
mat—shaped like the sail I had tried to use but smaller. I
reflected on the storm jib. It was the right shape and it
had a reinforced triangular clew-piece on the bottom,
designed to take the pull of the sheet, which meant that it
was very strong. It had an eyelet at one corner for the
sheet, and the strong tapes up each side could be used to
take hauling lines. I thought I could made something of
it and spread it out in the cabin. I unpicked the stitching
laboriously, for these excellent sails were not *meant* to be
unpicked—and then took it up on deck and clamped it
over the trussed-up hull with two more ropes. Going
below, I saw that, sailing as we were, hardly any water
now gushed in. I went back on deck and stared down
with amazement. Why had I not thought of this little
section of sail before? It was just right for such a leak.
Even if rough seas hit us now I believed this device would
remain fixed. Heartened, I made a thorough inspection
of the work I had got through during the last eight days,
and once again a kind of warmth filled me—the warmth
of admiration for my own improvisations. I had managed to get thirteen ropes taut around the boat over the
hole, and they created an almost solid barrier. This outer

binding made *Galway Blazer* very sluggish in the water, but what did that matter? I might even add more ropes and she would sail slowly, safely along in her coil.

On the ninth day, December twenty-third, the wind at last crept into the southwest and I dared turn the boat's nose toward Australia. Gingerly I tried (crossing my fingers) the starboard jibe with the damage *underwater*. Everything held in place. Very very little water seeped into the cabin. "I'm going to make it," I said to myself almost in disbelief. "I'll be afloat for that radio meeting tomorrow and I can tell my news. Rescue will come."

Day ten, December twenty-fourth, brought a frenzy of excitement which increased as the precious hour for communication approached. At five fifteen Perth transmitting station would be listening in on my wavelength. I had everything ready. I kept looking at my watch, thinking of the brief words I would use to describe my plight. But when the moment came, the wildly longed-for moment when I switched on the transceiver, expecting a clear voice to answer from Perth, I heard only the usual cats' chorus of atmospheric noises. I was sailing in a Force-6, 24-knot wind with the leak pressed down into the sea and canvas and ropes holding. For a quarter of an hour I shouted desperately into the handset. My precious prearranged rendezvous time ended without Perth answering. Had the station forgotten to listen, or was my voice too faint? With a feeling of frustration I laid down the handset. My only comfort was that on this day I could log that *Galway Blazer* had sailed one hundred miles in the *right direction*.

On the eleventh day, December twenty-fifth, I had to wish myself a Happy Christmas—no one else in the world knew where I was! But I felt everything coming right while the south wind held, and I knew I ought to be grateful. To increase this line of thought, I recalled other, even worse Christmases spent at sea! There had been that one, in *Snapper* grounded on a sandbank on an enemy coast, which made this jaunt seem a pleasure trip! Now quite a lot of nice things were happening to me, and I had to keep thinking about them. I could eat. I could sleep. And the boat looked as if she would keep going until we reached Australia.

On December twenty-sixth, Boxing Day, the wind moved back into the east, but I dared to sail on into it while nervously watching my repairs. Both outer coverings and inner wedges held firm. And I got a real Christmas Box—one that I did not expect—and it made up for the disappointment of Christmas Eve. At seven thirty the sun had risen and I had made what seemed a very satisfactory inspection, so I decided to make another effort to contact Perth on the radio. I had no scheduled meeting, but we were getting close and it seemed worth a try on the off-chance. To my surprise and delight, the voice of the Perth operator, using their call sign VIP, came on the air. I shouted my call sign and jammed the handset against my ear as I heard a clear voice repeating it. "Mike, Zulu, Delta, Tango I receive you." I was able to give my position and describe what had happened while stating that I did not now need assistance. How curious was the sensation of relief that flooded over me after contact had been resumed. A week before I would have hoped for rescue craft to come my way, but as things were, I felt certain I could make it on my own, and all this call really meant was that other humans would be ready for me. Whatever happened, my family would now know the story.

All during the thirteenth day, December twenty-seventh, I kept sailing fairly fast. I could record one hundred, then ninety miles from Fremantle. It seemed difficult to believe that I really was approaching land —that soon I would see the harbor, that harbor I knew so well.

In the early morning darkness of December twenty-eighth, I nearly ran into an oil rig under tow. Ten days back I would have welcomed any ship. Now I registered only irritation at a huge moving edifice which spelled danger for small boats. It was the final run up. I had taken only three days to sail out to the point where we got holed and fourteen days to sail back. The monster had attacked when we were four hundred miles from Fremantle but we had been forced out another two hundred miles by the adverse winds so *Galway Blazer* had to cover six hundred miles in her roped-up state.

In the afternoon a plane appeared and circled around me. I waved, elated at this final visual human contact. I was *found*. The friends who had cheered me off would be waiting, thinking of me. My heart thumped. I could risk sailing faster. By sundown I saw Rottnest Island—a sandy lump in the evening haze. The Fremantle fishing harbor entrance was not very far, but I did not want to enter after dark. At nine o'clock, I decided that the wisest plan would be to allow *Galway Blazer* to have a quiet night hove-to under the island's lee. This is the first time I had dared to let my boat sit upright, but no water seemed to be coming in and we were so near home. I hoped for a peaceful and tranquil night. It is always advisable to rest well before sailing into harbor after an arduous voyage; one seldom seems able to manage it, but I thought it most necessary not to be tired on this, of all occasions. I would need my wits about me on the morrow in a small crowded harbor, and simply had to try to rest.

I took what precautions I could and climbed into my bunk. Thus we reached the fifteenth day, December twenty-ninth, but a few minutes after midnight a Force 8 gale started to blow, which ended the "rest" program. As the unwanted wind roar woke me, I hurried up to investigate the leaks. Not too bad, but I realized that the inshore current would soon carry me out to sea and so far north that I would not be able to make Fremantle when morning came. Instead, I would have to make for

Geraldton, a port up the coast I did not know and for which I had no charts. Cursing this sudden storm which had chosen to descend just when I regarded myself as safe, I stumbled around in the dark hoisting sails and beat into the wind. Inevitably this put the whole damaged area under water, but there was nothing else for it unless I was going to get broken up on the reefs which lie around Rottnest. When not sailing the boat out into the middle of the sound I was jumping down below to run my fingers over that precious jigsaw of wedges—were they beginning to give way? Could I feel water trickling in? How bitterly I regretted having left that copper strip for radio connection running along the top of the damage, for it now prevented me from inserting my hand behind it to plug up the top fixing. Why had I been so keen on communication? *No* message could be worth weakening the hole in a boat. That little band of metal running along the top of the leak proved to be my Achilles' heel. If I put up sufficient sail to make headway water poured in. If I shortened sail, the boat, all trussed up as she was, could not beat to windward at all. There was no time now while moving off a lee coast in a full gale in the dark to start chipping away at the metal. And I had to keep pumping like a lunatic. Wrapped in her swaddling clothes of ropes, *Galway Blazer* simply could not press into a gale. She churned her way, zig-zagging pathetically up the sound all through the hours of darkness while I dashed from one task to another. Perhaps because I was so near home and had given up the tense expectancy of danger, the pumping absolutely exhausted me. In a trance, I remembered the plane which had welcomed me yesterday and I visualized the drama if my boat went down *here* just outside Fremantle Harbor, where joyous weekenders sped out in their small boats! If this occurred, I would, of course, be picked up in my little dinghy, but how cruel to founder at this stage! However, it *could* happen, and it very nearly *was* happening. And the real risk was created by that copper radio band.

My plan to rest in the lee of Rottness in order to be fresh to enter harbor could hardly have proved more of a fiasco. All night I sailed perilously down Gage Roads, and only with dawn did the gale lessen. When it was possible to see the reefs I sailed cautiously between them and found the tiny entrance of the fishing harbor. And then I was suddenly tacking between anchored boats! I really was very tired indeed. Having to end up with such a night must have made us look most inelegant—a bleary-eyed skipper on a tub of ropes! I sailed poor *Galway Blazer* carefully between two rocky moles and rounded up alongside the Fishing Research Vessel. They were half expecting me, but not in this plight. I threw out a line. And then suddenly everything became different. Eager hands were helping everywhere. I was no longer alone. A kind voice put it gently: "You look cut up. How about a good strong cup of tea?" I was surrounded by my own kind. *Galway Blazer* was being petted, examined, exclaimed at. Friends began to arrive on the jetty.

That night—or was it the next night—anyway, sometime when I'd slept myself out, Marko was sitting beside me and I was telling him about it. "All you need for the Horn," I joked, "is to be able to *get there!*" His huge strong hands were already jotting down notes. "We will repair her," he said. "You will go again, don't worry." A week later, when my boat had been unwrapped and was up on the slip so that various experts could peer at the great hole in her hull, I looked up and shivered slightly. The hole looked so much worse up in the air than when I was pounding through the sea. Optimistic my nature may be, but had I actually got a clear view from below of the size of that dent, would I really have worked with such confidence?

Then came discussions with marine biologists. What

animal had launched the attack? I had automatically attributed the impact to a killer whale because I had heard of packs of these black and white beauties—so popular in aquariums—sinking small boats, but fishy friends made a different assessment. After examining the angle of the hole which showed that the attack came from aft, they considered the culprit more likely to have been a great white shark— the biggest and fiercest fish in the sea. These huge devils travel alone; everything fears them and the water empties at their approach—a great white shark would follow and attack from behind just as this one had. The unpleasant stories produced concerning ditched airmen whose orange survival suits attracted both big sharks and killer whales made me resolve to paint *Galway Blazer's* hull green. There had, in fact, been red antifouling paint on *Galway Blazer's* underside, and this might possibly have suggested blood to a hungry denizen of the sea. As the great whales have been steadily decimated by man, the balance of nature has become upset in the ocean depths. A lack of their ordinary food supply might cause either killer whale or great white shark to attack a boat in hope of biting into flesh. Now that the incident was completely over, I could not help wishing that whoever had played me this dirty trick had lifted his head to reveal his species!

The brisk, unusual phrase, "Holed by a whale," traveled quickly by telegraph and phone. Newspapers had it in England before my arrival in Fremantle. Friends recorded the episode with raised eyebrows, but no one cabled: "I told you so."

Anita and my nineteen-year-old Leonie took the news magnificently—or so they said. On Boxing Night, twelve hours after I had managed to get through to Perth by radio and while I was still in the sound, they were dining with Lord and Lady Rosse at Birr Castle in Ireland. They had, in fact, after a long day on horseback, paid a visit to St. Brendan's Well, whose water accompanied me on all my voyages. That night, very weary after their galloping but refreshed by hot baths, they were prepared to enjoy a wonderful evening. Eighteen guests sat down to dinner at Birr Castle, and it was before the dessert that Anita was called urgently to the phone. She knew the voice of John Coote, managing director of the *Daily Express.* He seemed hesitant, wondering how to deliver the news his paper had just received from Australia. He tried to make my message sound as pleasant as possible and hoped it would not spoil her dinner! Anita returned to the dining room where seventeen expectant faces turned toward her in electrified silence. "Anything about Bill?" asked Anne Rosse rather nervously.

"His boat has been holed by a whale," was all my wife could say.

"Holed by a whale! It's too much. Smelling salts for all . . ." called her hostess.

"I wish Daddy wouldn't *keep* doing such things," muttered Leonie.

Conversation returned very slowly to the bewildered festive table. No one could think of anything to say, except one practical lady who remarked, "If only the whale would properly sink that old boat and bear Bill back to safety how happy we would all be."

During the next weeks in Fremantle I had to face a few decisions. Marko worked splendidly and fast at repairing the hull, and I reckoned there might just be time to reach the Horn before it grew too cold. But when all the work had been done and I tried sailing out, it was no good. I was just too tired to make sense. Ten days of incessant pumping had depleted my strength for a while. Letters poured in, begging me to cease "tempting fate," etc., but not from my family who were ready for me to go on to the end of this deep adventure. Among the letters was one from dear Francis Chichester who, of all people, best understood the lure of the Horn. As a seaman, he was, of course, immensely interested in my extraordinary adventure, but he did rather worry about Anita, and on this occasion he added, "I am sorry for your family, Bill. Why not come home and put *Galway Blazer* in the Transatlantic Race—it will be *the* race of the century because hereafter the boats will be too big and expensive for the ordinary man to compete?"

I thought of this; I used to love ocean racing, but it meant nothing to me now, and *Galway Blazer* was slow beating to windward. She had not been designed to race. So I stuck to what I still wanted—the experience of sailing right around the world alone. But next time my hull would be painted green and rendered, I hoped, unattractive to denizens of the deep.

Part IV

CHAPTER 17

Australian Memories

I had to leave it until the following year, but far from growing tired of attempting to reach the Horn, I found my spirits raised to a higher level on this fourth departure than at any other time.

The reason for this lightheartedness may not have been immediately apparent to my friends and helpers in Western Australia; but basically I think it stemmed from the discovery of how much I enjoyed the challenges of the Southern Ocean, and in my, by now absolute, assurance that I had the perfect boat for the job. I was more than ever interested in what *Galway Blazer II* could stand up to. Also I knew how much I liked being alone in seascapes of ever-changing beauty, and I suppose, in my heart of hearts, I plain liked finishing what I set out to do!

There were a few incidents connected with the trip which I had not liked at all—being capsized, being holed, and having raw hands. But I did not feel that the unusual bad luck of the first two episodes could strike again—an out-of-season hurricane and a killer whale attack could hardly occur twice to the same person! And I had taken precaution against my hand problem.

Another thing which certainly built up my morale during preparations was the kindness and hospitality of my Australian friends. We'd all had a taste of this during the war when even we brutalized submariners felt our hearts touched by affection and warmth. Now that I was on my own and had suffered formidable setbacks in a personal endeavor many individuals rallied round me. I really wondered how Western Australia manages to breed them like that! While I worked away at refitting the boat, those able to spare time from their jobs helped me as much as they could.

One blazing noon I was struggling alone to adjust the main rigging when a voice called down from the jetty. "Want a hand?"

"Looks like it," I replied, for although I kept myself burned mahogany brown so I could work in shorts only, I was sweating and gasping and cursing because I didn't have eight arms.

Down onto the deck came a strongly built man who looked about forty. The moment he started to handle gear I realized that he was a first-class seaman, the sort of man one prays for when looking for a crew.

When evening came and we relaxed over a cup of tea in the cabin, I asked Alex Koppen his story. How had he become so good at it all? He answered—and the accent was very slight indeed—that he had been born a Dutchman, and when war broke out, he happened to be serving in a German sail-training ship. He escaped to England and joined the British Merchant Marine where he served both as a gunner and sick-berth attendant when survivors were picked from the cruel sea. Three times torpedoed, he had himself spent long periods in open boats. No wonder he had become a first-class hand. It was quite a training!

When peace came, he qualified as an electrician and emigrated to Australia, where he married and raised a family. Now he found himself between jobs, and interest in my voyage impelled him to come to see if he could aid the preparations. By good luck he had arrived at a moment when I was desperate for a strong helper.

God knows how he managed to find day after day to spare, but for the last weeks Alex's happy sunburned face appeared every morning on the jetty, and he labored beside me while I blessed his many skills and agile strength. During the last few days he often ruefully glanced at lovely *Galway Blazer*, and I felt that he was really longing to make the voyage too, feeling the lure of the Horn! "When you get to Plymouth, I will be there to meet you," said Alex. He didn't say how, and I laughed, thinking his words just a friendly exaggeration and that the idea of waving me off in Australia and waving me in from Plymouth appealed to him.

So it was, that after all this friendly help, in an absolutely confident frame of mind I cast off from Fremantle on December 4, 1972. It was a relief to feel in no way hurried. Hurry is one of the worst agonies when planning a long voyage. I had refitted quietly, painted the hull in two greens to disenchant sharks, and chosen my own time to sail. A band of friends came to see me off, and my hostess, Pam Blackburne, rushed wildly back from the jetty to snatch last-minute mail from the postman. This mail and a final gift of ripe pineapple were taken out on the press launch and handed to me as *Galway Blazer's* sails filled—my final human contact until England.

Much as I enjoy good food and wine ashore I still could not be bothered with any form of cooking at sea. Quite frankly it bored me to think about food in these conditions, and I snapped straight back onto the steady diet of soaked sultanas, nut paste, wheat biscuits, and bean shoots. There is something very restful about not having to plan meals, and I always felt so well on this specialized diet. Like an animal in its element, I reached out for food when hungry, washed my tin mug in the sea, and concentrated on sailing the boat and assimilating philosophies which my mind could not take in clearly in the turmoil of land life. When, seven days out, I transmitted as arranged to Perth Radio Station and got through a message for the family, I never dreamed that this would be the last message they would receive from me for five months.

By now I had sailed some thirty-thousand miles in my little boat, and mentally it had done me a power of good. The waves and the winds had washed out those channels in my mind which wartime tensions and frustrations had blocked. I had myself always been considerately treated by the Admiralty, but friends of mine, men who had rendered tremendous service under terrifying conditions had through the quirks of senior officers suffered having their deeds deliberately unrecognized. One submarine skipper—who may laugh as he reads this was—seven times mentioned in dispatches for sinking ships in the Mediterranean yet never given any decoration. I do not think it possible for the most saintlike character to not mind such treatment after prodigious deeds of valor. I grew acid with resentment thinking of such men, and now with enormous clarity I realized what it had meant to me when *Snapper* and *Telemachus* had returned to harbor after important sinkings to be greeted by sirens from great battleships and lines of blue sailors giving a "cheer ship." This is the stimulus which a captain knows his crew needs. One can push men to the end of their endurance, but they have to be *noticed*.

By now Boethius was helping me to adjust my mind, to set my memories in order. Then I found myself growing injured and resentful because *he* with his perfect Roman mind, had been executed. I had to read and reread his "Consolation of Philosophy" to cool my indignation.

The passage out from Fremantle started with a thrashing beat against fresh winds. Then when we reached south of Cape Leeuwin came a period of strange tranquillity. Light winds and warm days calmed my reason. By December 15 we had reached the Roaring Forties, but the weather remained fair. One night I wakened with a sudden sense of danger. Looking out of the hatch, I saw two large red lights, which is the indication at sea of a "vessel not under control." The ship was closing in on me fast, and so bright were her red lights that I could not for a time pick out any green starboard light to give me the vessel's course. Eventually I spotted a dim emerald and was able to tack hastily out of her way. It had been a near disaster. In these deserted seas one did not expect to meet any ships whatever, much less one carrying out-of-control lights. When I had escaped and watched two other ships of the same size pass in the distance, I wondered about the cause of her two-light signal: Could it have been a defective engine? Or was this whaler towing her catch and therefore unable to steer? I would never know, but I *did* know that my sudden awakening was curious. As it is impossible for a small boat to carry enough fuel for lights while sailing around the world, I had to run most of the time in darkness, keeping my batteries for emergency time in shipping lanes. On this occasion, when danger approached, the old submariner extrasensory perception had waked me. Next time I might add to my antennae by an expensive purchase—one of those new bright electronic masthead lights. I am all for mingling commonsense aids to esoteric guidelines. It was, oddly enough, just after this incident that I laid down Boethius and took up John Bliebtru's *The Parable of the Beast.* I became riveted by his studies of the pineal gland—the "third eye" described in eastern religions. Used by the lowest forms of life for elementary conscious contact, the pineal carries awareness of cosmic forces and opens the door for mental illumination in man. Now racing between waves and sky, I enjoyed new speculation. Why had I suddenly wakened in what I believed to be a deserted ocean just in time to avoid collision with that out-of-control ship? Why, when the great white shark struck the boat, was I standing facing it, just over the position where it struck? How had I known over and over again when danger was approaching, in sleep or in darkness? There had been so many odd coincidences during my months of sailing that my interest in the esoteric was stimulated. And definite memories of submariner intuition crept back. There had been a particularly strange incident in 1944 when I was taking *Telemachus* across the Java Sea.

The whole history of my third submarine came flooding back. She was faster and bigger than the other two. I had given up attempts to persuade the Admiralty to devise any kind of snorkel, but at least we had the thicker bullet-proofed plating on the gun platform for which I had cried out ever since the war started, which meant we could effectively indulge in close-range gun action. Owing to heavy casualties, *Telemachus* had to sail with a half-trained crew. The senior engine-room rating explained that his only previous experience had been in railway engines! I hesitated to complain to the Manning Depot for fear of robbing less-experienced commanding officers. To work up this novice crew, I insisted on training in warlike conditions. Depth charges were dropped around *Telemachus* until the fledglings could work unmoved in the din, and we practiced the gun crews until they were able to shoot off their first round within eighteen seconds of the submarine's tower cleaving the surface. On our first foray out of Ceylon I was permitted to patrol an area I had particularly asked for; this was a narrow neck in the Malacca Straits known as One Fathom Bank. All the Japanese ships making to Burma had to run through this narrow channel. I had for many months secretly kept the place in mind. I had thought of it and thought of it, and eventually asked for a patrol there.

Eight days out from Ceylon we reached the channel. At first I withdrew northward from the straits each night to charge batteries on the surface and throw away incriminating waste and oil. But after a few days I reversed this routine, letting *Telemachus* spend the day sliding through the strait underwater, and when darkness fell, she rose to lie with engines stopped on the surface in the land-locked waters to the south, charging her batteries. At the same time we would off-load garbage and sewage. Then we would move away from the tell-tale gash patch and hang quiet for the rest of the night listening on the surface, drifting silently with the tides. Beyond the black jungle shore, a little starlight showed up the hills of Malaya, and I took occasional bearings of these hills to keep in touch with our position. The radar was switched off lest it betray us to any new listening device. Our lookouts stood on the bridge, searching the darkness with straining eyes, and night glasses. The watch remained with ears alert for any unusual sound. We moved but slightly as the tides swirled us to and fro over the sandbank. It was quite still, not a sound broke the enclosing blackness, no lapping water against the metal hull, not a seabird's cry, only the faint hum from our ventilation fans expelling oil. So passed night after night. Waiting. Watching.

Came the morning of July 17, 1944. Toward dawn, when silvery fingers of mist were stretching over the smooth water, I dived *Telemachus* as usual. False dawn lit the sky as we slid down. Normally, one dives out of the noisy flurry of diesel engines. Diving from a dead stop, after a night's silent listening, is extraordinarily eerie. The submarine slips underneath without a sound except the shish of air going out of the saddle-tank vents.

True dawn came as we checked our trim and took the first look around with the periscope. I found it difficult to see through the dancing wraiths of mist and handed over to the officer of the watch. It was time for me to snatch an hour's sleep.

We had been submerged for less than half an hour when the submarine's broadcasting system blared, "Captain in control room." I rushed to the periscope and took over the eyepiece, while the officer of the watch whispered in my ear "a faint shape sighted in the mist bearing three hundred and twenty-five degrees, steering southeast through One Fathom Bank Channel." Meanwhile the asdic operator reported propeller noises. "Diving stations" blared the klaxon. The crew streaked to their emergency posts. All was tense and expectant though hushed. While each man in *Telemachus* stood ready at his appointed place, I pressed the periscope to my face for a long careful look.

I saw a sea mirror-calm, metal-still. The fingers of mist half dispersed were moving in the morning light. My heart tightened as out of a curl of fog there burst a large Japanese U-boat. She was going for home top speed on the surface. Only four miles away. This was the joker, the card that you abandoned the rest of the pack to get. For twenty minutes I watched with my eyes glued to the eyepieces. There she sped. Only four miles away. Thinking herself safe. All set for Singapore, so nearly home. I sensed the mood of her captain. Although in a narrow channel without room to zigzag, he was confidently relying on his speed and the mist to keep him secure. The lookouts would be country boys with splendid eyesight, topline, alert, but excited at returning to port, not concentrating on every ripple or what might be a small black stick showing for a moment in the glistening water. Their very thoughts transmitted to me through the sunshine. How often I had raced back longingly to harbor just as they, eager for the lights and lemonade! I reckoned that the U-boat would, on its present course, approach to within three-quarters of a mile. I contemplated speeding up to close in a little, but the slightest swirl might alert them. Through the periscope I could not see any escort vessels, but they might be hidden in the mist. It was so still that I could see flies floating on the surface. At such a moment the captain of a submarine keeps an almost psychic relationship with the leading stoker who works the hydraulic control of the periscope rams. As the brass cylinder weighing several tons comes out of its well, the captain squats down, seizes the handles in both hands, presses his face to the eyepieces. His knees straighten as the periscope ascends, and by the briefest order or moving of a finger he dictates the height of that tip showing above the surface.

Taking frequent tiny popping-up looks, I concentrated on the U-boat. We had to estimate her speed and course very exactly for a certain hit. The course was easy to assess in that restricted channel. Her speed had to be guessed from reference to our intelligence reports on this big class of Japanese submarine. The third officer crouched beside me reading from his reference book. "Nineteen knots," he whispered. I reckoned she must travel more slowly after a long patrol because her hull would be fouled with marine growth. I gave her eighteen. Now we were so close that it had become dangerous to pop up the periscope for another look, but I had to risk it. Nearer and nearer she came. *Telemachus* waited ready thirty-two feet below the surface. I heard my men's confident voices reporting on the torpedo tubes. Something in me recorded pleasure that they were all working like well-oiled cogs; the tight nerves of training patrols had left them. My cheekbones pressed yet harder on the eyepieces as I checked my longing to raise the periscope just a little higher so as to be able to see the bow wave and measure her speed with absolute accuracy. That would be too dangerous. We must shoot by calculation of *probable top speed.*

Within *Telemachus* the whole crew action was so silent that it had a dreamlike quality. Although I had done all this before, it seemed eerie. The tubes ready. The men at diving stations. Twenty minutes of often-rehearsed work. And now all ready for a collected shot.

There are two methods of firing torpedoes; time shots when the periscope comes down after the first shot and the remainder are fired by calculation, and visual shots when the periscope remains up throughout the attack. Now was the time to keep the periscope above water to enable us to fire a series of visually aimed torpedoes. Perfect accuracy would be needed for so small a target, but I felt confidence, for *Telemachus* had so often fired practice salvos and maintained her depth correctly.

As the U-boat approached to within a mile and reached the firing point beam-on, my submarine hung steady in the water. There was a long silence. You could hear men breathing while they awaited the order. "Stand by to fire number one, two, three, four, five, six tubes." By each tube a pin was pulled. A valve opened.

"FIRE ONE! FIRE TWO! FIRE THREE! FIRE FOUR!"

But as the torpedoes shot out, I realized that the unbelievable was happening—*Telemachus* was rising unbidden out of the depths. My exceedingly competent first lieutenant could not hold her under. Something had gone wrong with her. Our top hamper clove the surface just as a shattering explosion rent the sea. One of our six torpedoes had hit. The final two had been abandoned because we were endeavoring, by flooding and putting planes to *Hard Dive*, to get back under the water. As the flooding of our forward tank finally enabled us to dive, I shot up the periscope. Swirling water blotted out all view. Our enemy had certainly been hit, but had she sunk? I could not tell my men the answer until our intelligence network announced the certainty. All I could do was to run down to sixty feet and try to work out *why* we had risen to the surface on firing. Could it be that our new Torpex warheads were heavier so that more compensation was needed on firing? We had never been advised about such a possibility. In this lethal moment we had to discover it for ourselves.

There is a tall pagoda-shaped lighthouse sticking up near One Fathom Bank and the man in this must have had an extraordinary view of the whole episode. I *hope* he was looking, for only once in history could anyone see a submarine plunge out of the water like a whale blowing up another of its species! It would have been a shame not to appreciate such drama—such theater. Yes I do hope the light-keeper was not just an inscrutable little Japanese gazing with indifference. So eager was I to catch the other important prizes, which I knew must pass through this strait, that after making our getaway and resting out in the open ocean for two days, I decided to take the risk and return to One Fathom Bank. It was unwise, and *Telemachus* was very nearly caught. Perhaps I had grown too sure of myself in these waters. Anti-submarine craft were waiting; we expected this, but they detected us immediately and my crew had to stand up calmly to a terrific depth-charging. Only I, the captain, realized the full danger. Out battery was getting low. We were in confined shallow waters and the enemy was determined to block the narrow passage back to the open sea. Our only chance of escape lay in scraping down the side of the one-fathom patch of sandbank. That long experience of shallow waters unpleasantly won in the North Sea now helped my judgment. We nosed delicately along, running the electric motors very slowly, making as little sound as possible, just touching the sand, fixing our position by asdic bearings of the sound of the tide swirl in the bank. It was always easier to do something like this if you have done it before. Your memory helps your nervous control.

In dawn light we slipped out into broader waters, and I brought the submarine quietly up to periscope depth so that I could assess our chasers. Now I had to face the nightmarish decision which sooner or later comes to nearly all submarine captains: Should we continue to slink away under the sea or rise and fight before lack of oxygen made us stupid? I decided to remain dived deep at sixty to seventy feet. All fans and air conditioning had to be switched off. Inside the submarine the temperature kept rising and the carbon dioxide increasing. I lay in my bunk in a puddle of sweat, trying to weigh alternatives. The crew lay at their posts motionless, slowly weakening. Then we heard more depth charges in every direction. The enemy, having surmised that we had escaped from the shallow channel, was now angrily sweeping the open sea for us. But they were just guessing. If we could last till nightfall, gently nosing seaward, we might escape. We began to suffer severely. Our breathing came in long slow gasps. I knew the effects this must have on my own thinking. As darkness fell, I gave the order to surface. There was not a ship or plane in sight. The foul blue haze of our breathing and engine fumes went up the hatch like smoke. *Telemachus* drew in great lungfuls of air for her batteries. The men revived as their lungs filled slowly, driving the carbon-dioxide poisoning out of their systems. Our brains cleared. We remained on the surface all through the hours of darkness, watching and listening.

As we returned to Trincomalee the verification of our sinking of the large Japanese U-boat I 66 would be given to my crew. We rode into the harbor flying the Jolly Roger on which a red bar with a *U* in the middle showed what we had bagged. It was indeed a moving moment for us when rows of sunburned sailors turned out to give a "cheer ship." I felt my men quiver with pleasure. For most the them it had been a first patrol in enemy waters, and they had tasted early the sweet fruit of victory.

CHAPTER 18

South Pacific

THE memories of *Telemachus'* first patrol took my mind away for a time from the alluring subject of subconscious intimation of danger. Getting around the southernmost tip of Australia almost always necessitates a long tack out toward Africa and then a still longer tack toward the South Pole—into the wind all the time.

The dramas of sail-changing faded into an even more emotional drama of smaller dimensions when I broke off a piece of tooth and had to indulge in do-it-yourself dentistry. Back in London I had taken half an hour's instruction and I felt most businesslike tying a mirror to the mainsheet winch and spreading out my tools safely. When I then stuck my head out of the hatch, the light showed up the interior of my mouth nicely. "Open please." It was fairly calm and I managed to work a small cement filling onto the jagged part. Feeling extraordinarily clever, I kept opening my mouth to admire my own workmanship. And the filling stayed put.

My Christmas present this year was a vast meteorological depression, the "eye" of which passed right overhead. *Galway Blazer* sat wallowing in big confused seas under a windless patch of blue sky. I reduced sail to a scrap of foresail, and then when a storm blew in from the northwest, I ran before it under bare poles. So strong was the wind that the vane steering could hardly compete, and I sat up all night nursing my boat out of the broaches.

Once again I was to pass a Christmas alone at sea, and I

had prepared special messages for the family when I got through to Sydney at the prearranged time on Christmas Eve. I knew that Anita would be expecting news, and although she accepted my assurance that no creature was likely to attack my boat a *second* time, especially with the hull painted green, it was very important to me to get through greetings because on the previous Christmas I had been floundering about, wondering if *Galway Blazer* was going to the bottom!

We were tearing down the Pacific, and when the time came for my rendezvous with Sydney, the distance for transmission had become eight hundred miles. Radios do not really like the ocean, especially when they are old. Mine had, however, been carefully overhauled, and when tested out in harbor, it seemed to work perfectly. It had never entered my head that when a big English-speaking transmitting station was trying to get my wave-length at a fixed hour the result might be silence. On and on I went for over a quarter of an hour with the handset clamped to my ear, but no voice replied to my call, I had to give up and hope that my wife would not worry. Maybe the next rendezvous would be more successful, although the transmitting range would be growing longer. How glad I was that I had at least told her that with the aerial necessarily rigged to foremast, which did not give it sufficient height, I might possibly not get through later on to my radio contacts in South America. Yes, it was something to remember telling her that. "The radio aerial gives me a lot of trouble, so don't worry if you don't hear." But had it really sunk in? I had not wanted to make her feel it was *very* likely she might not hear, only to warn her of the possibility. She and Leonie would then again be staying at Birr Castle and how nice it would be if instead of hearing that I had been holed they received a jolly message of the distance I had covered in this fast wind.

Although I could not establish contact, my boat

vibrated with loud Australian weather broadcasts which gave lurid descriptions of the havoc wrought by the storm I had been running in. It had flooded Brisbane, brought snow to Hobart's midsummer, and most disastrous of all, stopped cricket in Melbourne! And all down the Pacific I could hear Radio London, the long-range station, giving Stock Exchange results! A lot I cared when the index fell two points! It made me laugh.

The New Year found me belting along some hundreds of miles south of New Zealand. I knew now that *Galway Blazer* could ride the crests at fifteen knots, with her steering blade screaming but holding her true. At first I could hardly believe the speedometer, as it ran up the stops, but testing proved it was recording absolutely accurately. As *Galway Blazer*'s theoretical maximum speed in the water was eight and a half knots, when she moved at twelve knots it felt as if my beautiful boat had fallen in love with the petrels flashing above her and had determined to take off and fly with them. Such poetic imaginings ceased when the Honda generator started to leak fuel. This breakdown necessitated changing to the spare generator—a mechanical job which entailed complete dismantling and then reassembling of a complicated exhaust system mounted with tiny difficult-to-locate bolts. Four hours spent handling metal side-plates and mountings started my old hand trouble. But I had thought up precautions and took the greatest care of my paws. I used barrier cream all the time and two pairs of gloves for work on deck—surgeon's gloves and plastic gauntlets. I disciplined myself never to make a quick snatching movement, and I slept with gloves next to my body so that I could pull them on warmed and avoid the first chill. By day, gloves were always ready, kept carefully under the perspex skylights warmed by the sunshine. There was, of course, no place for any heater in a boat of this size, and I had to learn to use the sun as my valet as well as my ocean guide.

On January 3, 1973, I crossed the date line. It always gives me a certain childish amusement to write the same date on two days running. I spent half a day trying to contact first Sydney and then Wellington on the radio. While fiddling through the frequencies, I intercepted a New Zealand weather report warning of a fifty-knot gale coming my way, so I got the boat snugged down and prepared to enjoy myself watching it blow. *Galway Blazer* took off and rode the waves with the steering blade singing a high note as its edge cut the crests while I stood transfixed. This was sport indeed, but one you have to search the greater oceans to find! Riding the crests in a Pacific gale is an incredible sensation.

After four or five days of blue sky with the desired north wind sweeping us straight down the Pacific, navigation began to seem ridiculously easy. Out here, when the vast swells of the Southern Ocean died away, I could use a sextant, artistically sweeping the sun along the horizon just as one was taught in the long ago—instead of, as usually happened, wildly trying to catch the moment of contact on a boat lurching off a breaking wave with oneself performing acrobatic feats.

This was fantastic weather. The winds gave *Galway Blazer* a marvelously fast run down the Pacific. On January 14, with a clear sky and mild wind on the beam, I wrote: "We are just about to enter the uttermost mid-Pacific where, except for a few coral islands, the nearest habitable land is three thousand miles in any direction. But these regions are birdless. I miss birds."

Then I started to run down the forty-eighth parallel, and freezing polar air came billowing up from the South Pole. Angrily I wrote: "My life revolves around gloves: surgeon's gloves, rubber gloves, plastic and leather ones, gauntlets, half-gloves, mitts and silk gloves. A whole locker full of them. Artful dodges are employed to keep them warm and dry—God, what a bore!" Then I felt ashamed of going back to grumbles and forgetting the magic of speed in this boat with a following wind. I suppose I was desperately frightened of so small a thing as peeling fingers that might again interfere with the supreme adventure of my life.

By January 23, we were 120 degrees west, about two thousand miles from the Horn. We were racing along, and all I had to do was keep my hands in good condition so that I could repair rigging in the icy cold. When the day came that the mainsail needed a stitch, I found my gloved fingers could sew and my confidence returned. Now I busied myself merrily with navigation and sometimes burst out singing. People would ask me if after weeks at sea I ever talked to myself. Well, I did not indulge in this habit, although I always spoke orders aloud to myself.

For a time the vast blue bowl of my outer world changed to a bowl of mist a few hundred yards across. This increased the feeling of dreamtime. Mist is usually the bane of mariners, but out there in the middle of the Pacific with no other ships and no islands or rocks for thousands of miles, one could pile on sail and keep no lookout. The very vastness became one's nurse. And now that my goal was fast approaching, now that all the winds blew right, I let myself revel in this emptiness; alone, yet not alone, I became part of it. The last tormenting shreds of what I had thought frustrating war memories blew from me. I reassessed my final year in submarines and put it from me, or maybe it would be more exact to say I altered memory's form. The dud torpedoes, the obsolete guns, the thinly armored gunshield, the lost friends—all these I must remember but differently colored. Now I must face today's facts: Am I really sailing for Cape Horn because the armor plating on my submarine was thinner than I wished? Because *Snapper's* gun would not fire backwards? Because in *Trusty's* best attack her torpedoes dropped to the bottom? Because *Telemachus* could not exceed fourteen knots and the Americans' did twenty-two? Or am I yanking myself around the world in a four-and-a-half-ton boat because I just like doing it?

As the magnificence of the lonely Pacific and the sequence of strangely varying dawns soothed my spirit, I knew that it no longer pained me to recall submarining errors and I was just living for fun. All I had to do now was to keep alive.

Fremantle and Perth lay more than two thousand miles to the northwest. My friends there would be wondering why they did not get a message, would be imploring Anita not to worry, while badgering the big transmitting station to keep trying my wavelength. How I had appreciated Australia after our fifty-nine-day patrols. After she had scored the Japanese U-boat, *Telemachus* had been allotted to the American submarine base at Fremantle. This placed us in a most irritating predicament. Not having the power or speed of American submarines, we should have been kept for specialized work at which we were truly experienced —nosing around close to the enemy—a dangerous but profitable game, which those of us who had survived had learned in the North Sea and the Mediterranean. If only we had been based at Port Darwin three thousand miles nearer the enemy, what useful work we could have done. Our submarines were not built for the long-distance patrols necessary from Fremantle, but how many Japanese ships we could have sunk had we been allowed forays at closer range.

I had pulled a long face at being based so far from enemy shipping lines; my groans increased when I was told that while the big American submarines thundered off across thousands of miles of ocean looking for their prey, we were to be employed transporting cloak-and-dagger parties to faraway islands. This kind of work is the nightmare of any submarine commander, and I was about the most experienced left alive, but we were to fritter away our time on the odious activity known as special missions—in other words, we could regard ourselves as taxis for suicide squads. Eighteen extra bunks had to be fitted into the torpedo stowage compartment and tempting targets that came *Telemachus'* way would have to be allowed to slide out of the periscope while our load of commando passengers endured a fortnight's stifling hell. Eventually we would creep up at night to a secret destination and launch the wretched fellows on enterprises which were impossible to evaluate.

My crew—engine driver and all—had matured immensely during their first happily successful patrol. They were ready to accept any nonsense philosophically. But close to me there was one person for whom I felt sincerely sorry. This was the new first lieutenant. I should have liked to be able to give him a taste of what we had known in Colombo. When Johnnie Pope, my splendid Number One, returned to England to become commanding officer, he was replaced by a quiet character of great gallantry. Had the exigencies of my command not been so demanding, I should have paid much more attention to Bill Dundas when he joined my ship, for he was one of the three men who had survived out of nearly nineteen hundred when our greatest warship *Hood* had been sunk by the *Bismarck* three years before. A midshipman at the time, Bill had known the fantastic chase after *Bismarck* and *Prinz Eugen* when they sailed around Iceland, hoping to reach the open Atlantic and raid our convoys, which were already being severely attacked by U-boats. And from the upper bridge he had watched the short terrible battle when *Hood* and *Bismarck* with guns over twenty yards long, weighing one hundred tons apiece, lined up and opened fire on each other. Those who were able to look saw, as their own guns deafened them, a ripple of fire run down the length of the enemy ship as it fired each salvo—and the crews could *see* the shells in the air. Admiral Holland in *Hood* had been unlucky. He had hoped to surprise *Bismarck* in the night. Instead, he met her at dawn at a bad angle for attack. White fountains arose around *Bismarck*, but she was not hit. Her fourth salvo landed a shell right on *Hood* which penetrated deep down to explode amid her magazines. The forty-two-thousand-ton ship—elderly but the pride of our Navy—sank within a few minutes. Neither the Germans nor the British who saw her go could believe their eyes.

The battle had lasted twenty minutes. Then suddenly *Hood* had gone up in flamesand vanished. Ninety officers and more than fourteen hundred men went down with her. When, two hours later, the destroyer *Electra* reached the scene, hoping to pick up survivors, they saw nothing but a patch of oil and some floating debris. Could it be true—that this was all that remained of the great *Hood*? Then three small rafts were spotted, floating near one another. On each lay a single half-frozen human being.

Naval officers accustomed to action in wartime usually discuss what the more extraordinary moments have been like, but Bill seldom mentioned the battle he had lived through. He only remembered climbing out of the upper bridge window when he saw the sea come up to it. Then he was in the water swimming away from the huge bow as it pointed skyward, and then it was strangely silent—the roar of guns had suddenly ceased—and there was only the sighing of waves in the gray Arctic sea.

Midshipman Dundas, Signalman Briggs, and Able Seaman Tilburn swam around in the icy water until they found some Carley rafts floating. Each climbed on one, and for a time they tried to hold themselves together but their hands grew numb. Then they lay quietly, obsessed by the silence, until the *Electra* arrived and pulled them on board. Three out of nearly fifteen hundred.

It shows how hard the pressure was on British naval officers that after this traumatic experience young Dundas was considered suitable for submarine training.

He was very good, very diligent, very quiet. We respected his reserve. The loneliness of that freezing dawn, the slow realization that all those others had gone down, must have affected his nervous sinews—but not his courage.

I felt so sorry that he had missed our first exciting patrol when we knew what we were about, but he just had to buckle down to this maddeningly unsuitable work of ferrying commandos about the Pacific.

When *Telemachus'* new role was described to me, I had grimaced but I did not immediately understand why the American staff officer who handed me orders to transport commandos looked quite so rueful when he said, "I've never in my life so disliked sending a submarine on any expedition." *He* knew that the Japanese fleet was expected to leave its anchorage south of Singapore, that a submariner's dream might materialize. The Battle of Leyte Gulf, one of the decisive sea battles of the war, was about to break. Instead of doing her proper work, *Telemachus* was to be engaged in sideshows. I did not have to suffer the mortification of the skipper of *Porpoise* who had to watch an unescorted ten-thousand-ton enemy oil-tanker pass close to his sights and refrain from torpedoing her so that he could land a party of commandos (these poor devils were immediately captured and executed), but I always felt that *Telemachus* had the missed chances of Leyte Gulf scratched deep in her old tin heart.

It was during one of these broiling fifty-five-day patrols out of Fremantle that an episode occurred which linked up curiously with my recent escape from being run down. Each submarine patrol into the China Sea involved passing through the "Malay Barrier of islands," a hazardous passage against a contrary current, and past enemy opposition in the narrow Lombok Strait east of Java, then westward to nose up through the Karimata Strait which we regarded with trepidation, for it was shallow and easy to mine. One needed an accurate position from which to take off because there were no landmarks, and haze often prevented astronavigation, so with all these unpleasant hazards in dangerous enemy-infested waters, it was desirable to obtain an absolutely accurate position when passing the Kangean Islands in the middle of the Java Sea. After that one could expect no landmarks for a hundred miles.

Thinking over all my experiences of extrasensory perception, I remembered a tropical night when *Telemachus* was approaching the Kangean group and I was carefully trying to work out how to use their outline as a landfall. Careful study of the large-scale chart proper to inshore navigation revealed no dangerous shallows, so I reckoned that it would be sensible to set a course straight toward the islands until we were about twelve miles offshore. The islands would then show up clearly against the bright night sky and we could accurately fix our position before making for the Karimata Strait. As we thrummed along on the surface over the silvery tropic sea, the job appeared to be so easy that I hurried down for a brief sleep while the officer of the watch remained in charge. It really seemed that nothing could go wrong for an hour. Within minutes of drifting off, however, I awoke with a start. A sense of inexplicable danger filled me. Another close look at the chart revealed secure waters—no small islands, no rocks—in fact, no reason whatever to stop going straight ahead. Yet I was so deeply perturbed that, for no logical reason, I gave orders to alter course.

A few hours later, as we slipped around south of the islands on this new course, we saw the land clearly and fixed our position. Next day, when light had driven us under water, I went back to the small-scale chart used in the open ocean. To my amazement and horror I saw that *it* showed a reef which would have ripped *Telemachus* to pieces had we continued on our direct course on the previous night. By some incredible oversight this reef had been omitted from the wartime large-scale chart always used when closing land. We had been within minutes of disaster. Why did I wake up? Why did I feel impelled to alter course? No one could have suspected that a new chart, printed in wartime and issued to submarines, could omit a vital reef. Had some radar system within myself detected peril? What had pinged against my sleeping brain? Was this how the "pineal eye" functions?

The memory of that near-disaster came back to me now to compare with my sleep-time awareness of those ships where none could be expected. And of my body's instantaneous facing of the attacking monster *before* he hit the hull.

These could perhaps be coincidences, so could several other curious occurrences which had led me to regard extrasensory perception as an ordinary, useful aid. But there was no coincidence possible and no logical reason for me to suspect danger under the moonlit water that night in Java Sea.

And then, because one fleeting memory leads to another, I recalled *Telemachus'* final departure from Australia . . . a story in which no extrasensory perception whatever was involved!

We had ended our Pacific commission at Port Darwin and were all ready to leave for England. On the last morning I came on board with my last orders to find that my absolutely splendid coxswain had been entertaining two RAF pilots overnight. Good-fellowship had gone rather far—much too far, in fact—and his friends were now lying unconscious on the casing. There is a tremendous tide in Port Darwin and the submarine was at this moment floating some thirty feet below the jetty so that a long climb up a slippery iron ladder was required to get off the ship. It was time to go to sea, and the only method of removing our guests was by tying a rope around the waist of each slumped figure and using manpower to haul them up the ladder. The bodies were laid out on the jetty and a few minutes later we cast off. Now the coxswain had to stand, as always, just in front and a little below me on the bridge, steering out of the winding harbor. It was a lucky position. Aware that he might be prone to errors, I was able to correct these by secretly sticking my foot forward to press down on the spokes of the steering wheel. We made the open sea.

CHAPTER 19

Round the Horn

NOW I was tearing down the Pacific, making what I felt must be record time for a small boat. The winds blew hard from the west for over five thousand miles—an astonishing favor. Evening after evening for two months I knew the joy of reeling off the miles, and the peace of the huge ocean encompassed me—golden days, vivid ever-different sunsets, nights of brilliant starlight or bright moon. Once again the sense of being part of this vast beauty overwhelmed me. I would never be quite the same animal again—a man who has found this link to the rotating earth must change. I knew that I would always carry this wondrous knowledge with me. You cannot cover the whole Pacific alone and remain as you were before. Sunrise, sundown, stars, planets, singing waters, changing winds—the memory of these horizons would be imprinted deep inside me forever.

But the tranquillity could not last. As I drew nearer to South America, I looked ever more frequently at the charts. The South American continent is shaped like a big fist pointing southward and nearly touching the Antarctic landmass. Between the two continents lies Drake Channel, only three hundred miles wide and acting like the spillway of a dam. Through this gap runs the pent-up millrace of the eastbound flow of the Southern Ocean, carrying a ceaseless procession of weather change, each bringing the violent winds of alternating warm and cold fronts. It is a nasty picture the year around, for the continental high-pressure system and the vertical throttling of the Andes chain build up a funnel for the winds. The upthrust of the continental shelf creates a gigantic weir, and the whole region around the Horn resembles a wind tunnel around the South Pole. Drake did not know the passage existed. He was, in fact, trying to sail through the Straits of Magellan when the ships were blown back into the Atlantic, and then meeting a terrible gale from the East, they found themselves being driven south and eventually into what looked like ocean rollers—the Pacific! At this moment in time, the ice, which used to extend almost across the narrow Drake Channel, has receded (in living memory ice used to extend up northward beyond the Falkland Islands). Horrible weather conditions generally prevail, but a good boat can battle through almost any seas. The real threat—the one which I always had in mind—lies in hundreds of miles of rocky lee shore.

Down to about 40 degrees the Pacific coast of South America presents a smooth unbroken shoreline, but from there southward it is fractured into thousands of fiords, inlets, and rocky islands right down to the ultimate tip. No lee shore could be less hospitable, and the only comfort issued by the old Sailing Directions was a list of the islands where those fortunate enough to survive a shipwreck might find Indians who were only moderately hostile!

When a sailing boat strikes down the South Pacific to Cape Horn, she must try initially to keep somewhere in the region of 50 degrees south so that she may benefit from the strong following westerly winds and yet remain clear of the ice zones. When the final approach to Cape Horn is made, she will have to dip down to about 57 degrees south to pass around the cape. Along this leg of the course, the mariner cannot avoid being exposed to the danger of being caught up against that jagged coast with the wind slanting into a southwesterly and gusting up to one hundred knots.

I always had great respect for a lee shore, and those

uncomfortable moments in *Snapper* on the sandbank intensified this respect! I had never known the bump of a keel again and I never wished to. To be stranded in a submarine in enemy territory is a lesson that lasts a lifetime! My deepest instinct is always to fly to the open sea for safety!

Now, as I approached closer to those jagged shores, the lightheartedness I had known in mid-Pacific seeped out of me. I was constantly aware of the great South American continent—aware by day and by night of that landmass. Also it was becoming horribly cold. Midsummer had hardly passed but these regions never really warm up and I rather hated the increasing feel of ice in the air. This was a unique experience and precious to me, yet I was not enjoying it as I ought to! I didn't *like* the feel of all that jagged land. I had become accustomed to emptiness.

My polar outfit consisted of a padded nylon suit worn under oilskins, and when I rolled into my red quilted sleeping bag and pulled my pet red knitted cap down over my eyebrows, I made a colorful picture! The seas now became big, but not tremendous. The waves never even faintly resembled the mountainous breaking crests of the hurricane that had capsized me. That also was an experience which never quite left my mind—like the wartime stranding it was in its way the ultimate of unpleasant happenings.

On February 2, 1973, I wrote in the log:

> Now we are three hundred miles from the landfall of Diego Ramirez and Ildefonso. Will I see anything? I am keeping a constant check on position and progress in case the last run is done in thick weather. After the vast ocean I hate the thought of rocky shores.

So there I was, after that superb fast run of seven

thousand miles in sixty days, pulling a face as I neared my life's goal—because that was really what Cape Horn had become. Since boyhood I had craved for this particular adventure—it appealed to me above all other—and yet, as the moment approached, what did I do but beef about the difficulties!

One cannot hang about in those Antarctic waters hoping for good weather, though the curtains of mist and storm can clear for a few hours and then switch back to tremendous waves and conflicting winds. As I approached the tip of South America I reckoned the sooner I rounded it the better. But all the time I was sort of angry because, after being the spoiled darling of the Pacific, I was now in black seas and thick fog. Perhaps it was the bitter cold that made me feel ill-treated.

When we were one hundred and eighty miles from land, the barometer crashed down and a gale roared out of the northwest. With visibility nil, I became seriously worried about getting sights. One could have no peace of mind in this freezing mist and the sea became extremely rough.

On February 4—just two months after I had sailed out of Fremantle—I reckoned that Drake Passage must lie just ahead of me. Three hundred miles wide, this narrow strip of tempestuous water that beats between Cape Horn and the Antarctic continent would test my navigational skill to the limit if I could see nothing the whole way!

Anxious to keep wide awake and alert, I filled my two stainless-steel thermoses with hot black coffee to last me twenty-four hours. I had expected huge seas and constant wind change, but not this unremitting thick driving mist. All through that day I hoped for a shaft of sunlight somewhere to get a fix, but the low black sky never broke and I began to hate the invisible landmasses on each side of me.

Reefing right down, I tried to idle through the night.

Not only did I long to see the basalt fang of the Horn—because if you come all this way on a romantic whim the least you can expect is to get a *look*—but also by now I was anxious not to sail right *onto* the "damn thing"!

The hours went by, black and icy and wild. I stared furiously into the gray dawn and literally craved the moment when I could dare turn left. And then suddenly, out of the murk, slipped a golden shaft—just enough to give me a fix and determine my position. I found all correct on my dead reckoning. *Galway Blazer* pounded confidently on between invisible landfalls. I passed the islands of Ildefonso and Diego Ramírez without obtaining a glimpse of either. South America was just a name—an ominous presence in this fantastic Wagnerian setting.

I don't know quite what sort of emotional thrill I had been expecting when I saw the great basalt fang that is Cape Horn. I was all wrought up; perhaps it was even more dramatic to battle through these curtains of darkness in the roaring wind, running under bare poles against storm force hammerblows. But I began to be afraid. The black clouds were down to masthead, mingling with spume from the sea. I longed for the curtains to lift just for one minute to let me know where I was, but it went on for two days and two nights—hailstorms and flick changes of wind that kept nearly jibing my boat. In this stormy passage, with visibility never rising above a mile, the confused tempestuous waters hurled us around in ceaseless squalls, until suddenly the storm would die, leaving *Galway Blazer* overreefed and floundering. Then it would blow up again, gale following gale from opposing directions. I began to feel exhausted, reefing and unreefing. Such conditions were unusual even at the Horn. I felt that the Atlantic and Pacific oceans hated each other and were fighting here between the rocky islands, with my little boat being buffeted by their fists.

During the second night, after more than twenty-four

hours without sleep, I started to stiffen, both mentally and physically. In fact, I began to wonder if I was going to die of cold and exhaustion. Then came a strange sensation as if someone were in the boat with me. How can I explain it—not a mystical experience, just a calm feeling of assurance that *someone* was there helping and sharing the tasks. Looking back, I do not feel that my mind became deranged—I was just quite certain that I was not alone, and creeping slowly back half-frozen from the deck to do some repair work below, I paused in my hammering, suddenly thinking, "I must not make such a noise—*he* may be off watch and asleep." Who? I saw nothing; I only felt that radiation which comes from a good companion.

This curious mental warmth sustained me, my fatigue lessened and so did that nagging fear that in this total blackness with mast-high waves and roaring wind we might hit an island. Someone was up front keeping a lookout. In this most lonely hour of my life there was no sensation of being alone.

As we bucketed along through Drake Passage, another dawn crept up and the mountainous seas turned from jet to molten lead. But still the icy fog prevailed, and I felt somewhat outraged at being able to see nothing and having to make my turn up the Atlantic on calculations alone. At the moment of turning, the wind increased to storm force as if screaming angry warnings at me. Wearing my safety harness, padded suit, and oilskins, I worked away on the foredeck clearing the foreyard which had jibed itself round the topping lift. I was thinking now in prayers which my frozen lips were too stiff to speak. But the sense of an unseen companion stayed with me, and I felt I was sharing the elation of this wonderful if horrible moment—the moment in which hoping that I *had* rounded South America, I turned *Galway Blazer* left, up into the Atlantic!

Having made the vital decision, I could but trust that

my calculations were correct. If we weren't around we would soon know it! I got down all sail and ran under bare poles with the southerly storm behind me through another day and night of murk and mist. I was very tired by now, but obviously we *were* around the Horn. Had we not been, we would have hit it. The wind stayed steady, easing to gale Force 8. When it became possible to trust to vane-steering, I dropped below and went to sleep for twelve hours. My companion left me and never returned.

On the next night, while running past Staten Island, the wind eased. I cautiously put up sail and slept again—recovering from the turmoil and battering. Glad not to have run into South America, annoyed I had not had a glimpse of her.

On February 6 I realized that the great point of my voyage was over. I had done what I wished, and now all I had to do was concentrate on avoiding the iceberg zone and sailing northward to warmer waters. My hands had stood up to the cold but only just. The icy spray-filled air was making them painful. I reckoned it would be wise to try keeping to windward of the Falkland Islands by passing them on their western side. After running into exceptionally bad weather even for this part of the world, I now got a lucky break. A fresh southeasterly wind—rare in these parts—started to blow and it was just what I needed.

On February 8 I made a dart for it and wrote in my log:

> I have not pressed the boat at all up to now, trying to preserve the gear, but today I really *asked* her and she bounced across the waves like a mad racehorse. I want to do an end-around the islands while this wind lasts. Once I've got a bit of sea-room I can ride out storms or beat up against foul winds—just that little edge is needed, the direction and speed is perfect.

Now I was fleeing, fleeing from those dark raging icy waters which had been at the core of my craving for so many years. Alone, I had sailed around Cape Horn and God, I thought, I never want to do it again! That yen really is out of my system.

On February 9, four days up into the Atlantic, I wrote: jubilantly: "The wind pattern might have been carved out for me. The southeaster carried me round behind the islands; it then veered south to swoosh me up past them and then turned west to blast us out clear." When a northwesterly gale erupted, I was out of the Fifties and racing through the Forties like a frozen cat looking for a better climate.

By February 11 I had completely revived. The cold and exhaustion which had beset me round Cape Horn became blurred memories. I could sleep like a log, and a healthy appetite assailed me. In the middle of breakfast I heard a screech of wind and the anemometer began to spin around—thirty, forty, fifty knots. I scrambled on deck to douse and secure the already reefed foresail. Spray and rain stung me horizontally; this, I guessed, was a taste of the dreaded "Pamper" winds which used to surprise the old square-riggers and tear their sails out. The gale blew in heavy gusts but from the right direction, and we sped northeastwards before it, leaving the Falkland Islands far behind. Four days this gale lasted on and off with a steep lumpy sea and a strange countercurrent unmentioned in the charts. I tended, in my excessively good spirits to put out too much sail, and my boat lay right over and buried her starboard bow in a huge comber. Water poured through the deck ventilator as she hung poised for what seemed an extraordinary length of time. A quick reef-down eased her, but I recognized in myself the dangerous euphoria of narrow escape—having *got* round the Horn I was now sailing thoughtlessly.

On February 18 we left the Roaring Forties on a northeasterly course and I sang with thankfulness that I

could see beauty again. The Forties waved me a special
farewell—by day a huge flock of white birds flashed their
wings over me, and then came a sunset of coral pink and
jade green with a full moon of polished steel making its
pathway on the sea.

As I strengthened physically and the sea grew warmer,
I again began to look forward to radio contact but the
prearranged call-up with Radio Buenos Aires elicited no
response. All the way up the coast of South America I
could hear voices reminiscent of Donald Duck quacking
in Spanish, but my own shouts went unheeded. I could
not understand what had happened. It was, I knew,
impossible to carry a sufficiently tall aerial on my
foremast and the radio set was getting rather old, but I
still expected my wavelength to be picked up, however
faintly, at prearranged times. H.M.S. *Endurance*, the
Antarctic survey vessel, had arranged a radio time
schedule and intended to communicate with me between
the Horn and the Falkland Islands, but because I had
made such a fast passage to Cape Horn (I was a fortnight
ahead of anticipated time), this big ship never came
within fifteen hundred miles of me. I had to resign
myself to the knowledge that my wife would have to
continue to go without news of me. Had I not told her
that it was quite likely that South American stations
would not pick me up, she would certainly have been
extremely distressed. I thanked heaven that I had,
almost by chance, told her this. With luck I would get
within a few miles of some ship; I didn't *want* to—lone
sailors *hate* the proximity of vessels which can so easily
sink them. But, in order to establish my existence, I now
wildly hoped for a funnel on the horizon. All I wanted
was to say, "I've done it—I'm coming home."

By February 25, three weeks after rounding the Horn,
we were still getting half-gales, babyish imitations of the
real thing down in Antarctic waters. Gusty winds, steely
rain, and lovely breezes played ring-a-rosy around us.

Then the sky cleared and we sailed silkily for the point in mid-Atlantic where we would turn north through the Variables to meet the Southeast Trade Winds. What pleasure it was to skim over a blue, sun-warmed sea, even if, when the breezes lightened, we made little progress. By night we hardly moved at all, the boat sighing dreamily through the water; I could mark inches rather than miles in the log.

As my hands healed and my tired body put itself to rights in the warm air, various boat ailments started to follow suit. *Galway Blazer* evidently felt in good form, now she was back in sunshine. The galley seawater pump recommenced work (while going around the Horn, the boat had been lifted so much in the air that seawater fell out of the bottom of the pipe and airlocks constantly formed). And all through the Southern Ocean the generator of the radio ammeter had vibrated ominously. Now, without any action on my part, it returned to duty. With wry amusement I noticed the boat readjusting herself just like a person.

Then on March 3, when we crossed the thirtieth parallel, I stood looking up at the wandering albatross who had accompanied me thus far north to the very edge of his territory, and a sadness filled me, for this might well be the last albatross I would see on this voyage—perhaps the last I would ever see in my life! *Diomedia exulans*, the noblest birds of all—they had chosen to escort me for close on sixteen thousand miles; I was going to miss the splendor of their company, the great wingspan, the grace, the sense of life's power that always made my heart miss a beat.

CHAPTER 20

The Horn Lies Behind Me

AS though the thirtieth parallel were an enclosing boundary, the first flying fish swerved under the stern. Now we entered the warm-water belt, struggling up two hundred and seventy miles through the Variables to that goal of all the old clipper ships, the ocean crossroads where Trade Winds meet the Variables.

The sun became hotter, but the winds fell slack and it took a week to sail nine hundred miles. Irritation seized me. Now that I had rounded the Horn, now that I had done what I wanted, I began to chafe at the thought of all the months of hard sailing which still lay ahead. It was nine thousand miles in a straight line from Cape Horn to Plymouth, and with the wind playing me up, how many more miles in actual tacking? The winds who had been so good to me in the Pacific changed their game in the Atlantic. They never ceased to creep around, heading me off, never remained steady in force or direction, and sometimes as an ultimate tease died away completely. The set for the ocean currents which should, according to the charts, have been to the east, turned against me and came from the west. The nights remained squally, allowing little sleep and occasionally rain deluged as if from emptied buckets. Anything but pleased by this kind of sailing, I found my appetite for food doubled. Now I craved mugs of protein and raisins; was it real healthy hunger or psychological frustration? However, I could comfort myself with the thought that this slow progress meant a warm North Atlantic. We never actually had to

record a day's run "backwards," but sometimes it felt like
it. I turned back to my precious little library. Aristotle's
Ethics—so dry and logical—ought to have been the right
medicine, but self-improvement was not my mood at the
moment. I felt flat. The Horn was over and I couldn't tell
anyone about it—I tried not to think about my family
longing for news of my existence. There was nothing for
it but to slowly battle toward the Southeast Trades,
shouting my head off at intervals into the radio and
cursing the fact that my urgent messages went unheeded. By now three months had passed since Anita
had heard anything from me and she could not be
expected to like it. I tried to remember exactly what I had
said to her. I certainly had told her not to worry if the
Spanish-speaking South American stations did not get
me, but had I mentioned the possibility of missing
H.M.S. *Endurance* near the Falklands? How could I warn
her that every possible connection might ignore my
wavelength. She couldn't not be worried, but there was
nothing I could do about it. I only hoped that Tarka Dick
and Leonie would infect her with their youthful
optimism. They always said, "Let Daddy do his thing.
He'll get back."

The Atlantic Sea remained lumpy and confused. *Galway Blazer* seemed to be either pounding into it or
wallowing. Often it felt as if we were just going up and
down in the same hole in the water. We sat in a stationary
thundery front, parallel to the coast of South Africa,
bashing into a series of gray brick walls—creeping,
creeping, creeping northward.

Sailing always brings a few bonuses, however. There
came one night that would remain imprinted on my
memory for its sheer beauty. The wind had blown steady
for many hours, and I stood on deck giving hail to the
firmament. The sickle moon had set and the whole
jeweled canopy of stars spread overhead, with the Milky
Way arched over our course: ahead Orion like a giant

over the foremast, Sirius the Dog Star at the main, the Southern Cross astern, and close to it a black stain on the Milky Way, which I believe the latest astronomical investigators would call a cloud of cosmic dust.

I had been reading Marcus Aurelius—that most Christian-spirited of non-Christian emperors—and now I recalled his ruminations concerning the immortality of the soul. He had found it hard to believe that a man's life ended completely at death, but when the emperor stared up into the heavens, into the vast blue vault by day and the sparkling darkness by night, his cold reasoning persuaded him that *there was no room up there for so many people!*

We know better—but how much better? Since then the human species, to which I belong, has stretched its mind out to discover that we do not live beneath a hard inverted bowl, that there *is* room and plenty. It is not material space that we need. It is spiritual knowledge. And I, a man evolving alone on the ocean's face—caught in this moment of time, caught at this stage of scientific knowledge, between phosphorescence and stars as a child between sparkling blankets—felt the curiosity of my race stream out, wondering and in wonder. Marcus Aurelius could only surmise within the appearances of his time; he had to marshal his thoughts beneath a *hard* dome, blue or black. *I* can speculate further, using the knowledge of my era to help arrange the patterns in my mind. And after me come other men—knowing more. But never could the night seem more beautiful to them than to me, and I doubt if they will enlarge on Pascal's phrase: "The heart of man is the microcosm of the universe."

But with all this, I am ashamed to say I remained at the mercy of my moods. Neither Aristotle, Marcus Aurelius, Pascal, nor the rose bloom of each dawn could improve my bad temper as adverse winds and unwanted calms delayed my voyage home.

By March 11, when we should have met the Trades, *Galway Blazer* was still dreaming in a windless ocean, devoid even of birds, for birds dislike long periods of calm. They need high winds for gliding, and waves to stir up plankton. Disenchanted, I watched a few silvery fleets of flying fish. When one fell on deck, I picked it up ungraciously and fried it. On March 13, after being becalmed for four days solid, I played a few conjuring tricks with my little-used, special ghosting rig and moved seventy miles northward. This was a small triumph, but my log remained full of grumbles—I was missing the seabirds of the Southern Ocean, furious that no Trade Winds whatever seemed to move in this Trade Wind belt, and my whole odyssey was becoming too long-drawn-out. "Home seems forever away and *when* will I get a radio message through to my family," I wrote on March 14, and I started to play a ridiculous game with myself—guessing the date of my arrival at Plymouth. Then the blessed Trade Wind started to blow and I was full of glee again. There is one benefit to be obtained in lone sailing; you don't have to practice self-control—what you feel, you can show. The ocean remains unmoved by human sulks.

During those weeks in the wild Southern Ocean, when I had only been able to move around using stiff knees and tense arm holds, my ordinary leg muscles had weakened. Now I kept busy recovering muscle power by deliberately doing exercises that made my limbs ache.

From March 22 to 24, as we sailed through calmer waters, approaching the equator, a strange phenomenon occurred. When *Galway Blazer* reached about 5 degrees south of the equator, a two-day procession of electrical storms swept over us, some brief squalls, some lasting hours. Flashing of fireworks in the sky and angry thundery growls made the upper air seem to be alive with human passions, as if the gods were throwing temper fits.

On March 25, after a fortnight in which the boat hardly moved, the sky cleared of all cloud and I knew some ecstatic sailing as we traveled downwind fast in the Southeast Trades. I sat on deck and sang.

By March 29 we were clawing our way northward on little puffs, and my sights put us six miles north of the latitude of the one mountaintop which sticks up in the middle of the Atlantic—I was glad to pass without near-viewing that sixty-foot-high guano-covered jag which is called St. Paul's Rocks.

April 1 played tricks on me in the traditional way. A nice sailing breeze sprang up—Hurrah the Trades, I cried! Their unexpected absence had riled me. Hoisting full sail, I set myself to enjoy a fast run, but it was April Fool's Day all right. After twenty miles we were sucked into a rainstorm which killed the wind, and I went below to depress myself further by reading Somerset Maugham's *Rain*. Then I sighted a merchant ship due to cross my bows a mile off. She was obviously bound for Rio, and I radioed her frantically. There might be *someone* awake in the wireless room, I thought. But modern ships travel by radar; no one bothers to keep a lookout, and my efforts proved fruitless. She steamed on past me. If only I could have let the family know I was alive!

After this, the rains came and beat down—more in the fashion of a monsoon than a mid-Atlantic burst. At two in the morning a little wind splashing waves against the bow woke me, for I slept with ears open for any change of sound on the hull. "The Trades!" I cried again, pleased at the idea. When I got on deck, it looked good. A few torn clouds were scudding across the dawn sky, but the wind kept north instead of its supposed northeast, and this meant I had to keep on beating steadily to windward. I began to count the miles to the Azores as one counts days to the end of a school term. A twelve-hundred-mile sail at this rate could take a month.

On April 6 we crossed the ecliptic, the track of the sun's

overhead path. I had once been taught that you can't take sights when the sun is exactly overhead. But you can! At the moment of noon he rolls right around the horizon, within the sextant. If you are spot on to it, he goes from east to no bearing but absolute altitude. He is right overhead, and you can roll him 360 degrees around the horizon, touching it all the way. It is fun doing something you have been told is impossible. Contentedly I logged:

> My noon altitude was 89 degrees plus and the sun swiveled round into the south. This seems to constitute a mark in the voyage and helps to break up the slog to windward.
> Very few flying fish—they must spurn this deep central part of the ocean and keep to the continents each side—Africa and South America. And still hardly ever a bird.

As I fled from the equator, the Trade Wind improved. On April 12 it behaved perfectly, blowing just as the book says it should—Northeast Force 4—and I relaxed as we sped forward. I wondered at the lack of flying fish until suddenly coveys of them appeared leaping over the ocean. Several crash-landed on deck each night and my breakfasts became large and delicious. I have sailed four times through the Northeast Trades and have never ceased to wonder at their phenomenon—blowing moderate and warm and unremitting since the beginning of this planet's time. To be *let down* by the Trades when I was in such a particular hurry seemed a bit thick. But perhaps they heard my plaint, for now they began to blow fresh out of a clear sky as if in a hurry to get me and my discontent out of their territory.

On the thirteenth we crossed the track of a voyage I had made twenty-three years before in the first *Galway Blazer*. Leaving the Canaries, I had then been looking forward to meeting Anita with a tiny baby in a basket in Antigua. Now that son was a grown man—somewhere. I could only hope that his round cheerful face had kept its grin and that Anita's hopeful speculations had not worn thin. It was now four months since she had heard from me.

On April 16 I conceded that the Trades were turning civil. They carried me right on to nearly 25 degrees north, even curling out of their usual line as if to help me point north. When they died, I felt it was my duty to be civil in turn, and I took my re-becalming in good part, using up time by refitting the rigging and having a shampoo and bath on deck.

One early morning when I was coaxing *Galway Blazer* along under foresail, a tanker fizzed close by our stern, maybe taking a northern route on the Trinidad-Gibraltar run. Once again I tried and failed to obtain radio contact, while the danger of being run down at night for my small boat struck me afresh. I can carry only enough fuel to show lights when in the crowded shipping lanes. A full moon was helping me at the moment, but there would be many dark nights in which I had to take a chance.

On April 20, Good Friday, I reached latitude 27 north, longitude 44 degrees west.

> Although we are in the Horse Latitudes, today was halcyon. A light wind kept us going so that I could point just where I want to go—one hundred miles west of the Azores and I could even ease her a touch off the hard-on-the-wind position which we have occupied almost continuously since leaving the equator. I like this course. It takes me away from the main shipping lines and the danger of being run down. There is a great deal of sargasso weed around, some of it formed into solid rafts. I have to be

constantly clearing the vane-steering blade with
a boat hook. Once the steering picked up so
much that it jammed the rudder hard over, the
boat was gyrating in circles before I could get it
sorted out, luckily nothing broke.

Since wind and weather were fair, I intended to do an
end around west of the Azores—making constant
attempts to obtain radio contact as we passed. I heard on
my radio (which always worked perfectly in the ordinary
receiving sense) that a large merchant ship had been put
out of action. Although we got only the tail end of this
out-of-season gale in the North Atlantic, it traveled down
and the impact certainly nearly finished me! I had just
got the last lump of seaweed off the steering when it
suddenly started to blow cold and hard from the west,
and April 23, 24, and 25 brought stormy weather. I kept
on running under fully reefed foresail but not dead
before the wind which would have been the safest thing
to do as in heavy weather *Galway Blazer* ran best
downwind. However, I could not bear to swing out of
my homeward route and I kept on trying to poke up
north.

The incident which so easily did me in happened this
way. I was trying to snatch a sun-sight, and to do this, I
had to lean right out of the cockpit hatch with both hands
on the sextant in order to see under the rail. I noticed a
squall racing over the sea, turning the water from blue to
black, but I thoughtlessly hung on in this position
determined to get my sight. I succeeded, and within a
second of getting the sun-sight and slipping down to the
chart table to work out the figures, the squall hit us.
Galway Blazer was right over on her side. As the first big
wave burst, roaring over the forecastle, I was flung
spread-eagled over the chart table while a trail of
saucepans and cutlery showered the cabin. For an age I
thought that the boat would not come back, that once

again, as in 1968, she would roll right over and maybe break her masts. I suppose that that hurricane, in seas such as I had never seen before or since, played always in the back of my imagination. I never could have believed in such seas—they *had* come, they had smashed me, they might again. . . .

But it was all right this time. She lay flat for a moment, almost trembling like a dog, rolling on its back, and then swung back. I jumped to square her right off before the wind and then doused and secured the foresail with the winds still roaring past me. Then I put the hurricane hatches on and kept a perpetual eye on the tiller so that I could take over if she looked like broaching. It was the end of the gale—soon the winds lessened and I found myself sailing fast under blue skies with a fair wind, with ease, but I had to digest the fact that I had at this stage of the voyage nearly been wiped out. Had this squall hit a few instants earlier, when I was leaning out of the cockpit with both hands on the sextant, I would have popped out of the boat like a cork out of a champagne bottle! I had just gone down in time—pushed by the same hand that had sent me below deck just before the earlier capsize. Any man can make a thoughtless mistake, which at sea leads to death, but on these two occasions I was not doing anything rash, only going about my ordinary sailor's chores when danger struck. In each case I had just moved to safety below—it struck me as curious; and then with a pang I remembered my family, and a deep thankfulness filled me. Had I been washed overboard, they would never have known that I had rounded the Horn and was battling toward them—my aim achieved. They would have grieved for me—not achieving my ambition.

On April 28 I wrote in my log:

After that superb fast run down the Pacific which I had done in sixty-two days, this long-

234 ADVENTURE IN DEPTH

drawn-out beat up the Atlantic gives me a
feeling of anticlimax.

On April 28 I also wrote:

On the wind charts of this region there are no
gales marked for this time of year and precious
little Force 7 wind. But I have met a gale every
day and it never blows *less* than Force 7. We sail
fast until it gets too severe and then run before
it, under bare poles. The barometer is falling
steadily. Driven eastward by these gales, I may
have to go between the Islands of the Azores,
but I want to do that end around West.

Worse was to come. I spent nearly a week dodging
around the Azores, trying to move northward but
determined not to get close to a lee shore with winds
blowing forty knots. I was lined up to pass about thirty
miles west of Flores in a nice southerly wind when it
swung to east and then north. In an hour we changed
from a run to a reach, then we were hard on the wind,
and then not able to lay the course. I held on grimly for a
bit, hoping to weather the island, but the wind backed
farther and we had to run out south of the island, tearing
along under bare poles and away from home!

By May 3, when the gale had blown for twenty-four
hours, I found it had set me back ninety miles toward
Cape Horn! I bashed back into the gale, but it was a
particularly vicious one and twice great combers
knocked the boat down flat, breaking over her with a
roar like an express train. Then, as if it had exhausted
itself, the storm died.

On May 4 we lay all day in a flat blue sea within a sight
of the mountains of Flores. I tried to establish radio
communication, but though I could always *hear*, no one
registered a bleep from me. I found it infuriating to have

to keep shouting into the transceiver, and yet it would not be fair to others to miss a single chance. I tried to stifle my irritation by reading Milton. "The mind is its own place, and in itself can make a Heav'n of Hell, a Hell of Heav'n."

Gradually I seemed able to master my emotions. To be alone on the ocean is good character training. It does not matter how old you are—sixteen or sixty—it is equally important to be able to grasp one's own tempers and twist them into submission. I took the fancy of pretending each mood was like a costume hanging in a cupboard, which one can pull out and don at will. And then I found I could laugh at myself. All these years, since indeed I was a child, those costumes had been able to leave their cupboard without orders and fling themselves on *me*. From now on I resolved to choose my own mental raiment, and this idea amused me greatly while I gazed back longingly toward the south, hoping for a right breeze to whip up and bear me home.

It came at last—a glorious south wind which carried me fast all night. When dawn came blue and violet, we were well clear of the Azores—an island chain that seemed to have encircled my boat for days. Now I could almost see the finishing post—Plymouth. Only thirteen hundred miles away and my mind *was* my own place.

CHAPTER 21

Home!

BREAKING out of those fetters of the Azores was immensely stimulating. Now it would be a clean race for home—swift, I hoped. *Galway Blazer II*, who had sailed out of Plymouth harbor on a bright September day two years before, was back in a stretch she knew well. We were in the area of the Westerlies, the northern equivalent of the Roaring Forties of the Southern Ocean. It had always seemed extraordinary to me that north Scotland lies in the same polar latitude as Cape Horn—but the Gulf Stream gives all the shores a different climate, and the land formation blocks the swirl of the Westerly winds.

The Forties of the North Atlantic are pleasantly different winds from those of the Southern Ocean, and I expected to tear along the "home stretch" of the Western Approaches to the English Channel. It might be cool and squally, but it ought to be right fast, and I had a great feeling of admiration for my boat. She had battled so well over fourteen thousand miles of stormy waters through the Southern Ocean, and now her life should be simple—a last glorious spurt of twelve hundred miles, with the wind behind her or on her beam, just as she liked it.

Having got myself nicely attuned to moods when alone in the ocean, I now had to contemplate my forthcoming readjustment to normal life. I would not want to sail alone anymore. I had fulfilled my heart's desire, and what a time it had taken! Maybe I could keep a boat for the family. Tarka was tough, and Leonie seemed to have inherited my lucky immunity to seasickness—in fact, when she was a little girl in the Bahamas, I could remember her complaining on a rough fishing expedition, "I *wanna* be sick, too!" Her pink cheeks were getting no sympathy while other children turned green and their wretched mothers cosseted them. This was the only time in my life when I've seen anyone indignant about *not* being seasick!

"Normal life"—what was it? The loneliness of a city? The debauch of towns? Girls, bars, the patter of tiny feet which so quickly turn into the teenager's midnight tiptoe?

Maybe I am adjusted to the ocean and not quite in tune with earth vibrations. I always feel so well at sea and never quite as well on land. Never knowing seasickness, I knew landsickness only too well. Why I was made like this—to thrive in the brine and wilt on land—I don't know.

Although I was *longing* to get back and see my loved ones, I was not really longing to live on land again. But I couldn't go on like this; I'd had my fling and cooled down my submariner temperature. Now I had simply *got* to tighten up and face the future—a future without perilous ambition. When I stepped out of *Galway Blazer* this time, I had to be able to say "Solo sailing is out of my system—truly out." The long-drawn-out knockabout adventure was about to end.

And then I was going to have to meet a lot of people—none of whom now knew that I was alive! Some, no doubt, would give me hell for wanting to go off in the first place, and if Anita felt resentful at the long silence —it was now nearly five months—I could hardly blame her.

When you go to sea, each day overflows with its own happenings, and I had enjoyed a kind of foreshortening of memory which wiped away the feeling of having been alone for a long time. When I had set out from Australia, that family reunion seemed to be hours not months away. I felt I was sailing *toward* them, *not* as when I left England, *away*, which *did* give me a twinge.

When I returned from solitude to human hubbub, it was as if I had never left it. One just picked up the book where one had left the marker. On this occasion something different had happened. *I knew I was all right, but nobody else did!*

I had been so calmly busy out there in the Pacific under that vast clear canopy of stars and so horribly busy while rounding the Horn and trying to keep alive. All this made time go fast for me, but now, as the voyage neared its end, I wondered if the months had gone at the same speed for my family. They might guess that I was shouting my head off into a weakening radio set, but other possibilities might enter their heads, too. No, I repeated to myself, they can't be expected to like it.

I ironed out some rather hasty philosophy. After reaching harbor—and now it seemed extremely likely that I *would* reach harbor—I would no longer be allowed to stretch my mind in the way that amused me out here on the ocean, speculating on myself as a microcosm in the macrocosm of the heavens. Wonderful as it would be to be home, I knew that telephones, bills, daily post, and income tax forms awaited! There would be perpetual decisions to make—not just the purely simple decisions of what sail to hoist and how to keep alive, but complex emotion-motivated decisions on which other human beings depended. I dreaded the transition while yearning for it. For so long the galaxies had been my ceiling and the rolling sea mists the walls of my room. Now only a thousand miles away, over the horizon, my wife and son and daughter—who might not necessarily share my ability to shorten memory—would have spent a whole winter wondering. I had no idea that in April the *Daily Express* printed headlines about the general concern and had requested Lloyds to ask ships to keep a look out for

Galway Blazer. All I knew was that the two ships which had passed within a mile of me failed to respond to my frantic radio call. And I had raged at their lack of attention.

The last thousand miles of the voyage were not, however, as I anticipated. Just as I was getting excited and gearing myself for contact and explanations, a terrific anticyclone descended over the North Atlantic and all wind dropped. Instead of racing over the waves toward England at full speed, as she had every right to expect, *Galway Blazer* found herself sitting in a flat metallic sea. The barometer rose to 1040—the highest I had ever seen it—and fog covered the whole quiet ocean. We were absolutely becalmed. After May 11, for three days *Galway Blazer* rocked along in a dreamworld of silvery mist banks which occasionally broke to reveal shining colors of startling clarity—too clear to be real—a sea made of glass, a sky like a blue plate.

Below decks there was little to do. The cabin was in perfect order. Nothing needed tidying. I went over my few treasures. On the wall above the bookshelves my tiny "picture gallery" of holy pictures, medals, and prayers sent by people of all denominations remained firmly stuck. Johnnie Pope had sent me a St. Christopher medal at the start, and it remained on the petrol tank to which it had been relegated as the most dangerous area! I would pick the medal off to give back to my former first lieutenant after its long voyage. And the bottles of St. Brendan's water safely stowed could be returned to Anne Rosse for her garden well. And the Irish tricolor—which was, I believed, the first to be carried by a sailing boat around the Horn—was shaken out and put back into place. That I could give to Galway! All these small ideas gave me pleasure, while the huge memories of the Pacific had encompassed my mind with a beauty I could never give away or even try to share—the vast horizon, the multicolored sunsets, and the glittering nights with only the sea sounds and sail sounds as music.

While fussing at the lack of progress, I pored lengthily over the Routing Chart of the area, wondering at what point to make another shot at radio contact. This chart gives in graphic form the expected winds and ocean currents and main routes of the world's merchant shipping. It also designates the location of ocean weather ships which permanently keep station and feed information, from their allotted positions, back to the weather forecasters on land whose honeyed voices eventually transmit the likelihood of happy sunbathing, successful harvesting, or pleasant race-going over the radio.

As a little light wind moved us onward, I marked my track toward Plymouth onto the chart and noted with satisfaction that the line passed within sixty miles of a weather ship named *Kilo*, stationed off the entrance to the Bay of Biscay. The book said she was manned alternately by British and French crews, so if I got through, I would be understood!

Despite the feeble range power of the radio set, I reckoned it was worth a try at sixty miles, though not worth sailing out of my way to reduce the distance. Anxiously I waited until we reached the closest possible position to *Kilo* on my route. Then when I knew we would not sail nearer, I prepared the set for one serious all-out effort.

Once, in the past, when I was navigating in a transatlantic race, our great circle track had passed right beside one of these brave weather ships, and I recalled the exquisite pleasure of sighting her exactly on station. Now I began to feel elated and confident. There was hope of getting through, real hope at last.

The *Admiralty List of Radio Signals* is not a tome which usually caused the heart to beat and fingers to tremble, but mine did as I turned the pages searching for *Kilo*'s radio frequencies—and there they were. It was the

morning of May 12, just five months and one day since
my last radio contact. I picked up the headset, tuned in
the radio transceiver and started to call *Kilo* on her
frequency. "This is Mike Zulu Delta Tango *Galway Blazer
II* calling ocean station *Kilo.*" Three times I repeated
these words and then waited. No response. It was just
like those other occasions all up the South Atlantic. My
hopes sank, but I determined to wait a few minutes and
then switch on again. After rechecking all settings and
getting a little more power for the aerial output, I
repeated, "This is Mike Zulu Delta Tango" thrice over.
Then came a silent listening pause . . . the waves slap-
ping against the bow—the parrels creaking on the mast.
Suddenly a clear, cultivated voice with a slight French
accent filled the cabin: "Mike Zulu Delta Tango, I hear
you." I could scarcely believe it. After all these months I
had got an answer! My throat tightened so that I could
hardly speak. I was shaking as I went through the routine
of giving my position followed by the brief all-important
personal message. I asked the captain of *Kilo* to inform
my friend John Coote at the *Daily Express* in London of
Galway Blazer's position and to send Anita—here I
hesitated a moment, seeking a word less banal than the
usual "love"—"send Anita my affections" was the phrase
I actually used.

And it was lucky I chose it, though for a reason I could
not then have guessed. When the *Daily Express* received
this message from the captain of *Kilo*, they realized that
an efficient captain was relaying to them by radio telephone, but as they had for some months supposed a
disaster had probably overwhelmed me, they decided to
hold a conference concerning the authenticity of the
message. During April a lot of publicity had been given
to what was called my disappearance. John Coote, who
had been a submarine officer, knew me well; he thought
it quite natural that I should directly contact him, but
then a hoaxer, after reading of general inquietude on my

behalf, might well have guessed that I had arranged to
send messages to the director of the Beaverbrook Press.
What clinched the matter was the wording of my greet-
ing to Anita. John Coote and Mike Steemson reckoned
that only I would have used this particular old-fashioned
phrase. They said, "It's Bill all right." So the joybells were
set ringing from the *Daily Express* offices. My son in
Cyprus heard the news on return to his stables; my
daughter in London when she got home from her art
school. My wife, who had just gone to New York to
launch a book, was taking a Sunday walk when the telephone rang; her hostess gathered that the *Daily Express*
was ringing across the Atlantic to say *Galway Blazer
II* had contacted a ship in the Bay of Biscay. Afraid of
causing shock, this kind lady was herself shaking like a
leaf and could only whisper when my wife came in from
her walk. "A newspaper phoned. Bill is all right." Anita
sat down. "What sort of all right?" In the boat? In a
dinghy? On a desert island? Upside down? Right side
up? Holed? Rescued? There were all kinds of
possibilities, but the main thing was that she knew I was
alive.

   Daily Express wires buzzed across the ocean. She drew
what information she could. "*What sort of all right?*"

   "Absolutely all right. Sailing for Lands End."

   So Anita chucked everything she had gone to America
to do, and took the first plane back to England.

   None of this could I visualize. All I knew was that a
human voice had *answered*, the first voice that had spoken
to me for five months. A *man* had heard me. My message
had gone through. After the rapture of this encounter, I
hardly cared about being becalmed. The atmosphere in
the boat changed. It became live with people. I tried to
imagine where my wife would be when she received the
news. And Tarka Dick and Leonie? And were *they* all
right? Now that soft winds forced a respite on me, I
realized that five months was the hell of a long time.

Having been wild with anticipation at facing that Southern Ocean, I began now to be equally as wild with anticipation at seeing dear faces, and I looked around eagerly for winds as if I were in an ocean race.

The Westerlies always blow at this time of year, and they ought to have taken me fast to Plymouth, but this freak weather held. While I fumed with impatience, *Galway Blazer* either had to keep punching to windward or else sit becalmed in heavy swell. Then, as I approached the channel where it nearly always blows from the west, a stinking east wind arose and stayed put. I was to have a nose-ender all the way to Plymouth and thick fog in the dangerous shipping lanes. I'd had superb luck in the Pacific, but as I rounded the Horn and approached England, the weather couldn't have played me worse.

During the three days in which I sailed slowly over the Great Sole Fishing Bank, trawlers became my nightmare. In the dark their own fishing lights flamed so bright that they could not pick out my masthead light, and sometimes they seemed to be charging right at me. I knew the sea around here was teeming with fish and it would be possible to vary my diet by getting out a hook and line, but lookout work kept me too busy. It has always been my intention, when entering the Channel from the Atlantic in a small boat, to keep to the very middle which remains comparatively empty because Mediterranean shipping tends to hug the coast of France, and Atlantic shipping keeps close to England, but those strong southeast winds had pushed me much farther north than I wished so that I was forced to pass near the Scilly Isles and sail along perilously into the stream of Atlantic traffic. I knew that the press would be trying to pinpoint my whereabouts and I continued to send radio messages, but the only answer came from an Irish merchant ship named *Sligo*. For a moment I thought I was contacting the port which lies only sixty miles north of my home on Galway Bay, and I kept stupidly shouting, "Repeat, repeat." Then the operator explained clearly and took down my position for transmission onward, but there was not time for any further message.

On May 19, long after I should have reached harbor, there were still two hundred and forty miles to go, and those sleepless nights which are the bane of solo sailors in crowded steamer routes affected my temper and, I feared, my looks! Not usually interested in my appearance, I now developed a sort of determination to arrive after all those months at sea looking as smart and fresh as my boat. It was not easy to have a "wash and brush up" while concentrating on not getting run down by large ships. England, like the Horn, chose to shroud herself in fog as I approached.

Dotted all around the oceans are certain traffic blackspots—the graveyards of ships. The Scillies are high on the list. Throughout history they have been the scene of wrecks. An extensive archipelago bordered by thousands of sharp-fanged rocks, they lie adjacent to the landfalls which vessels must make when coming from the west into the English Channel. They also lie in an area where bad weather and low visibility are frequent, and, to add to the hazards close to the Scilly Isles, the tidal stream forks. One flood turns north into the Irish Sea, the other eastward for Dover. The spring tides run fast. Thus, if the navigator's reckoned position is slightly in error, he may swiftly find himself being set by a tide at right angles to that which he had calculated. In a sailing vessel this can prove disastrous.

Disasters probably started more than two thousand years ago when the Phoenicians sent their ships to Cornwall for tin. Up until 1750 most charts, through some extraordinary error, showed the Scillies ten miles north of their true position. The sale of these charts may well have been encouraged by Cornishmen keen on plundering ships as they foundered, but far more valuables than landsmen could loot went to the bottom. I had proper charts and a host of kind non-plunder-minded friends awaiting me . . . but all the same I felt a shiver when I realized the extent of my danger . . . now so near to the end of my voyage. I could not keep a lookout *all* the time. I had to sleep. And strong winds had driven me too far north while I could not check my position in perpetual fog. I had no fear of the open sea—we understood each other—but I had the seaman's real fear of fog and rocks. And I wanted, desperately now, to get *home!*

Navigational genius, like any other, is greatly composed of perspiration and only partly of inspiration. I believe that if you have done your training, prepared your homework thoroughly, when it comes to the push you may experience the psychic bid which makes you know what is a right decision. I don't aspire to be in a genius class, but as I beat slowly up toward the Wessex coast I recalled a Fastnet Race. We were trying to make a landfall, although I had had no celestial fixes, owing to bad weather. There were no radio aids then, so I took a fix of two cross-bearings—one, the course of a butterfly, which I reckoned *must* have blown over from the Scilly; the other, of the stern of a liner which I estimated was on the great circle track for New York. We made our landfall correctly and won the race!

Now once again I found myself, coming up for my landfall, in much the same position as in that Fastnet and without astro sights. However I had my reliable radio direction-finder. I took bearings of the Scillies northward to show when I was past them, and bearings of Ushant on the French coast to make certain I was well clear to the southward. I remained a little scared of this bearing; a very competent ocean-racing skipper had once told me he had received what he called "bounce back off the coast" from this direction, which put him in grave error. By this time I was getting desperately tired from sleepless nights on the fishing banks, and it is in fatigue that errors creep in. I simply kept beating up to the northward, straining my eyes in the mist. Suddenly a large merchant vessel burst out of the mist, steering *north*. I knew I must have got myself into the main channel up into the Irish Sea, *between* the Scillies and Lands End, and all the hair on my neck rose with horror because this meant that I had narrowly escaped running on the rocks south of Scilly! The shame of having made such a blunder right at journey's end crept over me. Devil take this fog—I was getting too tired to think. Disgusted with myself, I pushed the helm down to swing her about onto a safe course. It had been a near thing. I left the ghosts of Admiral Sir Cloudesley Shovel and his squadron of ships wrecked here some four hundred years ago, and beat up straight for Plymouth Hoe.

God, I wanted to sleep. But while I spent both day and night with the lights on peering into the mist, I knew that everyone who cared for me would by this time be peering wildly through binoculars from the coast around Plymouth!

Various planes came out to spot me, and the first to do so was a little white machine which emerged from a rainstorm. It buzzed overhead as if pleased at its own cleverness at finding me in this bad visibility and I emerged on deck to wave back in the downpour. They must have had an extraordinarily good camera on board because next day a newspaper photograph would be published looking as if it had been taken in perfect light from a few yards above my head.

A few hours later a couple of RAF reconnaissance machines reared out of the rain to find me well-reefed down beating to windward in half a gale. These great planes enthralled me with their airmanship, grinding round in tight turns at what seemed to be masthead level while brown smoke poured from their exhausts. I couldn't think how they managed to stay in the sky. The noise of them, deafening and so different from the ocean roars, brought me harshly back into the world of men and machines. What an odd audience those planes had —one man applauding from a little boat!

After the RAF had disappeared in the clouds, taking, I felt sure, another snatch of news to my waiting family, I sailed on along the coast until darkness fell. Then, feeling continually nervous in this shipping lane with lights suddenly appearing out of the murk, I took a turn out to seaward, hoping for less frequented areas. Visibility improved as we got away from the coast, but I had to remain on watch all night—my last night at sea.

After dawn I turned northward toward Plymouth with a delightful following breeze—the first following breeze since I had left the Azores. Once again I had to cross the traffic lane, but it was less harassing in daylight. I began to enjoy myself, for there was just enough wind to carry full sail and it blew me along at great speed. Having taken a morning longitude sight at about seven A.M., I got another sight at noon to give me an an accurate fix, and this accuracy was fortunate, for the coast remained hazy and the first land I saw clearly was the entrance to Plymouth breakwater!

Suddenly I was in the great harbor and dozens of craft seemed to be converging on me. Choosing the eastern entrance in order to avoid a jibe amid the milling boats, I could let *Galway Blazer* sail proudly in at speed.

Then things began to happen. A press boat was rushing around. Admiral Ruck-Keene who had greeted me on return from so many submarine patrols was waving and shouting from a launch. And—could I believe my eyes—there, beside him, having flown out from Australia as he said he would, was Alex Koppen! Then came a naval barge that kept steady pace beside *Galway Blazer*. On it I could see my wife and daughter. We waved wildly. One couldn't wave hard enough. The joints of my shoulders nearly came out of their sockets. A mooring had been allocated at the Royal Western Yacht Club where dear old Francis Chichester secured after his world circumnavigation—and there on the landing steps stood his son Giles Chichester, waiting with my sister to join the welcome. Within a flash it was all over. The sails rattled down. My long voyage had ended. Anita and Leonie were aboard, hugging me, examining the cabin, looking to see if things they had fixed up were still there. Other eager hands were stowing and securing sails and rigging.

My daughter kept dancing around in my kangaroo-skin fur boots with my red wool cap pulled down her long mane of dark gold hair—the cap used during icy naps around the Horn. "Can I have it, Daddy? Doesn't it suit me?" Yes, I was home.

By now there seemed to be crowds of people waiting on shore. I didn't have much to pack and I guessed my wife would have some clothes waiting. We slipped off into the launch together and landed near the stone steps. I hoped my legs were going to work all right. They did. Hanging onto the rail, and with Anita and Leonie pressed close to me, we made a slow progress upward and then advanced through throngs of kindly cheering people toward the clubhouse. People I didn't know embraced me. It took half an hour to cover a hundred yards. Leonie kept getting broken off and lost in the throng. I felt dazed—or perhaps "dazzled" would be a better word. There seemed to be so much of everything. So many people and cameras and voices. I went into the club and sat down at a big table with reporters and interviewers, to answer their questions as lucidly as I could. The TV lights blazed on stands overhead. One becomes diffuse when leaving the open sea—people seem to ask such curious questions. *Why* had I done it? Well, just because I wanted to—or perhaps to contradict John Donne and insist that each man *is* an island unto himself.

It was evening before they finished with me and the popping of corks began. Then I was being driven to the house of a naval friend, and Anita was saying, "There's just time for a bath and then we go out to dinner—and tomorrow the Admiral wants you to go for lunch and the Lord Mayor has asked you to. . . ."

On a chair lay the vests and underpants my sister had purchased just in case—and two good suits fetched from my tailor by Giles Chichester and pink grapefruits carried from America by Anita in her hasty return to meet me. "You couldn't have had *these* at sea!"

Hundreds of telegrams arrived. Tarka Dick was furious that he could not get back from Cyprus to share the excitement, but he would be coming home in a few weeks.

I pulled off my sailing clothes and sank into a hot bath. A big dinner party awaited. My hostess, Mrs. Peter Cobb, the wife of the captain commanding the submarine flotilla, had ordered a vast goulash because neither hour nor numbers could be certain. All depended on a fair breeze getting me here in time.

"Are you going to be able to eat all this after so long on raisins and nuts?" asked someone.

The answer was "Yes." After five months on my particular regimen, I could step ashore and tuck into this excellent repast and douse it down with a good claret. I hadn't slept at all for forty-eight hours and precious little in the week before that. But I did not feel tired, I just felt good.

The person who couldn't eat was my poor wife. "It's just been too much," she explained apologetically. "All that time with headlines about being missing and then suddenly popping up out of the sea when I'd just gone to America—sorry, I simply can't swallow"—and a weak hand stretched out for a glass of champagne.

Dinner was merry and unique. I left overwhelmed by friendliness, and it was a surprise to realize how many people really cared about me—an old salt who had done just what he wanted.

So there it ended—with Admiral Philip Ruck-Keene patting my back. "This is the best patrol I've ever seen you back from." And cheerful Mike Steemson who had shared my chagrin long ago after that capsize. "So glad you made it, Bill." And my impudent daughter, tired of looking through binoculars into the mist. "When are you going to take *me* out for a sail?"

Down in the harbor, *Galway Blazer II* rested at her mooring of honor—she had carried me so bravely through all our adventures. This was the first night for five and a half months that she had spent without me. I hoped she did not feel lonely while we were toasting her name.